A FIGHTING DREAM:
THE POLITICAL WRITINGS
OF CLAUDIA JONES

books

Published in February 2024 by
1804 Books, New York, NY

1804Books.com

Cover by Kalia Leon

TABLE OF CONTENTS

ANTI-COMMUNISM & REPRESSION

TOWARD A PEOPLE'S CULTURE

FOREWORD

GERALD HORNE

Though often forgotten today, during her days from the 1930s–mid-1950s, Trinidad-born Claudia Jones was a premier activist and theoretician who sank deep roots into New York City.

She was a leader of the Communist Party USA, which came into existence as a direct outgrowth of the Russian Revolution of 1917.

This was a turning point in world history insofar as it built upon the Haitian Revolution, 1791–1804, which marked the triumph of unpaid workers and set the stage for the class project—or socialism—that 1917 carried forward.

The Bolshevik Revolution, as Jones and her comrades articulated, was of profound significance for peoples of African descent. Beginning in the 1930s, one espies the ascendancy of a global campaign targeting Jim Crow—US apartheid—embodied in the crusade to save the lives of the Scottsboro Nine,[1] African American youth slated for execution in Alabama because of spurious allegations of sexual molestation of two Euro-American women. Backed ultimately by comrades of Moscow, the US-based International Labor Defense—headed by her comrade, Black attorney and activist, William L. Patterson,[2] fought this case in the courts at home and in the streets worldwide, in a manner not unlike the anti-apartheid movement which too was global and eventuated in democratic elections in 1994.

It is also true that the Soviet Union armed liberation movements in Southern Africa that buoyed Nelson Mandela.[3]

The editors and publishers of this worthwhile work, cogently term a section of this book, "Anti-Racism, a Class Struggle," which underscores the aforementioned. For, as noted, enslavement was the ultimate class question, marking the struggles of unpaid workers for liberation from this malevolent status, just as the triumph over apartheid meant a step forward for exploited African workers—a struggle that continues. It is no accident that the descendants of enslaved Africans in North America vote most heavily against the right wing and are more prone to be pro-union than any other demographic, exemplifying the living legacy of fierce class struggle.

Comrade Jones also had the perspicacity to sketch the story of Ben Davis, also a Black Communist—and an attorney and journalist as well—who was elected to the New York City Council in 1943, reelected in 1945, then like herself he fell victim to an anti-communist persecution in 1949 and, also like her, wound up in federal prison. Yet it was the Atlanta-born Davis who supplied his Georgia ally, the Dr. Martin Luther King Jr., with a timely blood transfusion when the activist-cleric came within a whisper of falling victim to a stabbing at the hands of a deranged New Yorker, fueling the canard that the future Nobel Laureate truly carried "Communist blood" in his veins.[4]

This Red Scare also represented a "Black Scare," insofar as it was not accidental that those most vigorous in pushing for socialism and the redistribution of wealth were those who had been consigned by rapacious capitalism to initially unpaid then poorly paid labor. The struggle of those like Jones and Patterson and Davis in conjunction with the socialist camp and national liberation movements compelled US imperialism to move away reluctantly and haltingly from the more egregious aspects of Jim Crow, not least because of the arrival on these shores of diplomats, students, and the like from Africa and the Caribbean with Washington finding it problematic to appeal to these emissaries as long as peoples of African descent in this land were treated so atrociously: Jim Crow had to go. This created a dynamic whereby a kind of desegregation occurred but a stiff price was paid in that the most resolute fighters—Black Communists and their allies, including the late, great Paul Robeson[5]—were marginalized and imprisoned, ideologically decapitating our movement, a point Comrade Jones underscores on page 182 and again, on page 209 in her invocation of Robeson. This contradictory process continues to haunt us, leading to the profoundly wrongheaded viewpoint that progress for African Americans arrives when the radical left is bludgeoned.

This piercing misperception facilitated wars abroad—particularly of the anti-communist variety—on the Korean peninsula by June 1950 and Indo-China thereafter along with spiraling of military spending—a murderous process that continues to this very day. This in turn laid the basis for the ascendancy of fascist trends (p. 140), shamefully including an onslaught of police terror, which too continues to this very day.

Yet amidst the gloom and doom were bright rays of sunshine, speaking of the Cuban Revolution of 1959, a complement to both 1804 and 1917 (see p. 253). When Havana dispatched its military in 1975–1976 to defeat the apartheid invaders on the battlefields of Southern Angola and Northern Namibia, vouchsafing Pretoria's shattering defeat, it was further evidence—if any were needed—that the socialism that Comrade Jones espoused was the ultimate deliverance for Africans.

Comrade Jones' analysis also includes a factor unfortunately ignored too often, referring to her sketching of "class collaborationist labor," (p. 177) an odious trend that inheres in settler-colonial regimes, like that of the USA, which were constructed in the first instance based on settlers uniting across class lines for mutual benefit against the interests of Indigenes and Africans. She also makes reference to a trait that is essential to Marxism-Leninism, the philosophy that guided her, i.e. a political "estimate" (p. 179), whereby comrades assay the battlefield and make an assessment of the correlation of forces—positive and negative—which in turn shapes strategy and tactics.

Comrade Jones in sketching the dilemmas of Negro women also can be fairly viewed as a foremother of today's invocation of "intersectionality," i.e. how she embodied class, "race," and gender simultaneously, as did millions of others.

Though buried in London—the city to which she was deported during McCarthyism's stained reign, Comrade Jones' words continue to live—thanks to this penetrating volume.

INTRODUCTION

EUGENE PURYEAR

Class, gender, and race are the categories that order our lives. Where your personal "identity" intersects with all three is a pretty good guide to what sort of life you are going to have. Hard or easy, rich or poor, buffeted by discrimination or blissfully ignorant of hatred. Claudia Jones lives on because she was one of (perhaps the) first to offer up an analytical framework that outlined the relationship between the three that was structured as a guide not simply to understanding, but to action. The analysis pioneered by Claudia Jones, rooted in a historical and contemporary analysis of capitalism, offers guideposts to navigating the complexities of the relationship between the ongoing oppression faced by many in the context of greater representation and recognition of the impact of bigotry on society.

Given the stakes, this alone would be enough of a reason to bring out a collection of works by Claudia Jones. For those who hold a similar desire for a future free of exploitation and oppression, her work through the years offers valuable lessons for how to transform our world today. Her views, however, could (and have been) summarized and packaged by others in an attempt to address the same issue. Bringing together a reader, then, has its own importance: meeting Ms. Jones on her own terms.

Writing about Black communists in the United States has exploded in recent years. A younger generation of scholars, themselves often rooted in radical social movements of the '60s, '70s, '80s, and '90s, have taken on the crucial work of unearthing the vibrant history of communism in the US and its role in the Black liberation movement, the labor movement and so on. The rise of a new generation of radically minded young people in the new century has also created a vibrant market for such texts and the historical distance from the Union of Soviet Socialist Republics (USSR) and the rise of "market socialism" have lessened McCarthyite fears among academic and major publishers.

As it concerns the relationship between communism and the Black liberation movement, however, the texts have been marred by the unwillingness of many scholars to meet Black communists on their own terms. Most of these works treat the "communist" element of that equation in a purely instrumentalist way. As the narrative goes, the Communist Party was the only vehicle for uncompromising Black protest, hence, they joined, but, at the end of the day, they were not terribly deeply rooted in Marxist-Leninist theory—just purely "utilized" or "adapted" it to some other primary purpose; "navigated" their way around party "strictures" on this or that; and mainly ended up relatively disillusioned.

Ultimately this stems from the fact most of these scholars work within a theoretical framework that is skeptical of many premises of Marxism-Leninism. Further, many of these scholars are actively engaged in fighting against capitalism, racism, and patriarchy and, logically, seek to place their own stamp on how past struggles are viewed in the present. That being said, the result is a (sometimes) subtle denigration of Marxism-Leninism as a framework for liberatory movements today. Whether one agrees it is an appropriate framework or not, attempting to round off the edges of the Marxism-Leninism of Claudia Jones, or whoever else, lessens our ability to engage critically with the philosophical underpinnings of Black communism in the mid-twentieth century.

For instance, Dr. Carol Boyce Davies, the most prominent Jones biographer, states that:

> Her writings, however, never defend hardline Stalinist programs. Jones was well read in Leninism, and recognized that Lenin had advanced views on the colonial question, as he did on the woman question. She would therefore have found Stalinist positions untenable . . . Claudia Jones, then, was not a Stalinist; but she also did not see

Stalin as the problem for her, the enemy was not Stalin but growing U.S. imperialism.[6]

Jones was a key party cadre whose writings in the '30s and during World War II conformed totally to the "party line" which was, in the final analysis, determined by Stalin. Further, Jones' analysis of the "National Question," is heavily tied up in a theoretical schema codified at the Sixth World Congress of the Comintern which solidified Stalin's ascendancy as the undisputed leader of the world communist movement, and which Stalin himself instrumentalized as a key element in his struggle against "the Right" at the Congress. While separating Jones' legacy from Stalin certainly helps create an atmosphere for acceptance in Western academic and literary struggles, it offers no insight into the relationship between the USSR and movements of oppressed nationalities.

Taking Ms. Jones' work on its own offers an opportunity for the reader to decide for themselves how relevant her theoretical framework may or may not be—particularly because her adoption of Marxism-Leninism does not seem accidental or incidental. The interplay between class exploitation and racial and gender oppression in her own early life speaks directly to a universalized critique of capitalism.

In junior high school, her mother died at the workbench of spinal meningitis. As she noted: "The conditions of nonunion organization of that day, of speed-up, plus the lot of working women who are mothers, and undoubtedly the weight of immigration to a new land where conditions were far from as promised or anticipated contributed to her early death at the age of thirty-seven."

The tuberculosis that would haunt her for life was contracted from the "open sewerage" running through the typical low-quality housing Black workers in New York were crowded into. In her high school, teachers recruited young Black students as maids and sought to humiliate them through racially tinged academic "lessons."

After high school: "I went to work . . . since college was out for me . . . I had to help support myself and contribute to the family . . . My first job was in a laundry, where I observed, under the incredible (to me then) conditions of overwork, speed-up, etc., in the heat of summer young Negro women fainting regularly because of the unbearable conditions. I didn't want to become like them, so I went to work in a factory."

The injustices of capitalism and their disproportionate distribution were not simply theoretical for Claudia Jones. Early on she took up the cudgel to resist. As a young person she worked with the NAACP, the Urban League, and a Harlem-based Black Nationalist organization around issues like the Scottsboro Boys and the Italian invasion of Ethiopia. Friends in the Communist Party, a major part of these movements sweeping Harlem, started talking to her more about the Party and its ideas, leading her to join in 1936.

Following her admission as a party member, Jones held a steadily ascending series of posts that involved her deeply in the work of the party. Her presence in the histories is, conspicuously, thinner than her actual role in the work. Without a doubt, sexism is the major reason for this, regardless of race, as female leaders in the communist movement are woefully neglected. Yet another reason this text is important. Jones' role has remained obscured for another reason as well: she was a true cadre, not simply a personality.

Her main roles were as an editor of various publications and an organizer on various bodies and commissions. This placed her in a position to shape and organize the work of others. The type of position creates a prominence at the time, but can be obscuring historically. The subtle and overt influences of an editor are less obvious to history than the byline. It's one thing to note the list of speakers at an event, another to understand who arranged the program, booked the venue, and supervised the promotional materials. It's clear who was on the National Women's or National Negro Commission, but not necessarily as clear how the discussions in the meetings shape not simply policy, but specific formulations.

Claudia Jones was the type of person necessary for an organization to run, but those can often be the types of people that fade into the background a bit as time goes on. In her time, however, Claudia Jones was a beloved member of the communist movement in the United States and the left-wing community nationwide. As documented by Augusta Strong—another pioneering female Black Communist—"hundreds" gathered at Jones' farewell party at the Hotel Theresa in Harlem just before she was deported. The Communist heavy-hitters were there: Ben Davis, Eugene Dennis, Claude

Lightfoot, Elizabeth Gurley Flynn, and more. W. E. B. Du Bois sent a telegram and Nadyne Brewer—who would later be a star at the Metropolitan Opera—sang.[7]

The US government, however, was not confused about her importance, hence their move to deport her. Undoubtedly their hope was that her influence would fade into obscurity, but, as this volume proves, Claudia Jones, her thoughts and experiences, are alive and well.

EDITOR'S NOTE

The following writings are transcribed from archival clippings, but due to the nature of their age and the condition of some of the records, some pieces are incomplete or have missing/unintelligible portions. We've strived to transcribe them as accurately and completely as possible, but we've noted pieces where there are parts we could not read or locate, and illegible/missing portions are denoted with a —— (sometimes we offer our best guesses in brackets).

FIGHTING WAR AND FASCISM

The following selections cover a controversial moment in time in the struggle against fascism. During this period, we watch Jones' and the communist movement's analysis evolve from the start of World War II to the beginnings of the Cold War, all the while adapting to a rapidly changing political landscape. From 1935 to 1939, the Soviet Union had worked to develop an antifascist front of the "democratic" countries, the labor movement, and national liberation movements worldwide. However, Western Europe and the US were skeptical of an alliance between communists, socialists, and liberals, preferring to encourage Nazi Germany to turn against the Soviets—an alliance that did not require any change to imperial policy in London and Paris in particular.

Once the Nazis invaded the USSR, the previous proposals for an anti-fascist united front with the "democratic" countries became reality. Communists and anti-colonial forces worldwide seized this opportunity to use the contradictions in the "War for Democracy" to strengthen their own struggle. The need for full mobilization and labor peace meant even the most reactionary "allies" made certain concessions and allowed popular forces to build broad support for various pro-worker, anti-colonial, and anti-racist policies.

After the war, the imperial leaders reverted back, working aggressively to contain the burgeoning labor and anti-colonial upsurge. They launched the "Cold War" to contain communists in Eurasia and create the basis for the mass demonization that would become known as "McCarthyism" to launch vicious attacks on left-wing forces in the Western "democracies." The articles that Jones penned around that time show the struggle against fascist powers and the fascistic elements—the Jim Crow and colonial dictatorships—embedded in the "Democratic" allied countries of the West.

Claudia Jones' pieces that follow cover this period and reflect the shifting emphasis of the communist movement, but also the consistent thrust of anti-colonial and anti-racist thought and practice she and other left-wingers displayed throughout the period.

ETHIOPIAN AIDE AND WIFE RALLY HELP HERE FOR PEOPLE

DAILY WORKER
JANUARY 26, 1937

Stamp Issued to Harlem Merchants Gets Funds to Carry On Work—Dr. Malayku Bayen Plans Nationwide Tour to Get Support

"The morale of the people of Ethiopia is high, and this reflects their determination and knowledge that Ethiopia has not yet been conquered." In these words, Mrs. Malayku Bayen, American wife of the Ethiopian delegate Dr. Malayku Bayen, expressed the feelings of the people of Ethiopia.

Working intensely at their offices at 2353 Seventh Ave, Dr. Bayen and his wife have been rallying the people of Harlem to the Ethiopian cause for aid in their government.

"The sympathy among the American people is gratifying," said Mrs. Bayen, "Unfortunately, however, the sympathy here in Harlem is largely among the persons unable financially to help Ethiopia."

Women Aided

Asked how the Ethiopian people responded to colored Americans coming to Ethiopia and to the cry raised here that they did not consider themselves Negroes, Mrs. Bayen said that this question was raised only on this side for the Ethiopian people: royalty as well as natives welcomed Negroes as brothers.

The women in Ethiopia played an important part in the earlier stages of the war. Bravery and courage were not lacking, for it has been reported that besides giving aid to the wounded, the women went on the battlefields with the pretense of helping the wounded, and fed and manned machine guns which enabled many victories for the Ethiopian warriors.

Was War Correspondent

Mrs. Bayen served there also, aiding the wounded and also as staff correspondent for the *Amsterdam News*.

Their main work at present is raising funds for the Ethiopian cause. It was bitterly denounced by Mrs. Bayen that during the worst stages of the war, many Harlem racketeers made their slice of profit by using the cry of aid for Ethiopia. Now, these same racketeers are trying to discredit the authentic work of Dr. Bayen for Emperor Haile Selassie.

Plan US Tour

The methods of raising funds have been confined largely to the buying of Ethiopian stamps by the Harlem merchants who in turn distribute these stamps free of charge to their customers. The slogan, "Harlem Merchants Aid Ethiopia," has been raised and to date, 170 stores have paid for their stamps. The original stamps were printed in Switzerland and sent to the Ethiopian consul who turned them over to the doctor and his wife. The stamp now being sold, however, is a souvenir stamp, printed here in the United States.

At present, Dr. and Mrs. Bayen are completing plans for a tour of the United States to raise funds for Ethiopia. They plan to tour for two or three months and will leave about February 1.

JIM CROW IN UNIFORM*

JULY 1940

Introduction

Already the blood of nearly a million men, women, and children has flown forever under the bridge of history. Twentieth-century history moves with seven-league boots by the hour today.

The warring imperialists of Great Britain and France, after seeking for seven months to make the so-called "phony war" into a "real" war against the Soviet Union via Finland, are faced with the fact that German imperialism has broken the stalemate on the Western front and let loose an inferno on the peoples of Europe. The small nations of Norway, the Netherlands, Luxembourg, and Belgium have been sacrificed on the false altar of "protection."

Today, those who sold out the national interests of France by building up Hitler by stabbing Spain, have signed a separate peace with Germany and Italy. The people of France now reap the bitter fruit of betrayal by the Daladiers, Blums, Petains, and Weygands. Such a peace is *not just*. It is the kind of peace which imposes the same solution as was imposed on the German people in the Versailles Treaty.

The betrayed French people must conduct a fight on two fronts— against their own rulers who have set up a military dictatorship against them and against the invaders of Germany and Italy.

A virtual dictatorship has been set up in Great Britain. Reaction, led by the Roosevelt Administration, follows the reactionary path of France and Britain, which today vies with Germany as to degree of

---

* Claudia Jones, *Jim Crow in Uniform* (New York: New Age Publishers, 1940).

5

oppression of their peoples. Roosevelt drives America to war with locomotive speed. "National defense" of America is being raised alarmingly at this time to prepare the ground for America's entrance into the war. In all this development, the Soviet Union stands firmly as the strongest force for peace in the world.

Only a few months ago, $500 million needed to finance the American Youth Act for jobs and education for five million unemployed youth couldn't be found, but today $4.5 billion have been found for armaments.

If soberly examined, it becomes clear that these huge sums are not for defense at all. They are calculated to speed America's entry into war on the side of the Allies at the earliest possible moment.

From the Wall Street and Washington circles, coupled always with talk of "defense," is talk also of these places . . . Dutch West Indies . . . British and French West Indies . . . Mexico . . . Canada . . . South America . . . Greenland . . . British and French possessions in the Atlantic. These are the far-flung colonial prizes, in which nearly twenty-five million Negroes live, which are making the yearnings of United States imperialism articulate, and for which they plan to plunge America into the arena of world war.

Who will pay for this mighty war machine?

The people, of course, but the "cost" is said by the President to be "minor."

Already the trade unions are being made the main targets of these burdens. And it is becoming clear that true defense demands greater safeguards if the rights of labor and the people are to be secured against the labor baiters who have now found in the phrases of "defense" the ideal mask for their labor wrecking.

Is it for "defense" that the American people must accept the unbridled rule of the sweatshop, the stark miseries of unemployment, the cruelties of profiteering, the loss and wrecking of all the social gains they have won? Is it for "defense" that the voice of Labor and the people must be gagged by police terrorism and a whole people imprisoned in the shackles of M-Day?[8]

Is it for "defense" that everyone who speaks of liberty and civil rights, for their own opinions, will be dubbed "Fifth Columnists" by the lynchers of American democracy, the real fifth column in America?

Anyone could be dubbed a "fifth columnist" if he or she protests the shameful sabotage of the Senate Committee against the passage of anti-lynching legislation!

True national defense is needed. But more and more it is becoming obvious that *peace is America's best defense!* The real traitors to the nation's security and national defense are the big rich people. The crime of these people is their plans to attack Latin American nations. For the real defense of the country, the American people demand that the government stay out of war. That it advance the living standards of its people, Negro and white. That it refuse all aid to the belligerents. That it feeds America and starves the war. Labor and the people have the united strength to save America from the horrors of M-Day and war.

The newest proposal of the president is for national conscription of all of America's youth—young men and women. This is a military dragnet for America's youth. The plan is for the development of youth as a cheap labor source for the munitions industries and for cannon fodder for Wall Street.

A necessary condition of real national defense is a free and prosperous people. This means an increase, not a decrease in the living standards of the people. This would mean the preservation and enlargement of the democratic liberties of all the people. Under such conditions, the youth of the country, labor, and the working people train for true defense against the enemies of the people—the monopolies, against all policies of military adventures for "protecting" the neighboring colonies or small countries in Latin and South America.

But, national conscription of America's youth, which is based on Roosevelt's policies of shattered neutrality—on a policy of Yankee imperialism for Latin America—cannot but mean a betrayal of America's youth.

This sinister proposal of the President, which should be fought against, more than ever shows the true hand of the Washington government in its plans for war, for slashing the civil liberties and rights of youth, and the working people who ask for peace, jobs, civil liberties, and education.

Peace hangs by a thread!

But you can help keep America out of war by raising your voices high. The youth of America want jobs, not cannon!

Pass the Anti-Lynching Bill!
Keep America Out of War!

—James W. Ford

Jesse Clipper, Negro Hero, 1895–1917

In the heart of the Fifth Ward, center of the segregated Negro residential section in Buffalo, New York, a monument stands erected to the memory of Jesse Clipper, Negro hero, who died in battle in the First World War of 1914–1918.

Jesse Clipper is so honored because of his bravery and his valor. Young Jesse Clipper died believing that he had done his share "to make the world safe for democracy." He must have died happily, too, at the thought that he and his buddies had given their lives "in this war to end all wars"—that the armistice which was signed would be a permanent one. But this belief was a shocking illusion.

Twenty-three years ago, in 1917, three years after President Wilson proclaimed the neutrality of the United States and had implored the citizens to "refrain from taking sides," America, at Wilson's advice, took sides, and Jesse Clipper enlisted.

Jesse Clipper died in battle. He had no chance to weight the aftermath of the war. How could he know, for example, two years later, when it was all over, that the war dead of America together with the rest of the world numbered some twelve million? How could he know that the war had given birth to some twenty-five thousand new millionaires? How could he read the same press which now blatantly confessed that many of the atrocity stories concerning the Belgians weren't true, after all?

No, Jesse Clipper could never know now. Even if he could come to life again, he would probably die again of disillusionment. He would see at a glance, that the very things he fought for and was promised—freedom, equality, opportunity—were still denied his people. He would see the tragedy of Natchez, Mississippi—in which over 240 Negroes died—the pyres of charred bodies which are symbolic of the half-slave, half-free Jim Crow oppression which Negroes in America still suffer from, economically, politically, and socially.

But the thing that would perhaps alarm Jesse most would be the realization that the Second World War was in progress. That reaction did "break faith" with those who sleep in Flanders Field. That already, the youth of three continents, Europe, Africa, and Asia, were in trenches again. That the threat to American liberty and freedom was becoming more real every day, by the studied build-up in the press of America of prejudices, hatred against countries, all under the similar guise "to preserve democracy."

He would hear the laughter of the Wall Street clique while they maneuvered in Congress, making loans and selling arms to belligerents, already cashing in on the blood money of the war. He would see the formation of a "national unity" among men, who only a few months ago were bitter enemies on both domestic and foreign policies. A "unity" designed to take us into war.

Whose War Is It?

The newspapers are saying in our time, some of the things they said in Jesse Clipper's time. They are saying that this war, between two of the major imperialist powers in the world, Great Britain and Germany, is a war "to preserve democracy." They say that it is a "holy crusade" which will decide whether freedom and democracy will forever prevail, or whether force and violence will rule the world.

The newspapers ask you and me to believe this. But how can we believe this when we are aware of the fact that democracy has been a farce to some five hundred thousand enslaved colonials under the domination of English rule? Can this was [sic] give the kind of real democracy which previous centuries did not give? We're sorry if we cannot believe this just because the newspapers say so. No, the colonial peoples, black and white, cannot support this war.

For it is a war that is imperialist in nature, which means that both England and Germany are out to get more territory, out to gain more influence in international affairs, are out to have a showdown as to who can exploit and enslave more peoples, small nations as well.

Colonial Folk against the War

British imperialist "democracy" in action, besides, has in each previous war made things *worse*, not better for the colonial peoples.

While pretending to be fighting for the rights of small nations and for democracy, the British ruling class denies to its colonies the most elementary democratic rights.

That is why the progressive forces in the West Indies take the stand as indicated in the editorial columns of the *Barbados Observer*:

> We colonial workers have not forgotten the last World
> War, when all kinds of promises were made to us . . .
> Therefore we are determined never again to allow our-
> selves to be used as cannon fodder by *either camp* in the
> war. (My emphasis —C. J.)

Some apologists for British imperialism argue that, under British rule, Negro colonials have fared better as compared with their status under German rule, and for this reason, beginning with the premise that cither side must win in the end, it is better for Negroes to support British imperialism in this conflict. Mr. W. A. Domingo, British export-import Negro merchant, openly supports this proposition.

This argument is fraught with danger for two reasons. First, it is a vicious acceptance of the status of Negroes as inferiors *who must be ruled*, regardless. Secondly, and perhaps more important, it is a statement designed to lull the actions of Negroes, who want peace, not war, and to offset their attempts to raise their voices and act to halt the war, now.

Besides, it is also a false premise, when it is assumed that either side *must* win. For the ever-present desire for liberty on the part of Negro colonials will never be achieved through a change of masters, both of whom are interested not in the freedom, but in the further enslavement of them. Only through organization, education, and struggle against reaction, against war profits, against reaction's drive on civil liberties, under the guise of war emergencies, can this new threat to the ultimate freedom of the colonial peoples be met. Only the abolition of imperialism, of the whole system of the war makers, will guarantee peace and security for the peoples.

Who knows that yet Ethiopia may not rise again soon in revolt against both Anglo-French imperialism and Italo-German imperialism, showing the path to all colonial peoples of Africa to freedom and liberation from imperialism as a whole? This is the real choice!

Lindbergh—Spouse of the Morgan Fortune

Sometimes the reactionaries themselves let the cat out of the bag as to the true situation.

Take the speech made by Colonel Charles A. Lindbergh, the lawful spouse of the fortune of Morgan, decorated by, and friend of Field Marshal Goering of Germany, for instance.

The speech is entitled simply "Aviation, Geography, and Race," delivered over a national network and reprinted in the *Reader's Digest* of 1939. He says:

> . . . Western nations are again at war, a war likely to be more prostrating than any in the past, a war in which the White race is bound to lose, and the others bound to gain, a war which may easily lead our civilization through more Dark Ages if it survives at all.

Lindbergh then goes on to warn that his "civilization" is menaced by "the infiltration of inferior blood."

It is clear that Mr. Lindbergh feels that the war is a white man's war—or more correctly—a war for white supremacy. That it is a war which, unless his Western nations win, will mean world domination by darker peoples, which will then be a civilization equivalent to the Dark Ages. Obviously, civilization as he sees it does not include the black man.

What contribution can "inferior blood" make? Ask George Washington Carver, Negro scientist and inventor of one hundred or more uses of the peanut, for instance. Ask Marian Anderson, outstanding Negro contralto. Ask Paul Robeson. Ask Joe Louis, who tore down the myth of "Aryan" supremacy. Ask all the millions of heavily pigmented people throughout the world, whose sweat and blood have been given for centuries to build up empires, profits, and wealth.

They have even contributed their "inferior blood" time and again in defense of democracy because they believed the cause was theirs, also. Ask the dead who fought with Crispus Attucks in Concord for American independence. Or the Negro soldiers who died on the battlefields with Jackson in New Orleans. Or the War of 1812. Ask a few Negro Civil War veterans who fought with Sherman. Ask the Negro dead who lie in Flanders Field.

The False Theory of a White Man's War

Prof. Rayford Logan of Howard University and Elmer Carter of *Opportunity* are bearers of a theory of ill-repute, the theory of the "white man's war." The fact remains that Negroes comprise a good bit of the cannon fodder for Europe's war-makers.

In our own communities, since the war, the bubble of the false theory of a "white man's war" quickly explodes amidst the rising cost of living, the corresponding lowering of income as a result of the Roosevelt war and hunger budget. The Negro population are delivered not only as cannon fodder, but the acute brunt of the war crisis is first felt by them. The falsification of actual fact as shown here is for one main purpose: to weaken the domestic front of Negro and white unity, to lull the Negro population against fighting the imperialist war, and to slander the white working population who want and have no part in this war. The theory must be fought against, for it is both anti-Negro and anti–working class.

The Administration Gives a War Deal to the People

That the New Deal has become a war deal is an ever-conscious growing fact on the minds of everybody. The few concessions of appointments of Negroes to hitherto unheld Federal, state, and city posts; [and] the integration of Negroes into the Federal program, in theatres, labor, and social service have been forsaken by Roosevelt.

Only two hundred thousand Negro workers are now left on the Works Progress Administration (WPA) rolls as a result of the Woodrum amendments and the Roosevelt war and hunger budget.

If the United States intends to keep out of war, why the huge armaments program as against social betterment for the people of America? And what kind of security can the people have, when even the temporary security of WPA, National Youth Administration (NYA), Public Works Administration (PWA) is taken away from them? The President's message offers neither peace nor security to the people of America!

The demagogic slogan of "national unity" means that Roosevelt has been promoted to full leadership of the rulers of America and they are nationally united against the people, to make more profits, by starvation, by clamping down on the civil rights of the people, on the basis of war.

The Anti-Lynching Bill—Touchstone of American Democracy

In urging unity of the nation behind his budget message, the President ended on the note that now is the time for everyone to come together, forget past quarrels, and so establish once and for all that democracy as a system still remains unchallenged as the best way of life yet devised by man.

For whom? might be the query of the Negro. How can he forget past quarrels when Negroes in the South still remain disenfranchised? How can he forget past quarrels when in the heart of the nation's capital, prejudice against the Negro abounds?

Only recently, at the premiere opening of *Abe Lincoln in Illinois*, Negro citizens in Washington picketed the theatre because Negroes are not allowed to mingle with whites in the unwritten laws of American democracy.

High in the annals of achievements of American progress for 1939 is the passage of the Anti-Lynching Bill in the House of Representatives for the first time. But reaction in the person of Representative Rankin of Mississippi recorded the typical yearly slander when he shouted in the House:

"You are trying to placate a few *nigger* communists who are infesting the gallery."

"Nigger Communists ... " And in this slander, the Tory Representative Rankin paid unwilling tribute to the Negro Communists who have, together with white Communists, fought for the passage of the Anti-Lynching Bill, fought against distortions of the role of Negroes in American history, fought against every manifestation of prejudice where the Negro was concerned.

Representative Rankin rants with the Bilbos, Ellenders, Cotton Ed Smiths, because his idea of democracy is being challenged by progress.

As it was challenged by Angelo Herndon, Negro Communist, who led the light for Negro and white unemployed workers in the heart of the deep South, in Georgia.

As it was challenged and brought to a new high by Ben Davis, young Communist editor of the *Daily Worker*, who, in the Senate caucus hearings upset the dignity of the "Democratic reactionaries" and "Republican hypocrites" by exposing the truth.

The President has never once raised his voice in support of the Anti-Lynching Bill. It is still the touchstone of American democracy, and it will require even greater mass support if it is to become law. Current reactionary lies to the effect that lynchings no longer take place, therefore there is no need for an Anti-Lynching Bill, must also be answered. In the year 1939, twenty "silent lynchings," the new technique of reaction, minus the mob, took place. Since 1940, already five lynchings have occurred. This—in face of the reactionaries' lie that this is a "lynchless year." That is why the voice of progress must be raised ever louder and clearer to Pass the Anti-Lynching Bill!

The 1940 Elections

Negroes constitute a balance of power in most of the major cities of the nation. Already there is being recorded in the press bids for their support by both the Democratic and Republican parties—twin parties of reaction. These old traditional major parties have today less of a division on real issues and political currents in American life, than in any former period of their existence. On a domestic scale both the Republican and Democratic parties fully agree to scrap all labor and social legislation as much as possible, to militarize labor, to drastically curb civil liberties, to lower the standard of living of all the people. They are both agreed on dubbing peace lovers and fighters for democracy "fifth columnists," because they both want to bring about America's entry in the present war. The real fifth columnists can be most easily recognized, because it is they who most openly sow the seeds of race prejudice, the seeds of Negro-baiting, or if they don't do it openly, they are in secret agreement with those who do. The leadership of both parties contains the real fifth columnists.

But Negroes cannot agree to such a program, for the Negro people want peace, want to keep America out of war. The Negro people want jobs, economic security, civil liberties, passage of social legislation, such as the Anti-Lynching Bill.

No, the answer is not in a return to support of either of these parties. The answer lies in independent political action of the people in 1940, aligned with labor, as expressed recently by Earl Browder when he called for a People's Platform for Jobs, Peace, Civil Liberties.

Such independent action will make the people's answer clear against the war and hunger budget of the Roosevelt Administration, against the policies of the Republicans who in effect give support to his policies.

Such independent action can be a powerful force for support of progressive congressional candidates regardless of their party labels.

This, coupled with day-to-day actions against America's entry into war, for peace, for social legislation, for an advanced standard of living, against step-by-step involvement policies of the Roosevelt

Administration, can be the means for making 1940 be symbolic of the people's will for peace and prosperity.

The only party which fights for the interests of all the people is the Communist Party. The only party which truly fights for the interests of the Negroes is the Communist Party. Vote Communist! Vote for Browder and Ford, its standard-bearers! For jobs, peace, and civil liberties! Vote Communist!

Historical Comparisons of Two Presidents

In 1917, too, the people of America had to make a choice on how best to keep America out of war.

Then, as now, Wall Street's profit-making men, under the guise of free trade, were pouring money and supplies into "little Belgium." Loans were followed with human security.

The recent historical analogy is "Little Finland." Remember the headlines. For months the typewriter generals in Helsinki issued thousands of dollars' worth of ink, paper, and type, in an effort to create the impression that here was a moral cause to be rightfully defended. Roosevelt and Hoover urged its defense with loans, with arms, with a huge "Relief" campaign.

Today, there is peace in Finland. Today, the same press which threw you off your balance candidly admits its lies. Why the lies? Why the fakery?

It was because the newspapers spoke the aims of the imperialists whom Roosevelt leads, who would drag America into war. There is peace in Finland because of the peace policy of the Soviet Union, which aims to defend its own borders, which aims to limit the sphere of World War and establish peace. There is peace because the Finnish generals have become convinced that they were being used as pawns of the Allies against Germany.

Herbert Hoover, Chief Egg in the Scramble of Finnish Relief

The truth about the Finnish-Soviet conflict is most clearly understood when we look at the person who raised the most noise about it. Remember Hoover of "apple a day" fame? Well, Herbert Hoover was the chief egg in the scramble of Finnish relief. Hoover, who couldn't help the millions of Americans, Negro and white who starved while he was President, headed the committee which raised loans and contributions for the "relief" of the Finns. What of the millions of Americans who are in need of relief today, Mr. Hoover?

But Hoover was well interested in this cause. Hoover, together with Roosevelt and the imperialists of America and England, was responsible for egging Finland on to perform aggressive acts on the Finnish border which resulted in the death of Red Army patrols there.

Yes, Hoover hopes to add to his fame his humanitarian efforts for the rich of Finland. But since we're talking of fame, let us not forget to give Hoover his due. He has one outstanding action to his credit, not often told.

Hoover may have sent your grandmother, or my aunt on a segregated freighter which was really a cattle boat to France. You remember the Gold Star mothers, who were Negroes, went over in a cattle boat provided by Hoover to see the graves of their dead sons.

Wasn't This a War for Democracy?

Thousands of sons of Negro mothers were also led to believe that joining the Army, fighting for Uncle Sam, would help to win them freedom. For after all, wasn't this a war for democracy?

It was no wonder then, that in 1917, when an NAACP editorial called for support of Negro Americans in the newly declared war, that Negro America, as in the past, "closed ranks" in support of American democracy.

Stories of Jim Crow treatment of Negro men in arms seep through even the most conservative journals. No matter what their qualifications, Negroes were given the most disagreeable jobs. Negro professionals were taken out of their ratings and given jobs as laborers, while white doctors were assigned to Negro troops.

Jim Crow in Uniform

Did you know that Negro soldiers in uniform were stoned, jeered, and mobbed on the streets? The Eighth Illinois, on way to Texas, suffered such treatment. When the Ninety-Second Division, at Camp Funston, Texas, refused to recognize the Jim Crow line at local theatres, the notorious Bulletin 35 was issued by the white commanding officer which read, *"Don't go where your presence is not desired. White men made the Division and they can break it just as easily if it becomes a troublemaker."*

It is a historical fact that in Houston, Texas, where the Twenty-Fourth Infantry was stationed, members of the provost guard had to endure the humiliation of going about their duties unarmed. Local white policemen disregarded their authority constantly. The famed "Houston Affair," which resulted in the killing of eighteen persons, is another example of Jim Crow in uniform. Court martial proceedings, which followed this incident, without War Department review, resulted in the hanging of thirteen (not even granted the usual military death by shooting), forty-one got life, four short terms, and five were acquitted.

The nationwide protests which followed this, and other "troublemaker" actions, forced the Wilson Administration to pass a statute which declared that soldiers were not to be executed without War Department review. But this was not the only verdict resulting from Houston. The people also gave one.

Significantly, many white soldiers from the North protested such treatment of their brother soldiers.

Anti-War Sentiment Among Negroes

But these protests only climaxed the great anti-war sentiments and agitation for Negro rights which punctuated the response of the Negro people to broken promises almost from the start of the war.[9]

Most of the historical books written about the Negroes' participation in the first World War give the impression that nowhere was there any anti-war sentiment expressed among the Negroes. This omission is designed to keep the false halo of complacency about the Negroes, wishfully expressed by reactionary historians.

Before America's entry into war, for instance, in 1915, great protest developed around the premiere of *Birth of a Nation*. Even the reactionaries argued—for their own purposes, it is true—that this play developed antagonisms between whites and Negroes. Already then, preparations for America's entry into war were on the way. Today, *Gone with the Wind* typifies the same, though subtler, slander of the Negro people and is designed to whip up the war spirit of hysteria and race prejudice.

One of the most significant protests, recorded in the *Negro Year Book of 1918–1919*, was the parade of some five thousand Negroes along Fifth Avenue in New York, held on July 28, 1917, in demonstration of the indignities which Negroes suffered in this war "to make the world safe for democracy." The parade bore such banners, with slogans: "Make America Safe for Democracy," "Taxation Without Representation Is Tyranny," "America Has Lynched Without Trial 2,876 Negroes in Thirty-One Years and Not a Single Murderer Has Suffered," "Put the Spirit of Christ in the Making and Execution of the Laws."

Further evidence of anti-war sentiments among the Negro people is unwittingly brought out in a letter written to George Creel, chairman of Committee on Public Information in Washington, by Trumbull White, of the Investors' Public Service in New York, informing him that:

> ... The big Negro colony in Harlem is badly infected with a series of rumors arousing great distress and disquiet . . . . The rumors are of various kinds . . . . One is that the Negro regiments are being terribly abused by their white officers. Another is that the Negro regiments are being discriminated against in the distribution of troops where the danger and suffering will be the greatest . . . . Another is that already more than two hundred Negro soldiers with eyes gouged out and arms cut off, after having been captured by Germans and then turned loose by them to wander back to the American lines have been sent home to this country and are now in the Columbia Base Hospital, No. 1, in the Bronx . . . .

He concludes his letter by making two recommendations. One, that a permit be arranged for a Negro preacher, doctor, and "intelligent" Negro woman from Harlem be sent to the hospital for complete inspection. And the other that, preferably Irvin Cobb, lecture in Harlem on the subject of Negro troops in France since **"Cobb has the Southern affection for the Negro and could do the thing right."**

It was obvious that things were not right either at home or in France and the Negroes were answering back with protest and signs of discontent.

Other outstanding examples of anti-war sentiment would include the work of William Monroe Trotter, progressive Negro editor of the *Boston Guardian* who, during the war, fought in his columns against America's participation in the war and the treatment of Negroes. Among the outstanding present-day leaders who protested against the injustices was James W. Ford, now an outstanding leader of the Communist Party, its present candidate for Vice President of the United States, then with the Eighth Brigade of the Ninety-Second Division in France in 1918. And foremost against the imperialist war was Earl Browder, now general secretary of the Communist Party of United States, and its candidate for President, who went to Leavenworth prison because he spoke against the war.

Commissioning of Officers and 'High Blood Pressure' Removal

Have you ever heard of Col. Charles E. Young, highest ranking Negro West Point graduate? But, even though it was before our time, you probably didn't hear of him, because he was suddenly retired, supposedly because of "high blood pressure" when America entered the last World War.

He was returned to active service soon after. You know, that after once having been retired, you need not necessarily be considered for promotion.

It is to be wondered if all the "high blood pressure" wasn't that of certain super-patriotic gentlemen, which rose at the thought of a Negro officer being promoted to a high position in their army over the heads of many white officers. Equality is at a premium even for black men in most armies.

Most of the 1,200 Negro officers who were commissioned during the war were in Jim Crow regiments. It was the pressure of the Negro and white progressives against quartering of troops in the South which led to the establishment of the first Negro officers' training camp at Ft. Des Moines, Iowa, from which 275 Negro officers were commissioned.

Such was the treatment accorded Negro men in arms at home in this "war for democracy." What could they expect fighting for American democracy abroad?

Men of Color Abroad

Negro troops in France numbered a small percentage of the American Expeditionary Forces (AEF), but they furnished 75 percent of the AEF's labor supply. Given stevedore jobs, in the main, they were used to do road building, loading and unloading ships, and cars, building depots, reburying the dead, and detonating scattered explosives.

The Negro troops who fought, however, were outstanding. The Eighth Illinois (part of Ninety-Second Division), officered by Negroes, received more citations and Croix de Guerres than any other regiment in France.

'Secret Information' and Slander Against Negroes in France

Carter G. Woodson, in his book *Negroes In The World War* exposes certain "Secret Information Concerning Black American Troops," August 7, 1918, issued in a document by American reactionaries in France. He writes:

> ... The Negroes were branded as a menace of degeneracy which could be escaped only by an impassable gulf established between the two races.

> This was an urgent need because of the tendency of the blacks to commit the loathsome crime of assault, as they said Negroes had already been doing in France. The French was therefore cautioned not to treat the Negroes with familiarity and indulgence, which are matters of grevious concern to Americans and an affront to their national policy. The Americans, it continued, were afraid that the blacks might thereby be inspired with undesirable aspirations. It was carefully explained that although the black man is a citizen of the United States, he is regarded by whites as an inferior with whom relations of business and service only are possible; and that the black is noted for his want of intelligence, lack of discretion, and lack of civic and professional conscience. The French army was then advised to prevent intimacy between French officers and black officers, not to eat with them nor shake hands nor seek to talk or meet with them outside the requirements of military service.

> They were asked also not to commend too highly the black American troops in the presence of white Americans . . . . The French were urged also to restrain the native cantonment population from spoiling the Negroes, as white

Americans become greatly incensed at any deep expression of intimacy between white women and black men.

The Returned Negro Soldier

The Noble Sissies, the John Henrys, all the Negroes who returned came back to learn that the percentage of lynchings had increased dining the war years. Total ninety-six: thirty-eight in 1917, fifty-eight in 1918! Five were Negro women! When five Negro soldiers were lynched in uniform, the last remnant of belief faded for hundreds of returned Negro soldiers and their families.

The post-war crisis, causing race riots, because reaction played Negro against white, native against foreign-born, lynched the returned Negro soldier economically.

To his great surprise, after fighting "for democracy abroad" the returned Negro soldier found it still had to be fought for at home. Democracy had to be won for Negroes too. Bitter, yet undaunted, he began to learn that it could only be won with the help of other workers. Negro and white workers began to organize while rebuilding the wastes of the war here at home.

Just and Unjust Wars

Today, with the Second Imperialist War raging in Europe and Asia, Negro youth face almost a similar situation as that preceding America's entry into the last World War.

However, unlike Jesse Clipper, we have a chance to contrast the experiences of Negroes during the First World War, and also in wars since then.

All wars, for example, are not fought for a false democracy as was the First World War for empire, or the present war between Germany and England. Didn't we support Ethiopia? It was because they were genuinely fighting for democracy, for their independence, against the intervention and brutal aggression of Fascist Italy. At that time the governments of France and England and the United States did nothing to stop Mussolini's brutal aggression.

Another such genuinely democratic war was the war of the Spanish people against the fascist Franco and his cronies, Hitler and Mussolini.

That is why the returned Negro and white youth speak only with pride of their service across in Spain. Ask such men as Walter Garland, who rose to the rank of lieutenant in that army. Ask the brave young Ethiopian fighter who fought in Spain "to get the murderer, Mussolini, in his lair." Ask Sterling Rochester, Negro machine-gunner and hero.

Today in China, Chinese people for over two and a half years have been heroically fighting a genuine war for democracy against Japanese imperialism, back by 80 percent of American products.

These are wars of national liberation. These wars are modern versions of the type of wars that Toussaint L'Ouverture fought for the independence of the black thousands in Haiti.

Enemies of Peace

There are many enemies of peace. There are those who cry peace and simultaneously stir up racial hatred and intolerance. There are those who cry "civil liberties for all" and proceed to deny to Communists and others their civil rights. Where was Dies in the case of Angelo Herndon? Or the Scottsboro boys? He has been a Congressman for some twenty-two years now.

We can record many instances of the rise of anti-Negro violence, to a higher pitch today. Only recently from South Carolina came reports of several vicious attacks on Negro citizens exercising their constitutional right to vote.

Yes, the KKK rides again with *Gone With the Wind* in the saddle.

But anti-Negro violence is limited not alone to the South. For over two years, John Williams, twenty-three-year-old Brooklyn Negro youth, was confined to prison on a trumped-up charge of rape, despite the fact that the decision was twice set aside by the Appellate Division of the Supreme Court.

The jury, which did not have a single Negro on it, found John Williams guilty and he was sentenced to from seven and a half to fifteen years.

At the second trial the presiding judge was the anti-Negro, anti-labor Justice Peter J. Brancato. In passing sentence, the judge declared: "*I would give him twenty years if I could. Remember she is a white woman.*"

On June 17, as a result of the mass fight against this northern "Scottsboro Case," John Williams was released.

This is a major victory for civil liberties of Negroes and for that matter, for all progressives today, in face of reaction's drive to war, led by the Roosevelt Administration.

That is why the reactionary District Attorney O'Dwyer of Brooklyn met the delegation of the Communist Party and Young Communist League, who brought ten thousand signatures to him, demanding the release of Williams, with the words:

Millions of American boys will shed their blood before this war is over, and there will be plenty of "black boys" too.

It is clear that the fight for civil liberties is inherently connected with the fight to keep America out of the imperialist war.

Just imagine what such action would mean on a national scale against the war. Remember reaction wants a divided people in order to drive more quickly to war!

Fight the War Every Inch of the Way!

We don't want to wait until the war is upon us. This was the mistake which the youth made in 1914. Whether it is a question of the high cost of living, whether it is a question of sale of arms and planes, whether it is a question of loans to the belligerents, to foreign registry, or attempts of British propagandists, on "visits" to America who are trying to sell us their cause, whether it is the apologists who speak for British imperialism while invoking the good name of the colonial people, whether it is the newspapers who would feed us a blind pro-Ally allegiance, we must fight the war-makers every inch of the way!

The young dead that lie in Flanders Field are telling us every day, "Don't Raise Another Generation of Poppy Sellers!" "Fight the War Every Inch of the Way." Young Jesse Clipper is telling us "Keep alive to get a job, to marry, to raise a family!" "Keep alive to demand passage of the American Youth Act, which would bring permanent federal aid to youth!" "Keep alive to free the four Scottsboro boys!" "Keep alive by fighting the war profiteers!" "Keep alive to get the Anti-Lynching and Geyer Poll Tax Repeal Bills passed!"

Young People Against the War

As a matter of fact, young people are already doing some of these things. All the major youth organizations have gone on record against the war as an imperialist war. The American Youth Congress, the American

Student Union, the United Student Peace Committee, and the Southern Negro Youth Congress have taken such a stand in their resolutions.

These anti-war resolutions of youth and of the Negro people are but reflections of the broad anti-war sentiments among the whole American people.

In Harlem, South Side of Chicago, and other communities, young Negro people have been active in declaring that they want no part of the European war. They have specifically pointed to the need for conducting a fight for civil rights, for jobs, democracy, and peace. This is the only war that they are interested in, as was so ably demonstrated in the historical Third National Negro Congress when they rejected the path of the former progressive, A. Phillip Randolph to choose support—of reaction by supporting the Roosevelt Administration, by supporting anti-Soviet schemes, by preaching segregation for the Negro—*and chose instead* the path toward working with labor, through Labor's Non-Partisan League, who has now agreed to make passage of the Anti-Lynching Bill the first job of labor!

What You Can Do

You can help spread the truth as to what kind of a war is being fought today. You can help to educate young people to the fact that the Roosevelt Administration and the Republican Parties, twin parties of reaction, are dragging America to war. You can help keep America out of war.

You will find that you are not alone in doing this, for right in your own community, you will find an organization, willing and ready to help you achieve this.

This organization is the Young Communist League, an organization of and for American young people, who look forward to a better future. There is no future in Flanders Field. All youth, regardless of race, creed, or color, belong to and are equals in this organization.

The Young Communist League fights for the interests of the toiling youth and the working class. It fights against imperialist war. It fights against the discrimination of Negro youth. It fights for the economic betterment of Negro youth for jobs and security.

The League opposes all measures aimed at the militarization of the youth. It opposes the militarization of the Civil Conservation Corps

(CCC) camps, the extension of the Reserve Officers' Training Corps (ROTC), especially on a compulsory basis: the proposed increase in the Army and National Guard, the M-Day plan. Its guiding slogan is:

Not a Man, Not a Cent, Not a Gun for Imperialist War Preparations!

We believe that our ideals can best be achieved by socialism, by establishing a new social order in which the working people will own and control all the vast natural resources and means of production and use them for the benefit of all the people, instead of the few.

The Soviet Union—Home of Free Peoples

Look here, fellows and girls, this system called capitalism, with all of its talk of free enterprise is free, all right, but for the bankers and Wall Street, for the German bankers, for the Bank of England, for the French bankers. Can you dream what it would mean to have the worry of a job eliminated? What if it was law that your security, your job, was guaranteed? Then you could finish high school, college. Then you could marry, raise a family, get that coat, that radio, that library you always wanted. This is what the youth of the Soviet Union have because they live in a socialist society. That is why the bankers want to take it away from them.

All roads are open to youth of the Soviet Union.

There is no national or racial oppression in the Soviet Union and in the USSR people of all nationalities, all colors, live as free and equal peoples.

All young people are guaranteed free education in the USSR to the age of eighteen. Equal opportunity exists for all.

For millions of us darker peoples, for oppressed people throughout the world, the Soviet Union stands as a beacon of light, hope, truth!

While the majority of people in America today are not for socialism, they are willing to work in common with those who similarly desire such things as jobs, security, democracy and peace. That is why we Young Communists stand together with the majority of American youth—Negro and white, who desire above all *PEACE*, so that they can pursue the American dream of "life, liberty, and the pursuit of happiness."

Negro America remembers the false promises of the last war. They are saying, "The Yanks Are Not Coming."

The dream we mentioned earlier can become a reality. In the course of the struggle for these things, we will learn that these can only be achieved and kept in a more permanent society—socialism.

We support no dreams of war abroad. We go to the wars at home. For jobs and civil liberties. For democracy and freedom!

Jesse Clipper, Negro hero, died believing he was doing his share to make the world safe for democracy. If Jesse Clipper were alive today, he would again fight for democracy. He would do it, however, not by following the loans of Wall Street to another Flanders Field, but by fighting for jobs, for relief, better housing, better health conditions—security for the people. We must make the world safe for democracy by making democracy safe for America. This is Jesse Clipper's dream now. We, the living, take our stand today on the side of *Life and Peace!*

QUIZ:

Since Great Britain and the United States are imperialist powers, how can we support them in this war? Since the Negro people suffer great discrimination in the USA, should we not first clear up this situation before we fight Hitler abroad?

WEEKLY REVIEW
SEPTEMBER 16, 1941

What is the situation today? All nations and peoples are menaced by the threat of Hitler fascism. Unless the Hitler monster is crushed completely, mankind, all oppressed peoples, face a return to the era of barbarism.

Why is this so? Because Hitler's attack on the Soviet Union represents a bid for world conquest which, if achieved, would decide the issue of world power in favor of Hitler and fascism. It would destroy the USA's independence.

This, the character of the war has basically changed, making all those who wage a fight against Nazi Germany today, fighters for a just cause.

Yes, it is true that the imperialists are still imperialists and that they retain their unjust aims. But the unjust aims present in the situation are subjective factors. The dominant character of the war is that it is a just war. There are no "pure" wars. In the unjust imperialist war, prior to the Nazi attack upon the Soviet Union, there were many just causes—the just fight of the Ethiopian, Grecian, and Yugoslav peoples.

But these peoples were small powers, and moreover, were used as fuel to fire the cause of the imperialist power. So today there are unjust causes in a predominantly just war. It is necessary of course, to be vigilant concerning the unjust aims of the imperialists. But they can only be offset to the extent that we understand that the main enemy today, of all nations and peoples, is Hitler fascism.

How can this enemy be defeated? Through unity of all forces who are interested, regardless of their motives, in the defeat of Hitler and Hitlerism. Only through the building of a gigantic movement of united peoples and nations will this be achieved. That is why we urge full unlimited aid to the Soviet Union, Great Britain, and all other nations fighting Hitler fascism. That is why we support the demands of the British people for the creation of a Western Front through the collaboration of Britain and the United States as the imperative need of the hour. Nothing would be more dangerous than to accept the argument which urges that we wait to see whether the imperialists are sincere about their present policies. Why? Because the threat is an immediate one. And because the only way we can guarantee correct policies is to build a gigantic movement of united peoples which can press for the full development and achievement of these policies.

Since the Negro people suffer great discrimination in the USA, should we not first clear up this situation before we fight Hitler abroad?

What is the main danger which faces the Negro people today? It is the danger which faces all oppressed people—all peoples of the world—the threat of Hitler fascism. The Negro people have always been overwhelmingly anti-fascist. It is precisely because they do suffer from great injustices that they understand perhaps better than any other section of the population the significance of this titanic struggle.

Why? Because a victory for fascism would mean a victory for the most reactionary forces in the world. It would mean the strengthening of the false Nazi theories of "race" superiority, of destruction of so-called "inferior peoples."

It would mean strengthening the lynchers in the United States. It would be a victory for the appeasers—the Lindberghs, Hoovers, Wheelers, those who hypocritically urge America to attend to their own problems first, who post as friends of the Negro people, but whose records show that they are the worst enemies of the Negro people, the advocates of racism.

No! The path to the alleviation of these injustices is a single path. To be concerned only with the problems at home is to fail to see the woods for the trees. A victory for Hitler would mean a defeat for the Negro people, while a victory for the anti-Hitler forces can only result in the unfolding of more democracy for the Negro people too. It is only through the unity of the people, Negro and white, through the defeat of Hitler fascism—this modern enslaver of humanity, that we

will be able to devote our full efforts to the complete alleviation of the
many evils which confront us at home.

This does not mean that we do not continue the struggle for full
equality for the Negro people. The fight for full economic, political,
and social equality of one-tenth of America's population is part of the
crucial struggle to defeat Hitler.

QUIZ:

*Is not the question of the struggle for Negro rights equally an
important issue as the defeat of Hitler?*

WEEKLY REVIEW
NOVEMBER 18, 1941

When Communists and anti-fascists proclaim that the main issue
today is the defeat of Hitler, they state what corresponds to the facts.
In saying this, however, we Communists have never and do not now
deny the important struggle for rights of the Negro people. How?
Today, the main danger that the American people face as a whole is
Hitler and Hitlerism. Hitler victorious would exterminate the Negro
people, as is proven in the case of the Jewish people and innocent
hostages murdered by Hitler's storm troops. Therefore, every vestige
of individual rights, of freedom and liberty, is threatened by Hitler's
drive for world conquest.

The Negro people have always won advancement and victory
through allying themselves with other peoples. This is true in every
crisis that America has faced. Therefore, today, the struggle of the
Negro people is part of the struggle against the main enemy of all
peoples—Hitler and Hitlerism. The Dred Scott decision ruled upon
by Judge Taney, represented the ideology which proclaimed that
Negroes have no rights which whites are bound to respect. This
ideology never took form because the democratic forces in America
together with the Negro people rejected it. But this ideology threatens
us today and the source is Hitler.

The Quislings of America, Lindbergh, and Hoover and Co., who
consciously state to the American people that their problems at home
are equally important, and more that they should tend to these problems first, are themselves the exponents of this Hitler ideology. A
Hitler victory would be the basis for making this ideology the law of

31

the land. It would retard the Negro people many years and would be the basis for reenslavement in a world where the predominant ideology would be that of Hitler's.

That is why the struggle of the Negro people today is a part of the struggle against Hitler. It is only in recognition of this fact that the Negro people and their allies can more successfully press for a solution of the problems today. In this manner victories can and will be won. Because the struggle for Negro rights cannot continue to advance unless Hitler is destroyed.

(Ed. Note: Our Quiz column has been answering questions for many weeks. Claudia Jones informs us that she can answer many more. Do you have any questions you want answered? Have your friends stumped you recently with a difficult question? This is to inform you that we welcome all questions. Don't be bashful. Sit down and write us a letter. You'll get the answer.)

WHERE DO THE COLONIES STAND?

WEEKLY REVIEW
MARCH 10, 1942

When Generalissimo Chiang Kai-shek appealed to India for "utmost exertion" in the cause of freedom and urged Britain immediately to give India "real political power," he again emphasized the character of this war as a just, progressive national war, and at the same time pointed to a practical measure for winning the war.

For it is indeed a critical moment in the history of civilization, to use the words of the Generalissimo. The growing threat of the Axis powers to the colonial peoples in the Far East and throughout the world have aroused a flood of questions and discussion as to what stand these peoples will take. Not only is their position vital but the homes and lives of more than two-thirds of the world's population are at stake in these countries.

What is the position of the national and colonial peoples in this peoples' war for victory over fascism?

First, it must be stated, that the main aspirations of the national and colonial peoples for freedom and liberation are today similar to all nations and peoples. All are threatened with national enslavement from the Axis powers. Hence, any correct approach to the question must flow from the realization that the national and colonial peoples are a vital factor in this war. More than that. This is a national war. A war for the liberation of all peoples and nations, a war to preserve and extend the freedom of those nations threatened with enslavement by the Axis powers. It is a war in which the United Nations have pledged that advancement will come for all peoples. And the national and colonial peoples, the world over, are in motion, correctly viewing this war as a war in which advancement must come for them. What the Indian, Chinese, Asiatic peoples, like all other peoples, want out of this war is their freedom.

This is likewise known by the Japanese fascists and the Hitlerites. And these enemies of all mankind are busily appealing to the colored peoples of the world, offering them free "gifts," trying to prevent them from uniting in the war against fascism.

Colonial Peoples Vital

The key question for the United Nations today is the proper integration of the effort of all anti-fascist forces to out-produce, out-fight, and defeat the fascist powers. The war is raging in regions, inhabited by victims of colonial exploitation. The native populations of these countries in the far east were only second cousins in any contract, which concerned the welfare of their own nation, their own lives.

In the specific case of India, directly threatened today, by Axis invasion from both Japan and Fascist Germany, the problem is that of unifying four hundred million people. India abounds in natural resources. In 1939, India turned out over 3 million tons of iron and steel, including 1.6 million tons of pig iron of which over 600,000 tons were exported. It has important coal deposits, cement, paper, wool and textile, and shipbuilding industries. India is strategically located, both with regard to the Southwest Pacific and the Middle East, and can thus serve as a nearby and key arsenal to a vast sector of the world front.

Why is India's participation so important? Because added to this, the Indian people are a powerful, anti-fascist force, having a powerful liberation movement, headed by Jawaharlal Nehru, a force which can have tremendous consequences for the victory of the United Nations. This can be achieved only if the Indian people are fully mobilized, only if the industrial resources of India are stimulated, only if this is accompanied by the recognition of the rights and liberties of its working class and its people, by working out steps to meet the independence demands of the All India National Congress, for a greater role within the cooperative war effort of the United Nations.

One of the main lessons of the Far Eastern war front is that the United Nations must immediately effect the mobilization of the colonial peoples to fight for the defense of their homes and land against

Axis aggression. We have but to look at the struggles of the Filipino peoples in the heroic battles of Bataan to illustrate the point, and if we look to Malay we also see the weaknesses of their inadequate participation, namely, the fact that they were not properly armed or sufficiently mobilized in the fight.

Need for Home Rule

This is one of the great lessons of this global war. The present security and future of India, Burma, [and] the Dutch East Indies, which are in the very path of Axis aggression and who are now preparing their defenses against attack, lie with the closest cooperation with the United Nations. And in terms of practical measures to draw in these populations into active, enthusiastic struggle, it is necessary that the United Nations grant greater autonomy and self rule, a greater recognition to these people who are capable of playing a heroic role in defeating the Axis in the Pacific and Middle Eastern state areas.

Pearl Buck, famous writer and champion of the Asiatic peoples, in a recent speech before the Book and Author club, raised sharply the question of racial prejudices as disastrous to the present and future of the war.

In the same spirit as Chiang Kai-shek, she showed the need for a real freedom for all peoples with mutual responsibility demanded of all to fulfill its conditions. Nor can we postpone such decisions for freedom, states Miss Buck, saying, "Let's win this war first!"

This is certainly in line with the need to utilize practical democratic measures to win this democratic war abandoning the old colonial policies of regarding these peoples as inferior.

However, Miss Buck erred when she stated concerning the loyalty of the American Negro people, that "the deepest loyalties may not be national." Even if it was her aim of shaking up her audience, of sharply putting the issue to them, such an approach is wrong, and only adds confusion.

What is the issue? Is it that the Negro people are not loyal to their nation? On the contrary. To assert this is to say in fact that the Negro people do not understand their national interest in this war, as do other Americans. It is a question the loyalty of the Negro Americans whose whole history has proved that in every crisis in American democracy, the Negroes have been among the most loyal supporters.

It is to confuse the correct and proper demands which Negros have today—for integration into war efforts, with their basic desire to win the war against fascism. Similarly, to urge granting of freedom and independence for the Indian people is not a condition for helping win the war, but is a necessity for winning the war.

Negros Loyal to the Nation

The ultimate result can only mean the unleashing of the full and total resources of the Indian masses, their enthusiastic and heightened morale which such freedom would release for battle. Applied here at home, the wiping out of all discrimination against the Negro people can only result in fuller mobilization and manning of American resources, to achieve the victory over the Axis.

Both the Indian and Negro people know that their stake in the present and future lies with the anti-Axis powers.

The Indian leaders, as the Negro people, have shown wise statesmanship in that they have not placed as a condition for their participation in the anti-Axis struggle their independence and freedom. In the same way, the British government could show their statesmanship, for they would be acting in their best national interest by giving concrete recognition to promote India's aspirations for national independence and freedom.

Another lesson of the war is that failure to mobilize the people who have a long tradition of freedom and independence and who possess the spirit of patriotism and nationalism, makes it easier for the powerful Japanese and Hitler fifth column demagogic lead to utilize "national liberation" and "anti-imperialist" propaganda to delay and immobilize the resistance against fascist aggression which arises spontaneously among oppressed peoples.

The great Soviet nation, the Chinese people, whose great victories against the war machines of Hitler and Hirohito are so admired by all, have shown that this policy of full mobilization of all people, of fully engaging the whole people for defense of their own security and independence, of equality, as is the signal case of the Soviet Union, is in good measure responsible for scoring decisive victories, even against superior military force.

The United Nations can show that the costly lessons of the Far Eastern front have not been in vain. The people of all the United

Nations, can as part of their anti-Axis fight, constructively urge on their governments the implementation of this lesson, the granting of the demands of the Indian people, as necessary to furthering the needed offensive struggle for victory over the Axis powers.

HITLER'S NEW ORDER: KNOW WHAT WE'RE FIGHTING!

WEEKLY REVIEW
JUNE 30, 1942

Many young Americans have been mentally chewing over the many stories in the daily press in popular magazines about Adolf Hitler. Hitler has been analyzed and psychoanalyzed. He is said to be insane and have queer quirks. The secrets of his life have been told. But from these columns of endless type, there is no mention of what fascism is. What is fascism?

Fascism is a ruthless terroristic dictatorship. It came to power in 1933—during the last decade of world history. It is a dictatorship of a special kind. This dictatorship is not the rule of one man, but of the most reactionary, aggressive finance capitalists in a given country. It is the antithesis of what we are fighting to achieve. Its gangster rulers are bent on conquest of the entire world—on imposing its ruthless system of force and violence on all but the ruling Nazi clique. Its history proves all of this.

Did not the fascists claim that they were bringing about freedom and plenty for the German and Italian people? Today, German, Italian, and youth of all other Axis countries, for since 1931 pour out their lifeblood supposedly to bring about "New World order" in Europe.

Reign of Terror

But what is this "new world order?" It is the rule of force and terror. Fascism's roll call of murder, plunder, and ruin from Ethiopia to Madrid, from Paris to Libya, from Kharkov to Sevastopol, is one unparalleled in the history of all humankind. The recent crimes of fascism as witnessed in the martyred Czech city of Lidice, wiped out by Hitler for the hangman Heydrick; the murder of sixty thousand Jews in the great cultural Soviet city of Vilna; the announcement by Herr Goebbels that he intends to wipe out every single Jew in Europe—all served to emphasize once again the ruthless, imperialist, aggressive common nature of the system.

Moreover, in all countries conquered and overrun by the fascist boot, trade unions and peoples organizations have been abolished. All parliamentary procedures: the right to speech, press, and assembly have been abolished. Labor and the people as a whole are chained to the concentration camp of forced labor for the profits of the fascist rulers. It is not the particular quirk of the fascist rulers that is behind all of this. The Nazi Party, financed by the German imperialist bankers, have employed these tricks—the better to hide their fat profits, which they have gained through the plunder and bloody conquest of the peoples of Germany, Italy, and all of occupied Europe and Asia. The leaders of the Nazi Party—Goering (who is a multi-millionaire), Goebbels and Hitler, exploit hundreds of factories and plants and have amassed fortunes. The Nazi regime is the dominant fascist power. One of fascism's favorite techniques is to divide and rule. Fascism always employs race, discrimination, making it the law of the land. It separates Christian from Jew. It persecutes communists and employees [by] red-baiting. It ruthlessly suppresses and wipes out all who protest.

Obviously, there is a world of difference between German fascism and American democracy, even though it is true that both are capitalist nations. America and Britain are capitalist states, in which capitalists exercise great influence, but here, elementary democratic rights still exist. The ability of the people to guide their own destiny exists to a greater degree. It is seen in the role of labor today which plays an important role in the war effort and on political issues affecting the war. There are trade unions and labor parties. Legislative and parliamentary governments exist while under Hitler rule, all these institutions and others have been replaced by "Ja" Reichstag. The wartime measures taken to suppress the fifth column by America, for example, are necessary military measures and not "fascist dictatorship," as the fifth column tries to make us believe through the mouth of a Herbert Hoover.

Fascism is out to destroy the independence and freedom of all nations by ruthless aggression, which menaces the freedom and independence of all nations including the Soviet Union as well as the capitalist nations.

Fascist Concepts Not Ideals

We young Americans have been told that the "ideals" given to the youth of Germany and Italy, by their fascist rulers are what has imbued them with their fighting spirit. There are others who say that the fascist "ideals" give greater inspiration to the fascist youth of Germany than do the democratic ideals to the youth of America. But how false are the so-called ideals of fascism! What "ideals" have the fascists imbued their youth with? The ideals of brutality and persecution? The "ideals" that meanness is nobility of race? The "ideals" that hatred of other nations and peoples is honor and pride? The "ideals" that morality is weakness? The "ideals" that women are "half-human, half-apes"? But these are not ideals! The ideals of democratic peoples everywhere is the ideal of independence and freedom of brotherhood and equality. But the fascists have banished these ideals by force from the lands they control. They have burned the books of the great cultural figures of Germany and Italy. Wherever fascism sets its foot, the perversion of science and education follow in its trail. The promise of a brilliant future to youth under fascism is incessant war and conquest by ruthless suppression of all culture and idealism. The concepts given the youth of Germany and Italy are not "ideals" at all. In fact, they stem from the loss of all ideals by the fascist rulers; from the degeneracy of fascism. To make such comparisons between the degenerate concepts that fascism promotes and the ideals of democracy is to elevate fascism to a place where it does not properly belong. It is to lose sight of the real weakness of fascism which claims it is invincible. It is to make more difficult the task of defeating Hitler in 1942. The ideals of democracy and the aims of the people everywhere are stronger, and more compelling than ever. What we must imbue our youth with is hatred of fascism and pride in the democratic ideals of progressive humanity everywhere. As Vice President Wallace said:

> The convulsive efforts of the dying madman will be so
> great that some of us may be deceived into thinking that
> the situation is bad when it is really getting better, but in
> the case of most of us, the events of the next few months

disturbing though they may be, will only increase our will to bring about complete victory in this war of liberation.

This is not by way of saying that the defeat of fascists is in the bag. The fascists are still strong. But the day of victory can be brought even closer once we understand that the sore of fascism can be removed and its concepts destroyed now. The growing revolt of the European peoples has roused the fascist rulers to the new desperate heights of terror. The balance of power rests in this moment in the hands of the United Nations. The so-called invincibility of the Nazi armies has been punctured by the scores of heroic deeds of Soviet youth and the great Red Army. It is for us to hold high the torch of victory by heightening our work and speeding the day of victory this year, 1942.

Socialist Democracy

Today it is no longer necessary to review the obvious lie that socialism is the same as fascism. The heroic Soviet peoples for a year now have written the answer in the stream of their blood and the scorching of their earth. But what is still necessary to refute is the misinterpretation which still exists in official circles that "the Soviet Union isn't a democracy, but it's OK if they continue to wipe out the Nazis . . . " The speech of Vice President Wallace before the Free World Association on May 8, has by implication, challenged this attitude. For the Vice President, speaking of the great democratic "march of freedom of the past 150 years" correctly included the great Russian Revolution. By doing so he places for the first time officially the great democratic achievements of socialist democracy alongside of the natural historic desires and urges of all freedom loving peoples, and nations. The Soviet Union's way of life, while it differs from the American or British way of life, is impelled by the same urges as all those who strive for liberty and independence. And the Soviet people fight in the spirit today only because their whole motivation has from birth been directed towards the advancement of its people on the great high road of history.

But in face of what is so obvious to all honest people, some defeatist and fifth columnists still try to sell mistrust about our ally—the Soviet Union. "What about Soviet Collectivism and Nazi Totalitarianism?" they say. This is an obvious attempt to say in other words that the Soviet Union is a "totalitarian power." But nothing is farther from the truth.

Fascist totalitarianism is the rule of the most reactionary terrorist aggressive clique who is out to conquer the world and who ruthlessly protects the rule of the most reactionary German fascists and bankers—and not the mass of the people—the farmers, workers, Negro, and the minority peoples. They are invaders and aggressors of the lands and peoples of other nations. Plunder and rule follow their train.

In the socialist democracy the masses of the people rule. The people elect their own representatives and officials. Under the Soviet Constitution, all people regardless of race, color, or creed, from the age of eighteen and up, vote. Its economic system is so geared as to provide work for everyone; and all factories, plants, and land are the property of all of the people. This is because socialism is a system in which the full equality of nations and peoples exists. The economic means whereby people make a living, belongs to all the people. But this also has been declared truth by Lord Beaverbrook, who in a tribute to the unity and heroic fight of the Soviet Union, declared:

> Communism under Stalin has produced the most valiant fighting army in Europe. Communism under Stalin has provided us with examples of patriotism equal to the finest annals in history. Communism under Stalin has won the admiration of all the Western nations. Communism under Stalin has produced the best generals in the war.

Against the fascist Axis dominated by Hitler Germany, all people, including those of the fascist powers themselves, must be bound in common struggle. For this will mean the liberation of the youth of Germany and Italy and other Axis nations. It is only the complete removal of fascism that opens up the possibility for the "century of the common man."

This is why all nations and peoples must speed the day for the final defeat of Hitlerism, this year, 1942.

WHAT WE MUST NOW DO ABOUT INDIA

WEEKLY REVIEW
AUGUST 25, 1942

**Four Hundred Million Strong, A Free Indian People
Must Be Mobilized for the Fight Against Fascism**

The world spotlight, focused on the India crisis, has brought about an unprecedented discussion about India. Among anti-fascists, such discussions do not conjure up mental pictures about a "FABULOUS, MYSTERIOUS" India; these do not call up visions of an India which is the "PEARL OF THE BRITISH EMPIRE"—rather such discussions are, in the main, based on viewing India and her nearly four hundred million people from the deep life-and-death relationship which she occupies today. The entire anti-fascist world has been shocked by the reviving of the old whiplash and terror rule of British colonial rulers and the British Cabinet against the Indian people.

It is all the more significant that the India crisis occurs at a time when the war has reached its overall crisis, upon whose victory depends the opening of the Second Front Now. It is doubly significant that the India crisis has come at a time when we celebrate the first anniversary of the Atlantic Charter which has as its declared aim "THE RIGHT OF ALL PEOPLES TO CHOOSE THE FORM OF GOVERNMENT UNDER WHICH THEY WILL LIVE."

Despite this realization, nearly the entire press of the nation has cloaked the real issues of the India crisis with the same attitude as that of the Colonial rulers, who under the guise of "law and order" are using guns and bullets against the Indian people. It is for these main reasons that it is important to establish what the real issue is in India; and why it is important for us to immediately act to bring about a

45

speedy solution of this crisis, which is inseparably connected with the whole cause of victory.

The cause of victory needs India, because India represents an important bastion for us both militarily and politically. India is in the path of Axis aggression. Hitler is moving in the direction of Asia Minor, helped by Rommel in the East, thus hoping to conquer the Caucasus. Japan is showing signs of moving upon Soviet Siberia and India. The consequences of such a juncture through India could not but have terrible results for the Indian people as well as the cause of victory. For the aim of the Axis powers is to separate the Soviet Union and China from their allies. Politically, India's importance lies in the fact that the mobilization of her nearly four hundred million people is needed now in our battle of freedom in order to stop Japan and Hitler.

India's fate is directly connected with the fate of the colonial peoples. Freedom for India may decide whether or not we will have on our side powerful allies to stop Japan and halt Hitler's advance in the Middle East. It is actually a test as to whether we will really fulfill our war aims—the freedom and independence of all peoples everywhere. It is for this reason the whole colonial world in Asia, Africa, Latin America, as well as the Negro people of our own country, anxiously watch to see what the position of London and Washington will be. By now we should have learned that the way to mobilize the peoples of the Far East, as well as the whole colonial world, is through the mobilization of the people THEMSELVES to defend their own homelands.

It is in this deep sense that we must recognize that freedom for India as well as the opening of the Second Front NOW, are two parts of the single key to victory.

Why then has India not been mobilized? The British colonial rulers and the continued stand of the British Cabinet to maintain the old policy of colonial rule (refusal to arm the people, etc.) are responsible. These colonial rulers, who, only six months ago, proved their complete inadequacy to mobilize the people for defense in Burma and Malaya, now are attempting through "law and order" to attempt to "organize" the people for effective resistance against the enemy. How can the colonial rulers, after three hundred years, proven incapable to solve the problem by "law and order," solve it now? We know that a people only fight if they are convinced that this is their war of liberation. It is for that reason too, that we cannot ask the Indian people to "put aside" their struggle for independence, in the interest of victory. In the first place, this war has proven, as in China and the Soviet Union, that only an armed people supporting the army is capable of defeating the fascists. Secondly, such an approach is the direct opposite to achieving full and complete participation of India against fascism, for the only way such mobilization can be achieved is through freely permitting India to mobilize in its own defense. Only then can we really win them as allies.

This, in essence, is the stand of the overwhelming majority of the All India Congress leaders and the Indian people. The Indian people have seen the effects of the colonial policy in Burma and Malaya. They have also seen the other road—in China.

Despite the confusion in the press, it is obvious that the All India Congress and the Indian people are aware of the fact that the Axis must be defeated in order to save India. This was shown in the rejection by the Congress Working Committee (prior to the All India Congress meeting) of Gandhi's resolution. This resolution was one which insinuated that the whole India nationalist movement is ready to sell out to Japan.

Moreover, at the time when British colonial rulers descended with their rule of terror against the leaders of the All India Congress and the Indian people, Nehru and other Congress leaders (as distinct from Gandhi) reemphasized that their demand for a National Government responsible to the people was a war demand, a military measure to assure the most effective mobilization of the people for the defense of India, in cooperation especially with China, the Soviet Union, England, and the United States.

Even more clearcut is the stand of India's Communist Party which has put to the fore as India's supreme need the defense of their country, calling on the people to unite and take their full part in the just war against fascism. Stating unequivocally that the "policy of the British government perpetuating the enslavement of India" is to be condemned, it points out that it should not be permitted to prevent the Indian people from adopting a correct attitude toward the war and from mobilizing the power of the people. They urge the recognition of the independence of India and state: "The establishment of a provisional National Government, enjoying the confidence of the people, and the realization of democratic liberties are essential to transform our general support of the war into an active and effective material cooperation."

From this we can see that Gandhi does not represent the All India Congress nor the sentiments of the Indian people. As a matter of fact, there has been going on for some time a sharp struggle against the dangerous "nonviolent resistance, noncooperation with Britain" stand of Gandhi. The suppression of the Indian people and the Congress, who are moving away from Gandhism, can only serve to strengthen Gandhi's hand, and thus endanger the whole course of India's freedom, as well as the United Nations.

An example of the bankruptcy of British colonial rule in India in this present crisis is to be seen in an article printed in the April issue of *The Student*, organ of the All India Student Federation.

Describing the situation in Calcutta which students found upon returning from the All India Students Conference in Patha, the article points out the "utter inadequacy" of the arrangements for defense of the city; the "insolence" of local British authorities to keep the PEOPLE out of it.

Entitled "If Moscow, Chungking, London Can—Calcutta, too, Can Take It," it describes the work of the students coming at the imminent fall of Singapore and Rangoon.

The description of what the students did, how they organized the Civil Defense, how they inspired the people, their belief and understanding of the issues involved, is stirring testimony of the ability and will of the Indian youth and their people to defend their nation, and in turn the cause of the United Nations.

> Students came back filled with the "New Life" the "New Line" had given them. One thought was in every mind. Will the fascist hordes overrun our fair land—when in the Russian snows, the Chinese loess caves, the desolate Balkan countryside, men, women, and even children were holding fast? Shall we lose the first round against the invader, when the Chinese people had not lost it in ten years?

> Calcutta was a dismal sight . . . . We got the "New Line" in a flash! We stopped trying to "understand" it through

tortuous clumsy efforts to "reason out" how this was the Soviet's war, Europe's war, and "therefore" "our war," in our interest. One look at our beloved city, where Bankin roused slumbering India to a flaming patriotism, where Rabindranath stood his full height, the tallest among men, where Deshbandhu Das, our greatest orator, commanded India's millions to remain forever true to unflinching patriotism—one look at the stark nakedness of our city was enough . . . We took a patriot's oath to keep the Japanese jackal out of the city . . .

Who said "Imperialism" was "our ally?" The Civil Defense arrangements were made by riff-raffs of questionable character for the most part, the imperialist's insolence made him keep the PEOPLE out of it. The utter inadequacy of these arrangements, the cynical indifference of the bureaucrats even at this twilight time, reduced our people to utter hopelessness. The panicky editorials in our dailies written by men who should have known better—added to the confusion. On top of it all, the silver-haired custodians of our education failed to stand their ground as fearless, dignified patriots. The result was crowded railway stations, deserted streets, deserted colleges and schools—for the authorities closed the institutions indefinitely and encouraged the students to evacuate.

The article goes on to describe how they issued a stirring appeal which ran:

For all self-respecting men and women, the issue is clear. For us there is no escape. Either we stand and FIGHT, or we go down in history as the blackest traitors. To remain at our post is the sacred duty, the task of the moment . . . to rouse the people, to organize and lead them into active resistance, we have to inspire them, awaken in them the spirit of resistance that is slumbering. We have the perspective before us of the day when hundreds of thousands of youth are in the streets educating and inspiring the inhab-

itants of this great city, when they have made every man
a soldier and every house a barricade against fascism . . . .

The results which they got, through carrying through study courses
on Civilian Defense within a week, were three hundred volunteers
enrolled within a week and one thousand to be gotten by the end of
the month!—showing the potentialities that India's millions have to
organize in defense of their own land.

Of course, this is not to imply that there aren't many complex
problems in India. We do not help by wringing our hands over
Gandhi or dwelling on "India's differences." For the path to the
solution of these inner problems are in the first place the job of the
people of India. Our role is to help to influence the direction of that
struggle, to help achieve what is needed now: the full mobilization of
the people of India for resistance to the Axis. For as proven by China
and the Soviet Union, national consciousness of a people grows once
they are given the perspective and means to accomplish that unity.

We know that there are two paths open to the solution of this
issue. We have already discussed some of the consequences of the path
being followed by British colonial leaders—the path of Burma. To
allow this to happen is to strengthen colonialism. It is to allow the
fifth column and defeatists to seek to use the India crisis as another
false argument against opening the vitally needed Second Front. The
very crisis in India has come at this time due to the delay in opening
the Second Front, enabling Hitler to freely continue his drives and
Japan to become more bold as a result. Not to enable a free India to
mobilize in her own defense is to renounce the aims for which we are
fighting—for freedom and independence of peoples everywhere.

On the other hand, we can play an important role in the crisis.
In fact, we must. That path is by action. By urging (as has already
been suggested by Pearl Buck, and increasingly being voiced by labor,
youth, and other progressive organizations) President Roosevelt to
intervene in the India Crisis, to urge the British government to
immediately resume negotiations with the Indian people. Such negotiations can result in the formation of a strong, unified, representative
national government in India against the Axis aggressors, and thus
enhance our common victory. Such negotiations, unlike the Cripps

Mission, must come to terms WITH India, instead of laying down terms TO India.

This is a test of everything we are fighting for. It is up to each and every one of us by boldly speaking—as we are doing on the Second Front—to speak out for India's freedom, to help pave the way for complete victory now.

THE EDITOR'S CORNER

WEEKLY REVIEW
JUNE 22, 1943

Last November, a great American who voiced the deepest hopes and aspirations of "the common man" for "the peoples' century" declared:

> It's no accident that the Americans and Russians like each other when they get acquainted. Both peoples were molded by the vast sweep of a rich continent. Both know that their future is greater than their past. Both hate sham ...

> When the Russian people burst the shackles of Tsarist absolutism, they turned instinctively to the United States for engineering and agricultural guidance. Thanks to the hunger of the Russian people for progress, they were able to learn in twenty-five years that which had taken us in the United States one hundred years to develop.

Today, the nation that "turned to us instinctively" is finding a deep response in all peoples of our own nation who "turn to 'them' instinctively" to know their courage and valor in the joint fight for victory and a better world.

Is it an "accident" that is responsible for this response? The Vice President was a thousand times right when he declared "it's no accident ... "

American-Soviet friendship dates back to more than a century ago. The great French author, Tocqueville, 107 years ago declared, "there are ... two great nations in the world which seem to tend towards the same end, although they start from different points. I allude to the Russians and the Americans ... Their starting point is different and their courses are not the same, yet each of them seem to be marked by the will of heaven to sway the destinies of half the globe . . . "

The French author could not have possibly dreamed of the close bonds that America and the Soviet Union would patriotically weld in the fires of war to death against slavery.

The importance of recognizing this is to be found in the wails of those who charge that some "magic" or "accident" can "explain" our alliance with the Soviet Union, or the Soviet's mighty achievements for our side.

But the contrary is the case. Soviet-American friendship is dictated by the deepest self-interest of our own nation; by its own needs in war and in peace for strong allies like the Soviet Union.

Far from being an "accident," the mighty achievement of the Soviet Union is something that springs from the deepest laws of human history. This is the essence of Vice President Wallace' statement that the Soviet Union is one of the great achievements of the human race in its long forward march, like our own 1776, the French '92, the Bolivarian Revolution of Latin America and like our own abolition of chattel slavery in '61.

The Soviet Union has a different—a Socialist system. Its valiant fight takes place because of, not in spite of that fact. It is upon the firm knowledge that everything in their land—its industries, land, and resources are their own, that hitherto undreamed of opportunities for advancement have unfolded before them—that the unparalleled national unity of the Soviet land is built. Racial hatred is unknown to the family of Soviet peoples. That is why its peoples are so united. The Soviet Union never has had and cannot have imperialist ambitions to conquer and subject other peoples.

Only Hitler and Hirohito fear Soviet-American friendship. They fear it because it spells the death of fascism; they fear it because it helps remove from their war arsenal, the powerful lie that the Soviet Union is a "mystery"; the "Bolshevist" Soviet Union "menaces the world."

No, there is nothing to fear about the Soviet regime. The roots of such fears are based on willful desire to lose, not to win the war.

As our own nation welds this friendship on this second year of Soviet battle, nothing better could be done than to seal that friendship in joint battle, now. To spread the truth about our Soviet ally is a patriotic duty. Such truth could be further enhanced, if like Britain, we enter into a pact with our Soviet ally.

THE EDITOR'S CORNER

WEEKLY REVIEW
JUNE 29, 1943

No one can read the stories which are coming out of Southern army camps and not be shocked and angered by the assaults against Negro soldiers by Southern bourbons and reactionaries. The same goes for the provocations by pro-fascist elements of riots between Negro and white workers.

Traveling from Buffalo to New York last weekend, I rode with a Negro officer for nearly six hours. We spoke about many things and naturally, our conversation took a turn to the war. The handsome young officer was bitter and cynical. He knew what we were fighting for—against Hitlerism he said, abroad and at home. But he told me what I already knew from the press stories that the morale of the men is at a dangerously low pitch; the indignities which they suffer are growing; they too are bitter as he was at such treatment.

These happenings are serious strains on our national unity provoked by the fifth column and defeatist Hearst press and the Ku Klux Klan "white supremacists" who want nothing better than to break up national unity to delay our fight against Hitlerism on the continent of Europe. These happenings are equal to a military victory for Hitler and Hirohito.

How can we stop these home front diversions—for that is what they are. We can stop them by an aroused youth population heightening their unity in the spirit of the tremendously significant June Negro Labor Rally in Madison Square Garden.

Negro young men and women are anxious to give their all to serve the nation patriotically. But it is not hard to understand why

Negro war workers, attacked by hooded thugs, and soldiers who want nothing more than to serve the nation in its fight for victory have low morale as a result of such incidents.

What I'm arguing for is a change in our War Department's statutes towards Negro soldiers. We are fighting a people's war in which all peoples have an all-out stake. Yet the War Department repeatedly has declared that it has found it "satisfactory" to segregate Negro soldiers and to induct them on a 10 percent basis into the armed forces. No other peoples or nationalities are inducted on any such basis. The fallacy of this policy is revealed in the indignation of the Harlem community a few weeks ago, when Selective Service Officials suddenly urged a 20 percent draft of Negro inductees in New York City.

The deeds of Negro servicemen and Negro production soldiers are replete with "extraordinary heroism." In Pantelleria and Lampedusa the first and only squadron of Negro pilots participated in the raids that helped bring this stepping stone to Europe to defeat. Yet training is all too small for Negro pilots, not to mention Negro bombardiers.

The tensions caused by segregation and discrimination of Negro soldiers are unnecessary. Mixed units, together with a policy of inter-racial education and training, following the pattern of the officer candidate schools and coast guard units, can solve the situation.

As declared by Judge William Hastie recently, "even where tensions are highest there are many citizens not bold enough to take the lead themselves but decent and patriotic enough to follow those in authority who will assume the initiative . . . "

All of these and more constructive demands are being put forward by the National Council of Negro Youth and NY State Conference of Negro Youth in their huge tribute to Negro Servicemen, June 27 at 4:30 p.m. at the Renaissance Casino, 138th Street and Seventh Avenue.

Tickets may be secured at 200 West 135th Street for only 55 cents.

All youth should give their support morally and better, in person to this great tribute of Negro youth and a galaxy of artists to their fighting men. For such tributes lead to heightening the understanding of all youth, routing the fifth column and welding unbreakable unity for victory over all the little Hitlers at home.

NEGRO REACTION TO CHURCHILL: 'NO'

DAILY WORKER
MARCH 18, 1946

Winston Churchill's speech certainly made no hit with the Negro peoples—or its press. He chose Jim Crow Fulton, Mo., and its backward Westminster College, which bars Negro girls and boys from its portals, to rattle his sabre for war.

It was a fitting setting to put forth his unsavory Anglo-Saxon military alliance for the "chosen people"—the English-speaking peoples. But Negro Americans have instinctively recognized the similarity of such a proposal to the Hitler myth of "Aryan supremacy." They know what Churchill urges Britons and Americans to do is exactly what Hitler's Germans were supposed to do.

Such is the tenor of the overwhelming majority of editorials and comment by Negro leaders in their press this past week. The unanimity of rejection of the Churchill speech by the Negro peoples, is unparalleled in any other section of the population. They all held that Churchill's speech by the Negro people, is unparalleled in any other section of the population. They all held that Churchill's speech was a "smokescreen" to cover the "real resolves" of British domination of colonial peoples. They took a forthright stand against Churchill's cry that Russia threatens world peace through an "expansionism of Communism."

Defender Calls on Negroes to Protest

They commented widely on the accepted fact that the Soviet Union is a proven friend of millions of black and brown colonial peoples. Many called on Americans to "indignantly rise up" to use the words of the

Chicago Defender "and force our government to reject Churchill's insane proposal."

It must be noted, of course, that few recognized that the real pied piper of disaster is American imperialism and its drive for world domination. But it is significant that their vigorous opposition to the Churchill anti-Soviet war mongering was based on their recognition that here is a desperate plea by British imperialism for American help in crushing the colonial millions, who are in motion, demanding the freedom which is justly theirs.

It is not accidental that the Negro press so widely commented on this phase of Churchill's speech. The connection lies in their inherent recognition that it is the Soviet Union to whom the colonial peoples—and increasingly they—look to as a beacon light example of the dignity of human freedom and equality of all peoples.

Negro People Vital Ally Against War Drive

What then, is the overall meaning of this reaction among the Negro people? It means, in my opinion, that (1) the Negro people are voicing the aspirations and determination of all mankind to live in peace and security; (2) they therefore represent one of the strongest allies of the American working class in its pursuit of security and peace; and (3) that important conclusions should follow these observations.

Mind you, such a reaction occurs in the midst of the most un-precedented wholesale attack against the economic, political, and social standards of the Negro people. Growing lynch terror in Tennessee, and Freeport, Long Island, following the defeat of the Senate Fair Employment Practices Committee (FEPC), bill, has served to sharpen the recognition of the Negro people and the nation as a whole, that bitter struggles will be needed to maintain their war time gains.

The Negro people are alert to these developments and are showing a temper and spirit that is best expressed in the words of the Columbia, Tenn., frame-up victims: "We are not backing up one inch." Negro veterans are organizing to gain their just desserts and to stop the terror directed against their kin by the Southern Bourbons and Big Monopolists, who fear their anti-fascist militancy.

It would appear that, above all, what is needed to strengthen this fight is (1) a response in volume a thousand fold its present size by labor in support of the struggles of the Negro people. This will serve to strengthen the front for peace, the alliance of the Negro people and labor.

Secondly, the opportunity exists as never before for the greatest unity against the war danger, and the growing lynch terror by the Negro people themselves. With such a wide unanimity of thinking on international and domestic problems there is no reason why this should not be done.

This is the way to isolate misleaders among the Negro people who fail to see this. Such is the way to strengthen the inner unity of the Negro people, and in turn, to bring a greater strength to their common allies at home and abroad.

Such thinking would be, it seems to me, a major conclusion from the reaction of the Negro people to Churchill's war mongering speeches and to the growing lynch terror in the US.

ANTI-RACISM, A CLASS STRUGGLE

Claudia Jones has become world-famous for her theoretical and practical contributions to the struggle for Black liberation—and the following section is just a snapshot of the urgent and lasting interventions she made. She spoke to the particular contributions Communists made to the Black liberation movement, rooted in one basic fact: the struggle for Black liberation was part and parcel of the struggle for socialism. As Jones outlines in her now famous essay, included here, "An End to the Neglect of Negro Women!," issues like "race," "gender," and "class" are not separate categories but essential parts of the broader capitalist "mode of production" and can only be understood in relationship to one another.

Looking more specifically at "race," Jones' work was resonant with the traditional communist views that eminated from a theory known as the "Black Belt Thesis." Developed in the 1920s, the thesis saw Black people in the United States as a distinct people, forged in the crucible of slavery in the South, and that this distinction was an inevitable development of the attempt to draw Black people from across Africa and turn them, regardless of ethno-religious differences, into a solid mass of unpaid labor. This continued "underclass" status given to Black Americans became so central to the foundations of US capitalism that it was impossible to uproot racism without uprooting capitalism, the two were too intertwined.

As a result, Communists put anti-racist organizing at the center of their work. As the following selections reflect, the Communists were at the forefront of the struggle against lynching, launched mass organizations that embraced tens of thousands, fought against the Jim Crow congressional bloc, elected one of their members as the first Black city councilmember in New York City, as well as produced original research about the realities faced by Black America. For the movement Claudia Jones was helping to lead, the anti-racist struggle was a class struggle.

NEGRO YOUTH PAMPHLET

DAILY WORKER
JUNE 17, 1938

OFFICIAL PROCEEDINGS. Second All-Southern Negro Youth Congress, 33 pages. Published by the Second Negro Youth Congress, 327 North First Street, Richmond, VA, Price 10c

The special significance of the Second All-Southern Negro Youth Congress, it is agreed by all observers, lies in the fact that in reality this movement expresses the economic, social, and cultural desires not only of Negro youth of the Southland, but of the entire Southern people, Negro and white.

Its second conference, held in Chattanooga, Tenn., April 1–3, attended by 355 delegates, registered approximately 381 organized Southern youth—an increase over the 250,000 represented at the first Conference in Richmond. Since the Congress was established in 1937 it has achieved a brilliant record.

The number of delegates this year, as compared to the five hundred of last year, was smaller. It is significant, however, that the composition of the delegates represents a considerable increase in qualitative representation, especially from the deep South. The credentials report records seventeen came from Georgia, twenty-two from Alabama, twelve from North Carolina, and so on.

The types of organizations represented show that a cross section of the main organizations among the Negro young people were represented—religions, fraternal, student, cultural, trade union, farm, athletic, social, and political.

The keynote of the conference was citizenship. Calling attention to the changing South, which is a reflection of the powerful currents of progress stirring the American people, the conference recorded the fact "that this powerful sentiment on the part of America to move forward the frontier of democracy is now entering our Southland."

The Conference resolved to "organize poll-tax-paying clubs . . . and registration centers in every neighborhood," thus assuring the maximum vote polled under existing conditions and helping to defeat poll-tax disenfranchisement and corrupt and anti-suffrage laws.

Other resolutions called for the right of Negroes to serve on juries, for more educational opportunities, for the release of the remaining five Scottsboro boys, for endorsing President Roosevelt's Chicago speech for "concerted action" for peace, for better interracial understanding, for support and passage of the Anti-Lynching Bill, for cooperation with the nationwide health campaign, and for support to the Second World Youth Congress.

The annual report of Edward E. Strong, National Executive Secretary and leader of the Congress, is printed in its entirety and stands out as a clear critical document on the major achievements and manifold problems facing the Congress if it is to achieve the great task of uniting the Southern youth.

The pamphlet concludes with the findings of the panels on citizenship, job security, Negro education, religion, rural youth, marriage, home life, and future. The reports reflect the earnest spirit in which these young people deliberated at Chattanooga.

The low price of the pamphlet will enable its reaching a wide range of young Negro and white people of the South, especially. It is a handbook not alone for the Negro people, but for all those who understand that the deliberations of the Second All-Southern Negro Youth Congress marks the historical beginning of a movement which is helping to rally the whole of the Southern people for freedom, equality, and opportunity.

RECENT TRENDS AMONG NEGRO YOUTH

WEEKLY REVIEW
JULY 1938

From the heart of the Southland to the industrial North, from the sunny shores of California to the rocky coast of Maine, conferences of Negro youth are signs of the times. Negro youth are coming together to discuss their common problems and find solutions like never before.

Significantly, these conferences are not only *forums* of youth, but *spokesmen* for Negro youth. These youth come together not only for "council" but "action" as well. It is especially necessary, therefore, to appraise these movements carefully, for they are but a reflection of the strong progressive currents among the whole Negro people.

The National Negro Congress has been in the forefront of the struggle to unify the Negro people for their democratic rights. During the past year, in its local councils, the Congress has more than often initiated and taken part in community movements for jobs, relief, and all the other local needs. And the youth divisions of the Congress have played an important part in rallying the youth in these struggles.

Picket Lines

But the activities of the Negro people are taking form and shape today in a different manner than heretofore. During the lowest point of the economic crisis, in 1933, in all of the Negro communities, picket lines were thrown around the local businesses, directed mainly against white people in the community, demanding jobs for Negroes.

Today, we are entering a new economic crisis and the picket lines are forming again in Negro communities. But this time, they are directed against Big Business, particularly, the utilities.

The outstanding example of this is the Greater New York Coordinating Committee for Employment in Harlem, which has initiated a Job Campaign that rallies hundreds of Negro people in Harlem in a fight against the utilities. Interesting methods of struggle are being evolved. For example, the entire community goes down to the utilities office together for the paying of bills. Before dialing a call, all telephone users call central operator first. Daily picket lines are thrown around the utilities local offices in Harlem. The Job Campaign Committee is getting results, uniting the people in a struggle which the progressive movement can well support.

Jobs for Negroes

Similiar developments can be noted in other Negro communities. In Newark, NJ, the campaign to secure jobs for Negro salesmen and shop girls in the local F&W Grand store is recognized today as the mainstream of the progressive Negro movement. Similar developments can be observed in Brooklyn, NY, where during the past year, the Citizens Civic Affairs Committee, representing the major organizations in the Negro community conducted a campaign for jobs in the local theatres, threw picket lines around the utilities buildings, and were able to secure jobs for the Negro young people.

Significantly enough, even the reactionary mouthpieces of big capital take note of the developing unity among the Negro people. An example of this is seen in the article "Black Omens" by Stanley High which appeared in the March 21 issue of the *Saturday Evening Post*. High declares that while no one knows where the Negroes of the North are going, it is certain "they are going there together." The main purpose of the article was to reveal the growing progressive outlook of the Negro people in every field of endeavor, in every sphere of their existence. Today, the Negro people have new heroes to worship and now more than ever these heroes are trade unionists and progressive clergymen.

These trends among the Negro people as a whole today are reflected among the Negro young people of America. Let us review a few of these conferences, their composition, their themes, their decisions.

Last fall, in Illinois, we saw the establishment of a broad, progressive movement, uniting all strata of Negro youth around their elementary demands: for jobs, educational opportunity, security, improved health facilities, against discrimination. This conference was called at the initiative of the National Negro Congress youth division in that state. This movement involved the major organizations among the Negro youth in Illinois: religious, fraternal, student, social, and political. Seeking not new frontiers, but new methods of uniting the youth to achieve their ideals, the Conference called for "Chicago's youth to reawaken the spirit of 'old Chicago.'" They established a permanent movement now symbolized in the Illinois State Youth Congress.

Missouri Conference

Further southwest, in the brewery city of St. Louis, Missouri, we find development of this same kind. There the St. Louis Youth Conference April 29–May 1 resulted, attended by approximately one hundred delegates, representing forty-seven organizations, with a total membership of 2,500 youth. These young people deliberated for three days on all questions facing the Negro people—and youth in particular. One of the things which created the most interest in the conference was a symposium led by the dean of the church cathedral in which the conference was held, who spoke on "If I were a Negro" with a young person taking the counterpoint, "If I were White." Thus brought out in a dramatic fashion the reality of what life is like for the Negro.

St. Louis Federation

Equally important to note is that in all these conferences, there is a general acceptance for white delegates and the feeling for further cooperation with white groups on specific questions. This, in itself, is a significant sign that Negro youth are aware of the need for more and more cooperation with other groups in order to broaden out their own movement for unity; in order to establish their proper relation to America's young people as a whole.

Labor and local church representation were also at this conference which established the St. Louis Youth Federation. Among its purposes, it wishes "to institute an educational campaign to educate the youth in intelligent usage of the ballot . . . that the Federation shall attempt to register all youth of whom the Federation can and will influence."

While the Federation is nonpartisan, it is not necessarily nonpolitical and is free to endorse and support candidates who deserve youth support by their actions and past records.

The outstanding development among the Negro youth is the Southern Negro Youth Congress which convened for the second time on the edge of the deep South in Chattanooga, Tennessee, April 1–3. This movement, speaking for 383,000 organized Southern young people, primarily of Negro youth, represents the growing unity among the Negro youth of the south to solve their manifold problems.

The answer to "Why a Southern Negro Youth Congress?" is the answer also as to why on a local scale many Negro youth today are coming together to "council and to action."

Edward E. Strong, National Executive Secretary of the Congress explains its purpose. In his annual report he declares:

> We wanted a vehicle of cooperation for Southern youth. This special instrument was needed because Southern young people face special problems, problems which arise out of the historical development of our nation. The peculiar feudal economy of the South was emphasized by President Roosevelt in his Gainesville, Georgia address of March 23rd. Only to the extent that there are sectional problems in the South, may it be said that the Congress is a sectional institution. Fundamentally, our horizon is as broad as all humanity.

The keynote of the conference was citizenship. Showing that it recognized the trends in the country, the powerful currents of progress stirring the American people, the Conference hails the fact "that this powerful sentiment on the part of America to move forward the frontier of democracy is now entering our Southland."

The Conference resolved to "organize poll-tax-paying clubs . . . and registration centers in every neighborhood," thus assuring the maximum vote polled under existing conditions and helping to defeat poll-tax disfranchisement, corrupt and anti-suffrage laws.

It was around such practical questions that the young people formulated a program of action for the coming year.

The Southern Negro Youth Congress expresses the social, economic and cultural desires, not alone of the Negro youth of the Southland, but of the entire Southern people, Negro and white. In every panel, the discussions and resolutions passed by the Conference were not alone concerned with problems facing the youth, but the adult Southern people as well.

In Harlem

In the largest Negro community in the world, in Harlem, too, young people are coming together to make their efforts more effective. On May 13–14, the first All-Harlem Youth Conference was held, representing approximately two hundred thousand youth from 102 organizations of every type of youth group in the Harlem area. Attended by 211 delegates, the main purpose of the conference was to evolve a program for cooperation and coordination of youth activities, for the creation of a better, more wholesome community life.

It is important to record the participation of the young people in the panel discussion groups, since this indicates the major trends among the Negro youth today.

The overwhelming majority of the delegates to the All-Harlem Youth Conference attended the job security panel. "Jobs" is the burning issue before all young people today, especially Negro young people and a struggle must be carried on to win jobs for the Negro youth, if we would win them to the progressive movement.

Resolutions

The Conference went on record endorsing the President's Recovery Program and urged the NYA, WPA, and CCC appropriations be increased. While the Conference delegates came overwhelmingly from religious organizations, the orientation was toward economic betterment and security.

The Conference rejected the idea that citizenship means formal citizenship or citizenship by birth alone. Citizenship was defined as the devotion to those ideals of democracy on which our country was founded and by which we hope to attain a better life for all people.

Resolutions were passed endorsing numerous progressive proposals on education, against discrimination in all fields, for support and joint action of those organizations working for adequate and just employment of Negroes in Harlem, for support of the efforts now being made within the American Federation of Labor (AFL) and the Congress of Industrial Organizations (CIO) for a unified labor movement. The Conference condemned the policies of those public utilities and private corporations which discriminate against the Negro in employment. They went on record, endorsing the O'Connell Amendment to the Neutrality Act, to lift the embargo on Spain.

A permanent committee for the coordination of youth action in Harlem was established. The committee represents a cross section of youth organizations, and it is assured that the expression of all points of view and coordination of efforts of all of Harlem's youth will result.

These are some of the main conferences that have been held withing the last year or so among the Negro youth. But these developments are not limited alone to Chicago, New York, St. Louis, or the South.

In Boston, a Negro youth parley was welded around planks already mentioned. In Southern California, Negro youth are coming together in an effort to unite the Negro youth on the coast. In Washington, DC, a national conference on the Problems of the Negro and Negro Youth, was held on January 6–8.

The Washington Conference was restricted however, "to formulating objectives which can be accomplished in whole or in part by action of the executive and legislative branches of the Government." It requested "that the Federal Government as a guardian and protector of all the people take the lead and set the example by abolishing racial segregation in all of its departments, divisions, and branches . . . Meanwhile, wherever racial segregation exists at present under authority of law," the conference asked "assistance of the Federal Government in obtaining for Negro citizens equality of opportunity with other citizens of the United States."

New Developments

What conclusions can we draw from these developments among the Negro youth? What do they show?

These movements have three things in common. The movement for the right to vote—the most elementary right of citizenship is an inherent part of all the movements, but is especially symbolized in the Southern Negro Youth Congress. It shows that Negro youth are more politically minded than they were two years ago. Negro youth are standing up and fighting for their right to live today, for full citizenship rights, as never before.

Secondly, this movement of youth for democracy embraces the fight for economic security, for jobs, and against discrimination.

RELATION BETWEEN WAGES AND HOURS OF WHITE AND NEGRO YOUTH

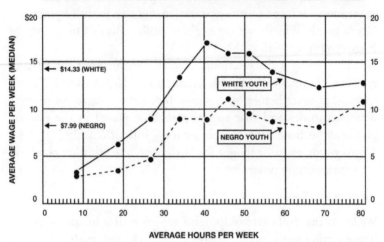

AVERAGE HOURS PER WEEK

From *Youth Tell Their Story*, American Youth Commission

Thirdly, we see the orientation the Negro youth towards culture, "youth's common heritage." This medium that will bring rich rewards to the Negro youth movement, since glorious traditions of the Negro people are evident, not alone in the field of song and dance, but in folk art, folk lore, and other cultural fields.

If we take all these movements and analyze them carefully, we see that today on a national scale, that Negro youth are moving in the direction of a unified national movement. While it is true that they have not yet been brought together, we see a developing movement for national unification among them.

Is it not possible, therefore, to call together these and other movements to really form a united front of the Negro youth of America? The similarity of purpose and aim of these movements certainly gives them this possibility.

Moreover, because of this broad movement for democracy on the part of the Negro youth, to make wide gains among them and win them for our Young Communist League (YCL) is now possible.

In our united front activity, we always are able to contact and work with the progressive and active young people in the progressive youth organizations. But we do not go far enough. Our failure to recruit our progressive and active contacts into the YCL is more than often the case. We are known among the young people in our community as the most advanced youth organization, fighting for full equality for Negro youth. Why do we not begin to utilize this fact to recruit the Negro youth we work with?

The coming 1938 elections, of major importance for all progressives of America, is doubly important to Negro youth. We will witness, as never before, the coming forward of Negro youth organizations to demand that special planks be placed in the election platforms to benefit them. Job security, full citizenship rights for Negro youth, must be fought for as vigorously as all other planks in the youth election programs.

Democratic Front

We know that full citizenship rights are impossible for all the people if one section of the people are oppressed. The rich traditions of the Negro people, in building America to what it is today, the best traditions of Negro culture, their folk art and heroic struggles for emancipation, should be familiar to every YCL'er and progressive person.

It is our task to help this Negro youth movement to achieve the ideals that they cherish. That is why it is necessary that white youth become informed of the struggles of the Negro youth in order to make for the closest cooperation between Negro and white youth organizations.

No longer do Negro youth accept the position as stepchildren of this rich, resourceful nation. To the extent that we bring into our organization such people, to that extent will we be able to rally the Negro youth for continued progressive action.

These movements of the Negro youth, with their advanced programs for citizenship, the right to vote, abolition of poll-tax laws, for job security, for peace, puts them in line with the developing Democratic Front.

'LYNCHLESS YEAR' LIE EXPLODED

WEEKLY REVIEW
JUNE 10, 1940

Mystery shrouds the dastardly crime of lynching today. Reaction's new technique of "silent" lynchings minus the howling mob is the real action behind the pen pusher flagrant statements concerning a "lynchless year." For while these pen pushers try to create a false optimism that lynchings no longer exist, the henchmen of reaction continue to lynch Negro and white workers in the South.

The International Labor Defense (ILD) in a letter published in the *Daily Worker* of May 16, refuted the statement of the Southern Women's Association for the Prevention of Lynching, which declared that during the year from midnight May 8, 1939 to midnight May 8, 1940 no lynchings had taken place. The fact of the matter is that five known deaths from lynchings have occurred since the beginning of 1940 alone. The ILD letter signed by Anna Damon, Secretary, said that the 1940 lynch victims include two Negroes, Richard Johnson and one known only as "Texas Red," and three whites, Sarah Rawls, Benton Ford, and Ike Gaston. Coupled with this an NAACP survey of 1939 reported that there occurred in 1939, in Mississippi alone, at least twenty "quiet" lynchings.

Since this statement of the ILD was published, the day following, from Birmingham, came reports of two Negroes in jail in State Line, Mississippi, and in danger of being lynched as the result of a fight in front of a country store in which two white men and a young Negro were killed. According to the report which came from the Birmingham Communist Party, it was said "that there are threats of lynching in certain circles although among a majority of the whites in the community, it is common talk that the white boys are the starters and cause of the trouble."

Why Is This Said?

The purpose is to lull the vigilance of the people, Negro and white, labor and progressive, by such optimism at a time when mild anti-lynching legislation is once more threatened with death by the reactionary southern and northern senators. Its purpose is to support those whose contention is that legislation to stop lynching is unnecessary. Its purpose is to support, consciously or no, those who are unwilling that mob rule which breeds the strange and bitter fruit of lynchings be crushed by law.

The *Herald Tribune*, which owes a debt of gratitude to Mark Sullivan, its columnist who first put forward the lie that lynching is today nonexistent, again shows why the press play up false "lynchless year" statistics. Editorially, the *Herald Tribune* writes, "Perhaps now we shall hear less of those anti-lynching bills . . . "

But in the teeth of such wishful deceit, the National Negro Congress together with Labor's Non-Partisan League, as a result of their working agreement, on May 7 went on record for passage of the Anti-Lynch Bill as the first goal of Negro and labor unity, and "will instantly and simultaneously use their full energies in a crusade to pass the Anti-Lynching Bill and to save the Wagner Act from amendments."

Recently the Young Women's Christian Association went on record for passage of the Anti-Lynching Bill. These, moving with all progressive women, youth, and Negro organizations together with both houses of labor are on record for passage of the Anti-Lynching Bill.

NO GAVEL NEEDED AT NEGRO YOUTH PARLEY: NATIONAL MEETING MARKED UNITY AGAINST HITLER

WEEKLY REVIEW
DECEMBER 2, 1941

The chairman did not use a gavel. He had no need to, because the young men and women assembled there were attentive, hanging on his every word. It was the Plenary Session—"Negro Youth Versus Hitler"—of the historic National Conference of Negro Youth, November 14–16, in the Nation's Capitol.

Miss Winifred Norman, attractive, alert, young woman from Delta Theta Sigma Sorority, was completing the keynote address.

"Either," she stated emphatically, "we destroy Hitler and his legions, or we will be destroyed and placed under conditions worse than slavery. This, I believe, is the supreme issue confronting us— defeat Hitler, or be engulfed by Hitlerism."

The discussion was on. During that plenary session, Negro young men and women rose to their feet, aggressively, to state their case against Hitler, to propose what should be done to make more effective the fight of the Negro youth against the cardinal evil of Hitlerism today.

Delegate after delegate went on record against Hitler. Some differed in the manner in which the question of the struggle for the rights of the Negro people today should be placed in relationship to the fight against Hitler.

Like Miss Elaine Bailey, Hunter College student who stated, "Of course, we are against Hitler. But we must also demand a practical democracy, now as well as after we defeat Hitler."

Others arose to amend her statement. Miss Anna Daniels, pretty and stirring speaker from Fiske University Chapter of the NAACP, was speaking.

"I believe that we must choose. That choice, if we are to continue to make progress, must be against the greatest evil of all mankind—Hitler and Hitlerism. It is only in this way we can have a new birth of freedom, and government of the people, by the people, and for people shall TRULY GOVERN the earth!"

America Cross Section

They represented a cross section of Negro youth of America. They spoke with conviction and with clarity that was inspiring on questions which many people had said Negro youth were not thinking of. But they were speaking, with notes and without, when the very eagerness of their audience forced them to do away with notes. Just as the delegates from church groups did on Sunday at a plenary session following the Religious Youth Convocation.

Rev. Joseph Haskins, young Baptist minister from Washington, sounded the keynote.

"Church youth," he told the audience, "are not afraid to face problems. They will stand up, as long as you stand up. We are not different. The role of Christian youth in the national crisis, is the same as all youth. We feel the fight, we feel the struggle, against Hitler and we want victory against Hitler as much as you do."

Walter Payton, young delegate from the Church of Master, in New York, refuted the charge that is sometimes made against Christian youth.

"Christian youth are not sissies. The Christian Church has been the binding post to progress for the Negro. We must not wait until we are in a position like a man who comes to dinner after being sentenced. We cannot allow Hitler to run over a country—our country, in which we have a chance of achieving something."

Upon conclusion of the plenary and panel discussions, they chose.

The delegates went on record against Hitler and Hitlerism. They stated, not as a condition, but as an aid to that end, that the nation must recognize and integrate Negro youth into the economic, political, and social life of the nation. Thus, the delegates proved in life, and in their statements that the only road towards achievement and struggle for Negro rights today, is within the framework of the struggle to defeat Hitler.

They chose and took their place on the side of the growing anti-Hitler forces in America and in the world.

The conference was a testament to unity as well as to the historic traditions of struggle on the side of progress of Negro Americans. It was seen in the overflow mass meeting on the opening night.

It was present when the Virginia State College Hundred Voice A-Capella Choir of young Negro men and women, brought wave on wave of emotion from an enthusiastic audience. It was present in the Cultural Festival, when Richard Wright, W. C. Handy, and Joshua White, brought their talents to the fore. The struggle for expression and freedom of a people was dramatized in the play production, *Sing Me a Song* by Thomas Richadson.

With Added Purpose

The delegates went home as they had come, in all kinds of vehicles. But they went back with something added. That something was a determination and a new faith in their strength—the conviction that they had taken a stand against Hitler and Hitlerism, had evolved with a program and a Continuations Committee of Fifty, headed by Miss Winifred Norman, whom, along with the others, they had elected to execute that program.

BEN DAVIS: SYMBOL OF
NEW YORK PEOPLE'S UNITY

DAILY WORKER
SEPTEMBER 22, 1945

A negro mother wished her blessing on Councilman Ben Davis a few weeks ago when she called at his office. Her soldier son had been freed after sixty days under false arrest in Columbus, Ohio. She had come to thank Ben for his intercedence with the Red Cross, Army officials, and Columbus authorities, together with other leaders of the community. And another rung was wrought out in the battle for equality for our Negro servicemen in the armed forces.

A few months earlier, several Negro firemen called on the councilman. They called to thank Ben for his almost single-handed efforts and success in ending the practice of the Fire Department of having special Jim Crow beds for Negro firemen. This fight resulted in the promotion—the first in twenty-five years—of two firemen who testified to the veracity of such a practice.

Many other "firsts" can be attributed to the presence of Councilman Ben Davis in the City Council; such as the unanimous adoption of his resolution demanding an end to Jim Crow in big league baseball; the indignant and unanimous resolution of the Council castigating Bilbo and Bilboism as an insult, not only to the Negro people, but to the entire citizenry of New York and the nation; his significant voice and vote in increasing the city budget which resulted in the long overdue wage increase to city employees.

With such "firsts" it is difficult to imagine New York's City Council without Ben Davis. It is a City Council today that is more attuned to the needs of the people and to the times we live in.

But it is precisely of this that the Dewey-Liberal reactionary Social-Democratic coalition wish to rob the people of New York. Bedecked in sheep's clothing, they cry to the four winds that their aim is "solely" to defeat Ben Davis "the Communist," and to as sure "adequate" Negro representation in the City Council.

Does the fact that Davis may not be reelected disturb these self-proclaimed "champions of the Negro people" one whit? Of course not! It matters little to them whether or not there is any Negro representation in the City Council of New York. As the "best quali-fied representative" of the Negro people, in the words of the influen-tial Negro newspaper, the *Chicago Defender*, and, as a Communist, whose very name symbolizes an uncompromising fight for complete equality of the Negro people, the reactionaries are finding it difficult to toss around the double-edged sword that Davis represents. Hence, their task is divided. On the one hand—give begrudging credit to his record. (What else can even they do?) On the other: confuse the issues of his reelection through red-baiting.

But this still does not fully expose their real aim. It is to foist "white supremacy" on one of the most important legislative councils of the land: it is this that they hope to achieve by robbing the people of New York of what the New York CIO Council termed when it endorsed Davis as being "above all—the symbol of the unity between the Negro people and the people of all races" as well as an ardent and zealous fighter in the interests of labor. This is the chief significance of their summary entering of three other Negro candidates in the field who have no possible chance of election. It is their hope by splitting the Negro vote and confusing the issue on red-baiting lines to elimi-nate Negro representation, and therefore give unbridled reign to the Bilboic attacks against Negroes, Jews, Italians, and other minorities.

Failure of labor, the progressive white citizenry, and the Negro people to recognize this cardinal truth could only result in a go-signal for the "white supremacy" forces of the nation!

Is it too early to speak of Davis' reelection in such terms? On the contrary. Historically, in our country, the resurgence of reaction has come in the form of "white supremacy." It was true during the close of the Civil War, when the Black Hundreds instituted a reign of terror which all but wiped out the Negro people's gains following a war to unite the nation and to free it from chattel slavery. In the anti-Semitic, anti-Negro, pro-fascist slanders against America's minorities by the Bilbos and Eastlands, this same drive is evidenced today, particularly against the heroic and dauntless sons and veterans of the Negro people.

Davis represents the challenge to "white supremacy." He represents the challenge to all pro-fascists and reactionaries, and the struggle to reelect him might well be compared to the fight of the immortal hero of Howard Fast's Freedom Road, Gideon Jackson. As true as was Gideon's fight to stop the reactionaries of that day, so is Ben's reelection the stop-gap to the reactionary coalition who would run riot over the people's gains of the last decade!

Although there is this similarity, there are also key differences. Chief of these is the recognition that it is possible—nay necessary—to reelect Davis in this crucial period in which the full results of our victory, security, and peace, and America's role and future history is being shaped.

Therefore, it might be stated, that Davis' reelection is the No. 1 national example of labor and the peoples' responsibility to maintain and extend the democratic wartime gains of the Negro people. If it is an example, then it is also a challenge. For in the deepest sense, maintenance and extension of these gains represent the essence of the nation's unity; the fruits of our hard-won victory, future peace, and security.

It is this that underlies the widespread national response to his reelection by the Negro people themselves. Inherent in the response is not only that the Negro people desire that New York's City Council should not be without a Negro Councilman; it is that the Negro people are demanding that the times we live in make it necessary for their representative to be a spokesman for their interests, particularly against racial discrimination and pro-fascist "white supremacy" ideologies and practices; as well as a spokesman for the interests of labor, the progressive white citizens, and their organizations.

There are manifold lessons to be drawn from this development. One is that the Negro people are evidencing their deep political maturity and are serving notice to reaction that they will not be split on nationalistic or divisive-baiting lines. (The sanguine observation of the *Chicago Defender* editorial should be voiced for all who have ears to hear—namely that Negroes recognize "that red-baiting is akin to Negro-baiting.") Second is that such recognition is based on their experiences in their struggle for equality in the last decade.

The key aspect of this struggle was that labor and a significant section of white Americans played an outstanding role in supporting the demands of the Negro people—demands which they are learning more and more is in their own fundamental self-interest!

This solidarity will have no greater test than in the coming councilmanic campaign around the reelection of Ben Davis.

As a fighter for Negro-white unity, as a champion of the interests of labor and all the people, Davis represents the symbol of the people's unity and their strength in the coming elections.

It is this fundamental understanding that has led the Communist Party to attach signal importance to the reelection of Davis in Manhattan, and to marshal all its forces for an all-out campaign to assure his reelection. For it is based on the recognition that Communists are the staunchest and uncompromising fighters for the rights of the Negro people, for the alliance of labor and the Negro people, against the fomentors of "white supremacy" and fascist reaction, and for achieving the complete fulfillment of the people's victory over Nazi-Japanese fascist militarism.

To consider Davis' reelection in these basic terms, therefore is to recognize that this understanding must be brought to the Negro and white voters of New York, to make them grasp the deep significance of the oft-used phrase: that Davis is not only a fighter for the Negro peoples but of labor and the progressive white citizenry as a whole.

There is reason to feel confident that deepening of the understanding of the voters as to the issues involved, the Davis record and the symbol that his reelection represents, can be the best weapon that we can and must use to defeat the splitters in the Dewey-Liberal-Social-Democratic reactionary coalition who hope to rob the people of New York of the champion fighter and unity symbol in city government in the nation.

The people—Negro and white—did it before. They can do it again, under new conditions, with a recognition that it's an all-out fight; for our city's future and therefore, that of the nation!

A NEGRO LEADER FROM BILBO'S STATE

DAILY WORKER
JANUARY 10, 1946

In famous Paseo Park, in the heart of Kansas City, Mo., thirteen years ago, a twenty-one-year-old Negro youth stood before an immense crowd listening to white and Negro speakers tell about the fight to free the Scottsboro boys.

On the speaker's rostrum were Herb March and Abner Berry. They mirrored in their words what was then becoming an international fight, led by Communists, not alone for justice, but for the full economic, political, and social equality of thirteen million Negro Americans.

Two kinds of petitions were passed among the crowd which this Negro youth signed. One was a Communist Party petition to free the Scottsboro Boys; the other an appeal to join the Communist Party. The Negro youth, known as Henry Winston, signed them both.

Saw Terror

From then on, Henry Winston's life reads like an American working-class saga. For eleven years a member of the National Committee of the Communist Party, veteran of World War II, and Secretary of the National Negro Commission of the CP, he is one of the scheduled speakers at the forthcoming Lenin Memorial Rally, next Tuesday, Jan. 15, at Madison Square Garden.

Winston, born in Hattiesburg, Mississippi, not far from Bilbo's home, had himself been witness to terror and injustice of the feudal poll taxers and lynchers in the Black Belt; he too had experienced the plight of Negro sharecroppers and workers.

These were the days of hunger marches; the days of the fight for unemployment relief. And "Winnie," as his friends call him, was in that fight. He told me with pride how deeply he felt when Negro youth in Texas, Barney Ross, framed much like the Scottsboro boys, had his life sentence commuted by the Governor of Texas, as a result of the activities of his Communist coworkers. "We could both fight and win," he said.

Henry became active in the YCL. Holding many posts, not alone in Kansas City, but in Ohio, in Harlem as director of the YCL, and in Brooklyn, he was elected to the National Committee of the YCL in 1935. Shortly before this, he went abroad to visit the Soviet Union, France, and England.

"I found in France and England much of the same kind of problems as those faced by the American working class," said Winnie. "In the Soviet Union I saw how socialism works. I brought back a lasting impression that freedom of all peoples and internationalism—true interracial brotherhood, has been achieved there since racial discrimination is punishable under Socialist laws and customs."

Author of many pamphlets and articles, Winston pioneered in the movements which developed in the last decade, as a result of the growing political maturity of the Negro people. He helped found the Southern Negro Congress, the National Negro Congress, participated in both the American and World Youth Congresses.

Winston enlisted in the Army shortly after Pearl Harbor, serving over three years, in the American and European war theatres. He received the Certificate of Merit, highest regimental award, and the Certificate of Proficiency. He served as army correspondent, and as assistant to the Educational office. He was responsible for orientation classes, helping to prepare the men for return to civilian life.

In an interview on the coming Lenin Memorial meeting, Winston emphasized Lenin's contributions to the fight against national oppression.

"Lenin," he said, "was first of all an internationalist. The cornerstone of his teachings is that of proletarian internationalism. It was this that led him to understand not only the problems of Russia but those of oppressed peoples everywhere. As far back as 1913, he made a study of the national oppression of the Negro people which had within it the elements of solving the Negro question in the

United States. Today in our country, Lenin's internationalism lies in the unity of Negro and white—a unity against monopoly capitalist oppression of the working class and its imperialist oppression against the Negro people."

LIBERAL OUTLOOK ON LYNCHING

DAILY WORKER
MARCH 11, 1946

PM's editors recently asked Jennings Perry, editor of the Nashville *Tennessean* to do a "behind the scenes" story on the anti-Negro violence in Columbia, Tennessee.

Undoubtedly, this is in line with *PM*'s taking up some issues affecting the Negro people. But since no editorial comment accompanied Mr. Perry's piece, it leads one to suspect that this is *PM*'s "line" on this vital issue.

Perry complacently notes that there was nothing unusual for the Tennessee highway patrol to be rushed in to devastate and invade the Negro community. Of this Gestapo-like terror, he simply says that the same thing was being done "ten days ago" by the same state patrol "on the report that the sheriff was being lynched" in another county where no Negroes live.

Here we have a typical bourgeois-liberal (acceptance of the status-quo) approach to the terror against the Negro people. To put it another way: Mr. Perry is saying, "What is so bad anyway with the 'inexcusable nastiness' (his term for death and lynch terror against Negro citizens) on the part of the highway patrolmen and the government officials of Tennessee? They were only performing their duty."

Aids Whitewash

This is nothing but an aid to the official whitewash of the lynchers of the Negro peoples in Tennessee, Freeport, Long Island, and elsewhere. It is an "equalization" of responsibility. It is a go-signal to the terrorist, pro-fascist hoodlums that they can expect protection from the powers-that-be in city and state governments.

Mr. Perry darn well knows that it is the Jim Crow conditions under which the Negro people live, that explains why, though in the nearby county, he so glibly mentions, there was no terror, there was terror against the Negro community in Columbia.

Mr. Perry's own comment further clinches this observation. He states: While it is true that all large cities in Tennessee "have their Harlems" a Negro "is seldom seen" in certain parts of Tennessee.

Well, why do we have "Harlems" in every city of the land? Is it because the Negro people want it so? It is because of Jim Crow and ghetto living conditions; of forcible exclusion (through written and unwritten laws) of Negroes from political, economic, and social life. Hence, Mr. Perry's reference can be nothing more than a complete acquiescence and propping-up of the Jim Crow status of the Negro people.

'Good Relations'

True, Mr. Perry takes pride in the ordinarily "good relations" between Negroes and whites in his state. He would not go so far as "the type of white politician" like US Sen. Herman Ross who advocates "depriving the Negro of all civil rights till he can be sent back to Africa."

To say the least, it quite escapes Mr. Perry that Bilboism and imperialist propaganda are abetted by his "liberal" acceptance of the Jim Crow conditions under which the oppressed Negro people live. No wonder Mr. Perry can say "there is very little political discrimination . . . though Negroes never get elected to office."

It follows therefore that Perry's (and also *PM*'s?) major conclusion is: there is really nothing to worry about in the spreading anti-Negro violence.

After all, Perry argues, the "race question has been here ever since the two races have." It is "an ancient inherited problem." And what has "edged it?" The drive perhaps on the part of American imperialism to destroy the wartime gains of the Negro people and the working class? The use by American imperialists of the Hitlerite scapegoat tactic of lynch terror against the Negro people as they drive towards World War III?

No indeed! Perry considers "the worst fly in the ointment of race relations" the "departure of Negro women from the white kitchens" which has "stirred quite a white fury on the distaff side."

True, he says—and quite rightly—that Negro women "do not mean to go back if they can help it." But his whole polemic really grovels before the gods of imperialism and "white supremacy."

It is too late in history, even for Perry and *PM,* to be making light of these incipient seeds of fascism in our own country. Instead of placing "equal blame" it is time to demand the speedy enforcement of official responsibility of the Deweys and others for punishing the lynchers of Freeport, Long Island and Columbia, Tennessee.

Let us remember the lesson of the German people: history will not excuse those who help fascism either by "liberal excuses" or by the conscious use of the ideological weapon of "Aryan supremacy."

NEGRO CONGRESS MAPS WIDE FIGHT TO END JIM CROW

DAILY WORKER
JUNE 4, 1946

Detroit, June 3.—The one thousand delegates to the Tenth Anniversary Convention of the National Negro Congress (NNC) wound up their parley here yesterday after adopting a militant program against oppression.

Endorsements were given [to] labor's Southern organizing drive. The delegates urged the NNC, AFL, and CIO to draw closer together to organize southern Negroes and whites by "fighting for full political and economic freedom of Negro and white workers as an integral part of the campaign."

The convention reelected Dr. Max Yergan as president and Revels Cayton as executive secretary. C. Lebron Simmons, assistant to the District Attorney in Wayne County (Detroit) was elected treasurer to succeed Ferdinand Smith, Vice President, National Maritime Union.

Raymond Tillman, an international representative of the CIO Transport Workers Union of New Orleans, called for support to the Southern organizing drive which was pledged in a resolution "recognizing the great need for organizing the South in the interests of all Americana and especially in the interest of the political and economic needs of the Negro people." "Full support to the campaigns of the AFL and CIO," were resolved.

Nine points make up the objectives of the NNC as embodied in its constitution:

1. Full citizenship rights as guaranteed in the Thirteenth, Fourteenth, and Fifteenth Amendments to the Federal Constitution.

2. The right of the Negro people to be free from Jim Crowism and mob violence and enactment of Federal anti-lynch legislation.

3. Employment for the Negro people, free from any job discrimination by government agencies and private industry.

4. Promotion of the cause of trade unionism among Negroes and organization of Negro workers into trade unions on a basis of full equality.

5. Effective health, educational, and housing needs for Negroes without discrimination and for security against old age unemployment and want.

6. Cultural development and expression of the Negro people regarding their traditions and contributions to American democracy, and a fight on all falsifications and distortions of their historic role in American life.

7. Promotion of the cause of peace, furthering of the aims of the United Nations, aid for the liberation of the oppressed colonial and semi-colonial peoples of the world, opposition to imperialist wars, and a realization of a genuine brotherhood of man.

8. An end to discrimination and segregation in the armed forces.

9. A spirit of unity and cooperation between the Negro and white people in a common struggle for their mutual welfare.

A spirit of enthusiastic cooperation pervaded the discussion. Delegates pledged financial support. Delegations from Chicago, Michigan and California offered to raise $4,000 in the next thirty days.

More than $60,000 was pledged in the form of outright contributions by individuals, trade unions, religious, and civic organizations.

Major provisions of the new constitution are to establish the National Negro Congress "based primarily upon chapters or branches composed of individual members in local communities, trade unions, churches, and other local organizations, which chapters shall be chartered by the National Executive Board."

BILBO IS NO LAUGHING MATTER & MASS STRUGGLE WILL HALT LYNCHINGS

DAILY WORKER
AUGUST 25–26, 1946

[These two articles appeared in succession from August 25 to August 26]

The startling admission of Klan membership by Theodore Bilbo, Mississippi's Seven-Percent Senator, has caused little more than a ripple in anti-fascist America.

A senator of the United States, sworn to uphold the "noble" principles of American democracy, boasted on a nationwide radio hook-up that he holds his oath to a fascist body higher than American laws, its Constitution, and its Bill of Rights! Such is his boast at a time when everyone knows that fourteen million Negro Americans are involved in the deepest political struggle for their very lives, below and above the Mason-Dixon line, facing the most vicious lynch-terror drive in the history of the land.

Yet, up to the present moment, the United Auto Workers (UAW-CIO) international board is alone among the great trade-union bodies who have demanded action to impeach Bilbo! This is the same Bilbo who has repeatedly ranted in the vilest fascist manner against Italians, Jews, Puerto Ricans, and organized labor—to say nothing of his "white supremacist" election incitements to violence against Negroes.

How can we explain the indifference that civilized anti-fascist America and its great trade unions have shown to this open admission of Klan membership on Bilbo's part? By the fact that in our country the rotten "white supremacist" race theories, consciously nurtured by the American imperialists, have so long prevailed.

These "white supremacist" ideas and practices are today part and parcel of the technique required by "our" imperialists to brutalize the American people, the "better" to prepare them for an anti-Soviet atomic war for world conquest.

It has become almost axiomatic to expect periodic demonstration to the world of the unique American pogrom lynching of Americans with black skins. But now, such lynchings and such "race supremacist" theories and practices have become the crass and boastful means through which a fascist system can be foisted on America. Hence, Bilbo's admission of Klan membership is tantamount to the early boastful admission of Hitler's Bund and Stormtroopers who pillaged and raped Germany; who terrorized and murdered six million European Jews; destroyed labor unions and other democratic institutions; brought death and destruction and terror to millions.

Let it not be forgotten that a German paperhanger, once the laughing stock of the world, moved more and more openly, to strengthen his power, until he destroyed the democratic liberties of a whole nation, in his aim to achieve world conquest. Nor should it be forgotten that our South, with its backward feudalist practices and conditions, its systematic denial of even the most elementary civil and democratic rights to ten million Negroes and poor whites, is fertile ground even as was Germany—for nurturing the fierce fascist terror, spawned by the German Junker landlord class and aided by the most modern scientific techniques of German Imperialism.

FOR BILBO IS NO LAUGHING STOCK!

It has long been the technique of the American capitalist press and its leaders to present the Bilbos, Eastlands, and Rankins as "amusing" figures. So long as this continues unchallenged, just so long will such fascist characters utilize every inch of immunity from the serious measures required by the body politic against their polluting sores.

Bilbo counts on this, as does the imperialist bourgeoisie and its mouthpiece.

The imperialists count on open familiarity with the Bilbonic plague to breed a special kind of contempt—a light, inactive one.

Even our own paper—leading anti-fascist paper of the country— recently reflected this light manner of dealing with Bilbo and allowed a "cuckoo's egg" to creep into our pages. "At least he's out in the open," stated a caption under Bilbo's picture, which accompanied an excellent piece by our popular columnist, Mike Gold, on lynch terror against Negroes! Does it make it "less" dangerous, or more so—that "he's out in the open?" It's unnecessary to belabor the point.

Suffice it to state that, while we learn from our self-criticism and take rapid steps to self-correction, we likewise stress the same for all anti-fascists—especially labor. For much of this thinking has served to court inaction—on this issue, based on lack of fundamental appraisal of the anti-Negro drive. This we shall analyze in tomorrow's article.

(Continued in Monday's *Daily Worker*)

❃ ❃ ❃ ❃ ❃

The Wall Street Bourbon lynch drive against the Negro people has ceased to be sporadic. For seven months, each new outrage has shown that this lynch drive by the Wall Street monopolists and their Southern landlord henchmen is a sustained one.

What we are witnessing are the lengths to which a corrupt capitalist system aims to go, its brutality—as well as its objectives.

Consider in this wise [sic] the complete breakdown of the federal and state processes of law and order, so recently admitted by the head of the Georgia FBI—where lynchers freely roam like hunters on human prey! Despite this, an assistant attorney general, from the office of US Attorney General Tom Clark, told a youth veteran delegation that the Department of Justice would take no positive action against the Ku Klux Klan and that it had no positive result of the one thousand cases of violent attacks against the Negro people!

Consider, too, the refusal of the President of the United States to give protection to white and Negro anti-lynch witnesses in Georgia, or to demand that the evidence thus far secured be immediately used to prosecute those known to be involved in the brutal mob murder of four Negro citizens!

Yet, this is the same kind of "justice" for which certain American "liberals" recently spent millions of dollars to "save" the hanged Yugoslav traitor, Mikhailovitch. Noticeable in contrast, too, is the manner in which the government of liberated Poland swiftly moved to execute the nine anti-Semites who perpetrated violence against Jews in postwar Poland.

It is not amiss to tell anti-fascists that once before it was their cry which rang around the world to "Free the Scottsboro Boys!"

Millions moved into action then—as millions must, and can, move now—because we knew that involved then as now—was not only the future of those nine boys, but the future of a whole oppressed people, the liberties of each and every one—of the entire nation.

A tremendous outline of this mass movement is in the making.

Negro women, meeting in the nation's capital, who never picketed before, threw a cordon around the White House in the dark hour following the Monroe, Ga., lynchings.

Thousands, embracing an entire city—as in Philadelphia—mourned the lynched dead of Georgia, unitedly, cutting across class and neighborhood lines.

In the largest single Negro community in the nation—in Harlem —the night after the Georgia Ku Klux fascist crimes, thousands of Negroes packed an entire city block, to hear Communist and non-Communist spokesmen, in unity, express their deepest emotions—that our very lives were at stake.

At the Lincoln Memorial and before the White House, two mass gatherings, embracing tens of thousands, protested in anger under the auspices of the Southern Conferences for Human Welfare, the National Negro Congress and the National Association for the Advancement of Colored People, supported by organized labor.

In Winston-Salem, NC, in Alabama, and in Georgia itself, the Negro people, supported by AFL-CIO labor leaders and other democratic organizations, hurled their protests in the teeth of the lynchers.

As in Scottsboro, the voice of the youth of the world, through the World Federation of Democratic Youth, urged US capture and trial of the lynchers from across the seas—in Paris, as from Havana, Cuba, when their protests were heard through the National Federation of Cuban Negro Organizations. These and other actions finally compelled the President of the United States to speak out after six months of silence against lynch terror. But the record of lip service of the Truman Administration tells us that words are not enough. With the prime exception of the Communist Party, not a word has been uttered by either major party—Republican or Democrat. The Communist Party, moreover, is the only party who has matched its words of protest with its deeds.

AN END TO THE NEGLECT OF THE PROBLEMS OF THE NEGRO WOMAN!

POLITICAL AFFAIRS
JUNE 1949

An outstanding feature of the present stage of the Negro liberation movement is the growth in the militant participation of Negro women in all aspects of the struggle for peace, civil rights, and economic security. Symptomatic of this new militancy is the fact that Negro women have become symbols of many present-day struggles of the Negro people. This growth of militancy among Negro women has profound meaning, both for the Negro liberation movement and for the emerging anti-fascist, anti-imperialist coalition.

To understand this militancy correctly, to deepen and extend the role of Negro women in the struggle for peace and for all interests working class and the Negro people, means primarily to overcome the gross neglect of the special problems of Negro women. This neglect has too long permeated the ranks of the labor movement generally, of left-progressives, and also of the Communist Party. The most serious assessment of these shortcomings by progressives, especially by Marxist-Leninists, is vitally necessary if we are to help accelerate this development and integrate Negro women in the progressive and labor movement and in our own Party.

The bourgeoisie is fearful of the militancy of the Negro woman, and for good reason. The capitalists know, far better than many progressives seem to know, that once Negro women undertake action, the militancy of the whole Negro people, and thus of the anti-imperialist coalition, is greatly enhanced.

Historically, the Negro woman has been the guardian, the protector, of the Negro family. From the days of the slave traders down to the present, the Negro woman has had the responsibility of caring for the needs of the family; of militantly shielding it from the blows of Jim Crow insults; of rearing children in an atmosphere of lynch terror, segregation, and police brutality; and of fighting for an education for the children. The intensified oppression of the Negro people, which has been the hallmark of the postwar reactionary offensive, cannot therefore but lead to an acceleration of the militancy of the Negro woman. As mother, as Negro, and as worker, the Negro woman fights against the wiping out of the Negro family against the Jim Crow ghetto existence which destroys the health, morale, and very life of millions of her sisters, brothers, and children.

Viewed in this light, it is not accidental that the American bourgeoisie has intensified its oppression, not only of the Negro people in general, but of Negro women in particular. Nothing so exposes the drive to fascization in the nation as the callous attitude which the bourgeoisie displays and cultivates toward Negro women. The vaunted boast of the ideologists of Big Business—that American women possess "the greatest equality" in the world is exposed in all its hypocrisy when one sees that in many parts of the world, particularly in the Soviet Union, the New Democracies, and the formerly oppressed land of China, women are attaining new heights of equality. But above all else, Wall Street's boast stops at the water's edge where Negro and working-class women are concerned. Not equality, but degradation and super-exploitation: this is the actual lot of Negro women!

Consider the hypocrisy of the Truman Administration, which boasts about "exporting democracy throughout the world" while the state of Georgia keeps a widowed Negro mother of twelve children under lock and key. Her crime? She defended her life and dignity—aided by her two sons—from the attacks of a "white supremacist." Or ponder the mute silence with which the Department of Justice has greeted Mrs. Amy Mallard, widowed Negro school-teacher, since her husband was lynched in Georgia because he had bought a new Cadillac and become, in the opinion of the "white supremacists," "too uppity." Contrast this with the crocodile tears shed by the US delegation to the United Nations for Cardinal Mindszenty, who collaborated with the enemies of the Hungarian People's Republic and sought to hinder the forward march to fuller democracy by the formerly oppressed workers and peasants of Hungary. Only recently,

President Truman spoke solicitously in a Mother's Day Proclamation about the manifestation of "our love and reverence" for all mothers of the land. The so-called "love and reverence" for the mothers of the land by no means includes Negro mothers who, like Rosa Lee Ingram, Amy Mallard, the wives and mothers of the Trenton Six, or the other countless victims, dare to fight back against lynch law and "white supremacy" violence.

Economic Hardships

Very much to the contrary, Negro women—as workers, as Negroes, and as women—are the most oppressed stratum of the whole population.

In 1940, two out of every five Negro women, in contrast to two out of every eight white women, worked for a living. By virtue of their majority status among the Negro people, Negro women not only constitute the largest percentage of women heads of families, but are the main breadwinners of the Negro family. The large proportion of Negro women in the labor market is primarily a result of the low-scale earnings of Negro men. This disproportion also has its roots in the treatment and position of Negro women over the centuries.

Following emancipation, and persisting to the present day, a large percentage of Negro women—married as well as single—were forced to work for a living. But despite the shift in employment of Negro women from rural to urban areas, Negro women are still generally confined to the lowest-paying jobs. The Women's Bureau, US Department of Labor, *Handbook of Facts for Women Workers* (1948, Bulletin 225), shows white women workers as having median earnings more than twice as high as those of non-white women, and non-white women workers (mainly Negro women) as earning less than $500 a year! In the rural South, the earnings of women are even less. In three large Northern industrial communities, the median income of white families ($1,720) is almost 60 percent higher than that of Negro families ($1,095). The super-exploitation of the Negro woman worker is thus revealed not only in that she receives, as woman, less than equal pay for equal work with men, but in that the majority of Negro women get less than half the pay of white women. Little wonder, then, that in Negro communities the conditions of ghetto-living—low salaries, high rents, high prices, etc.—virtually become an iron curtain hemming in the lives of Negro children and undermining their health and spirit! Little wonder that the maternity death rate for Negro women is triple that of white women! Little wonder that one out of every ten Negro children born in the United States does not grow to manhood or womanhood!

The low scale of earnings of the Negro woman is directly related to her almost complete exclusion from virtually all fields of work except the most menial and underpaid, namely, domestic service. Revealing are the following data given in the report of 1945, *Negro Women War Workers* (Women's Bureau, US Department of Labor, Bulletin 205): Of a total 7.5 million Negro women, over a million are in domestic and personal service. The overwhelming bulk—about 918,000—of these women workers are employed in private families, and some 98,000 are employed as cooks, waitresses, and in like services in other than private homes. The remaining 60,000 workers in service trades are in miscellaneous personal service occupations (beauticians, boarding house and lodging-house keepers, charwomen, janitors, practical nurses, housekeepers, hostesses, and elevator operators).

The next largest number of Negro women workers are engaged in agricultural work. In 1940, about 245,000 were agricultural workers. Of them, some 128,000 were unpaid family workers.

Industrial and other workers numbered more than 96,000 of the Negro women reported. Thirty-six thousand of these women were in manufacturing, the chief groups being 11,300 in apparel and other fabricated textile products, 11,000 in tobacco manufactures, and 5,600 in food and related products.

Clerical and kindred workers in general numbered only 13,000. There were only 8,300 Negro women workers in civil service.

The rest of the Negro women who work for a living were distributed along the following lines: teachers, 50,000; nurses and student nurses, 6,700; social and welfare workers, 1,700; dentists, pharmacists, and veterinarians, 120; physicians and surgeons, 129; actresses, 200; authors, editors, and reporters, 100; lawyers and judges, 39; librarians, 400; and other categoric likewise illustrating the large-scale exclusion of Negro women from the professions.

During the anti-Axis war, Negro women for the first time in history had an opportunity to utilize their skills and talents in occupations other than domestic and personal service. They became trailblazers in many fields. Since the end of the war, however, this has given way to growing unemployment, to the wholesale firing of Negro women, particularly in basic industry.

This process has been intensified with the development of the economic crisis. Today, Negro women are being forced back into domestic work in great numbers. In New York State, for example, this trend was officially confirmed recently when Edward Corsi, Commissioner of the State Labor Department, revealed that for the first time since the war, domestic help is readily obtainable. Corsi in effect admitted that Negro women are not voluntarily giving up jobs, but rather are being systematically pushed out of industry. Unemployment, which has always hit the Negro woman first and hardest, plus the high cost of living, is what compels Negro women to reenter domestic service today. Accompanying this trend is an ideological campaign to make domestic work palatable. Daily newspaper advertisements which base their arguments on the claim that most domestic workers who apply for jobs through US Employment Service (USES) "prefer this type of work to work in industry," are propagandizing the "virtues" of domestic work, especially of "sleep-in positions."

Inherently connected with the question of job opportunities where the Negro woman is concerned, is the special oppression she faces as Negro, as woman, and as worker. She is the victim of the white chauvinist stereotype as to where her place should be. In film, radio, and press, the Negro woman is not pictured in her real role as breadwinner, mother, and protector of the family, but as a traditional "mammy" who puts the care of children and families of others above her own. This traditional stereotype of the Negro slave mother, which to this day appears in commercial advertisements, must be combatted and rejected as a device of the imperialists to perpetuate the white chauvinist ideology that Negro women are "backward," "inferior," and the "natural slaves" of others.

Historical Aspects

Actually, the history of the Negro woman shows that the Negro mother under slavery held a key position and played a dominant role in her own family grouping. This was due primarily to two factors: the conditions of slavery, under which marriage, as such, was nonexistent, and the Negro's social status was derived from the mother and not the father; and the fact that most of the Negro people brought to these shores by the slave traders came from West Africa where the position of women, based on active participation in property control, was relatively higher in the family than that of European women.

Early historians of the slave trade recall the testimony of travelers indicating that the love of the African mother for her child was unsurpassed in any part of the world. There are numerous stories attesting to the self-sacrificial way in which East African mothers offered themselves to the slave traders in order to save their sons and Hottentot women refused food during famines until after their children were fed.

It is impossible within the confines of this article to relate the terrible sufferings and degradation undergone by Negro mothers and Negro women generally under slavery. Subject to legalized rape by the slaveowners, confined to slave pens, forced to march for eight to fourteen hours with loads on their backs, and to perform back-breaking work even during pregnancy, Negro women bore a burning hatred for slavery and undertook a large share of the responsibility for defending and nurturing the Negro family.

The Negro mother was mistress in the slave cabin, and despite the interference of master or overseer, her wishes in regard to mating and in family matters were paramount. During and after slavery, Negro women had to support themselves and the children. Necessarily playing an important role in the economic and social life of her people, the Negro woman became schooled in self-reliance, in courageous and selfless action.[10]

There is documentary material of great interest which shows that Negro family life and the social and political consciousness of Negro men and women underwent important changes after emancipation. One freedman observed, during the Civil War, that many men were exceedingly jealous of their newly acquired authority in family relations and insisted upon a recognition of their superiority over women. After the Civil War, the slave rows were broken up and the tenant houses scattered all over the plantation in order that each family might carry on an independent existence. The new economic arrangement, the change in the mode of production, placed the Negro man in a position of authority in relation to his family. Purchase of homesteads also helped strengthen the authority of the male.

Thus, a former slave, who began life as a freedman on a "one-horse" farm, with his wife working as a laundress, but who later rented land and hired two men, recalls the pride which he felt because of his new status: "In my humble palace on a hill in the woods beneath the shade of towering pines and sturdy oaks, I felt as a king whose supreme commands were 'law and gospel' to my subjects."

One must see that a double motive was operative here. In regard to his wife and children, the Negro man was now enabled to assume economic and other authority over the family; but he also could fight against violation of women of his group where formerly he was powerless to interfere.

The founding of the Negro church, which from the outset was under the domination of men, also tended to confirm the man's authority in the family. Sanction for male ascendancy was found in the Bible, which for many was the highest authority in such matters.

Through these and other methods, the subordination of Negro women developed. In a few cases, instead of legally emancipating his wife and children, the husband permitted them to continue in their status of slaves. In many cases, state laws forbade a slave emancipated after a certain date to remain in the state. Therefore, the only way for many Negro wives and children to remain in the state was was to become "enslaved" to their relatives. Many Negro owners of slaves were really relatives of their slaves.

In some cases, Negro women refused to become subject to the authority of the men. In defiance of the decisions of their husbands to live on the places of their former masters, many Negro women took their children and moved elsewhere.

Negro Women in Mass Organizations

This brief picture of some of the aspects of the history of the Negro woman, seen in the additional light of the fact that a high proportion of Negro women are obliged today to earn all or part of the bread of the family, helps us understand why Negro women play a most active part in the economic, social, and political life of the Negro community today. Approximately 2.5 million Negro women are organized in social, political, and fraternal clubs and organizations. The most prominent of their organizations are the National Association of Negro Women, the National Council of Negro Women, the National Federation of Women's Clubs, the Women's Division of the Elks' Civil Liberties Committee, the National Association of Colored Beauticians, National Negro Business Women's League, and the National Association of Colored Graduate Nurses. Of these, the National Association of Negro Women, with seventy-five thousand members, is the largest membership organization. There are numerous sororities, church women's committees of all denominations, as well as organizations among women of West Indian descent. In some areas, NAACP chapters have Women's Divisions, and recently the National Urban League established a Women's Division for the first time in its history.

Negro women are the real active forces—the organizers and workers—in all the institutions and organizations of the Negro people. These organizations play a many-sided role, concerning themselves with all questions pertaining to the economic, political, and social life of the Negro people, and particularly of the Negro family. Many of these organizations are intimately concerned with the problems of Negro youth in the form of providing and administering educational scholarships, giving assistance to schools and other institutions, and offering community service. The fight for higher education in order to break down Jim Crow in higher institutions, was symbolized last year by the brilliant Negro woman student Ada Lois Sipuel Fisher of Oklahoma. The disdainful attitudes which are sometimes expressed—that Negro women's organizations concern themselves *only* with "charity" work—must be exposed as of chauvinist derivation, however subtle, because while the same could be said of many organizations of white women, such attitudes fail to recognize the *special character* of the role of Negro women's organizations. This approach fails to recognize the special function which Negro women play in these organizations, which, over and above their particular function, seek to provide social services denied to Negro youth as a result of the Jim Crow lynch system in the US.

The Negro Woman Worker

The negligible participation of Negro women in progressive and trade-union circles is thus all the more startling. In union after union, even in those unions where a large concentration of workers are Negro women, few Negro women are to be found as leaders or active workers. The outstanding exceptions to this are the Food and Tobacco Workers' Union and the United Office and Professional Workers' Union.

But why should these be exceptions? Negro women are among the most militant trade unionists. The sharecroppers' strikes of the '30s were sparkplugged by Negro women. Subiect to the terror of the land-lord and white supremacist, they waged magnificent battles together with Negro men and white progressives in that struggle of great tradi-tion led by the Communist Party. Negro women played a magnificent part in the pre-CIO days in strikes and other struggles, both as workers and as wives of workers, to win recognition of the principle of indus-trial unionism, in such industries as auto, packing, steel, etc. More recently, the militancy of Negro women unionists is shown in the strike of the packing-house workers, and even more so in the tobacco workers' strike—in which such leaders as Moranda Smith and Velma Hopkins emerged as outstanding trade unionists. The struggle of the tobacco workers led by Negro women later merged with the political action of Negro and white which led to the election of the first Negro in the South (in Winston-Salem, NC) since Reconstruction days.

It is incumbent on progressive unionists to realize that in the fight for equal rights for Negro workers, it is necessary to have a special approach to Negro women workers, who, far out of proportion to other women workers, are the main breadwinners in their families. The fight to retain the Negro woman in industry and to upgrade her on the job is a major way of struggling for the basic and special inter-ests of the Negro woman worker. Not to recognize this feature is to miss the special aspects of the effects of the growing economic crisis, which is penalizing Negro workers, particularly. Negro workers, with special severity.

The Domestic Worker

One of the crassest manifestations of trade-union neglect of the prob-lems of the Negro woman worker has been the failure, not only to fight against relegation of the Negro to domestic, menial, and similar work, but to *organize* the domestic worker. It is merely lip service for progressive unionists to speak of organizing the unorganized without turning their eyes to the serious plight of the domestic worker, who, unprotected by union standards, is also the victim of exclusion from all social and labor legislation.

Only about one in ten of all Negro women workers is covered by present minimum-wage legislation, although about one-fourth of all such workers are to be found in states having minimum-wage laws. All of the arguments heretofore projected with regard to the real difficulties of organizing the domestic workers—such as the "casual" nature of their employment, the difficulties of organizing day workers, the problem of organizing people who work in individual households, etc.—must be overcome forthwith. There is a danger that Social-Democratic forces may enter this field to do their work of spreading disunity and demagogy, unless progressives act quickly.

The lot of the domestic worker is one of unbearable misery. Usually, she has no definition of tasks in the household where she works. Domestic workers may have "thrown in," in addition to cleaning and scrubbing, such tasks as washing windows, caring for the children, laundering, cooking, etc., and all at the lowest pay. The Negro domestic worker must suffer the additional indignity, in some areas, of having to seek work in virtual "slave markets" on the streets where bids are made, as from a slave block, for the hardiest workers. Many a domestic worker, on returning to her own household, must begin housework anew to keep her own family together.

Who was not enraged when it was revealed in California, in the heinous case of Dora Jones, that a Negro woman domestic was enslaved for more than forty years in "civilized" America? Her "employer" was given a minimum sentence of a few years and complained that the sentence was for "such a long period of time." But could Dora Jones, Negro domestic worker, be repaid for more than forty years of her life under such conditions of exploitation and degradation? And how many cases, partaking in varying degrees of the condition of Dora Jones, are still tolerated by progressives themselves!

Only recently, in the New York State Legislature, legislative proposals were made to "fingerprint" domestic workers. The Martinez Bill did not see the light of day, because the reactionaries were concentrating on other repressive legislative measures; but here we see clearly the imprint of the African "pass" system of British imperialism (and of the German Reich in relation to the Jewish people!) being attempted in relation to women domestic workers.

It is incumbent on the trade unions to assist the Domestic Workers' Union in every possible way to accomplish the task of organizing the exploited domestic workers, the majority of whom are Negro women. Simultaneously, a legislative fight for the inclusion of domestic workers under the benefits of the Social Security Law is vitally urgent and necessary. Here, too, recurrent questions regarding "administrative problems" of applying the law to domestic workers should be challenged and solutions found.

The continued relegation of Negro women to domestic work has helped to perpetuate and intensify chauvinism directed against all Negro women. Despite the fact that Negro women may be grandmothers or mothers, the use of the chauvinist term "girl" for adult Negro women is a common expression. The very economic relationship of Negro women to white women, which perpetuates "madam-maid" relationships, feeds chauvinist attitudes and makes it incumbent on white women progressives, and particularly Communists, to fight consciously against all manifestations of white chauvinism, open and subtle.

Chauvinism on the part of progressive white women is often expressed in their failure to have close ties of friendship with Negro women and to realize that this fight for equality of Negro women is in their own self-interest, inasmuch as the super-exploitation and oppression of Negro women tends to depress the standards of all women. Too many progressives, and even some Communists, are still guilty of exploiting Negro domestic workers, of refusing to hire them through the Domestic Workers' Union (or of refusing help in its expansion into those areas where it does not yet exist), and generally of participating in the vilification of "maids" when speaking to their bourgeois neighbors and their own families. Then, there is the expressed "concern" that the exploited Negro domestic worker does not "talk" to, or is not "friendly" with, her employer, or the habit of assuming that the duty of the white progressive employer is to "inform" the Negro woman of her exploitation and her oppression which she undoubtedly knows quite intimately. Persistent challenge to every chauvinist remark as concerns the Negro woman is vitally necessary, if we are to break down the understandable distrust on the part of Negro women who are repelled by the white chauvinism they often find expressed in progressive circles.

Manifestations of White Chauvinism

Some of the crassest expressions of chauvinism are to be found at social affairs, where, all too often, white men and women and Negro men participate in dancing, but Negro women are neglected. The acceptance of white ruling-class standards of "desirability" for women (such as light skin), and the failure to extend courtesy to Negro women and to integrate Negro women into organizational leadership, are other forms of chauvinism.

Another rabid aspect of the Jim Crow oppression of the Negro woman is expressed in the numerous laws which are directed against her as regards property rights, intermarriage (originally designed to prevent white men in the South from marrying Negro women), and laws which hinder and deny the right of choice, not only to Negro women, but Negro and white men and women.

For white progressive women and men, and especially for Communists, the question of social relations with Negro men and women is above all a question of strictly adhering to social equality. This means ridding ourselves of the position which sometimes finds certain progressives and Communists fighting on the economic and political issues facing the Negro people, but "drawing the line" when it comes to social intercourse or intermarriage. To place the question as a "personal" and not a political matter, when such questions arise, is to be guilty of the worst kind of Social-Democratic, bourgeois-liberal thinking as regard the Negro question in American life; it is to be guilty of imbibing the poisonous white chauvinist "theories" of a Bilbo or a Rankin. Similarly, too, with regard to guaranteeing the "security" of children. This security will be enhanced only through the struggle for the liberation and equality of all nations and peoples, and not by shielding children from the knowledge of this struggle. This means ridding ourselves of the bourgeois-liberal attitudes which "permit" Negro and white children of progressives to play together at camps when young, but draw the line when the children reach teenage and establish boy-girl relationships.

The bourgeois ideologists have not failed, of course, to develop a special ideological offensive aimed at degrading Negro women, as part and parcel of the general reactionary ideological offensive against women of "kitchen, church, and children." They cannot, however, with equanimity or credibility, speak of the Negro woman's "place" as in the home; for Negro women are in other peoples' kitchens. Hence, their task has been to intensify their theories of male "superiority" as regards the Negro woman by developing introspective attitudes which coincide with the "new school" of "psychological inferiority" of women. The whole intent of a host of articles, books, etc., has been to obscure the main responsibility for the oppression of Negro women by spreading the rotten bourgeois notion about a "battle of the sexes" and "ignoring" the fight of both Negro men and women—the whole Negro people—against their common oppressors, the white ruling class.

Chauvinist expressions also include paternalistic surprise when it is learned that Negroes are professional people. Negro professional women workers are often confronted with such remarks as, "Isn't your family proud of you?" Then, there is the reverse practice of inquiring of Negro women professionals whether "someone in the family" would like to take a job as a domestic worker.

The responsibility for overcoming these special forms of white chauvinism rests, not with the "subjectivity" of Negro women, as it is often put, but squarely on the shoulders of white men and white women. Negro men have a special responsibility particularly in relation to rooting out attitudes of male superiority as regards women in general. There is need to root out all "humanitarian" and patronizing attitudes toward Negro women. In one community, a leading Negro trade unionist, the treasurer of her Party section, would be told by a white progressive woman after every social function, "Let me have the money; something may happen to you." In another instance, a Negro domestic worker who wanted to join the Party was told by her employer, a Communist, that she was "too backward" and "wasn't ready" to join the Party. In yet another community, which since the war has been populated in the proportion of 60 percent Negro to 40 percent white, white progressive mothers maneuvered to get their children out of the school in this community. To the credit of the initiative of the Party section organizer, a Negro woman, a struggle was begun which forced a change in arrangements which the school principal, yielding to the mothers' and to his own prejudices, had established. These arrangements involved a special class in which a few white children were isolated with "selected Negro kids" in what was termed an "experimental class in race relations."

These chauvinist attitudes, particularly as expressed toward the Negro woman, are undoubtedly an important reason for the grossly insufficient participation of Negro women in progressive organizations and in our Party as members and leaders.

The American bourgeoisie, we must remember, is aware of the present and even greater potential role of the masses of Negro women, and is therefore not loathe to throw plums to Negroes who betray their people and do the bidding of imperialism.

Faced with the exposure of their callous attitude to Negro women, faced with the growing protests against unpunished lynchings and the legal lynchings "Northern style," Wall Street is giving a few token positions to Negro women. Thus, Anna Arnold Hedgeman, who played a key role in the Democratic National Negro Committee to Elect Truman, was rewarded with the appointment as Assistant to Federal Security Administrator Ewing. Thus, too, Governor Dewey appointed Irene Diggs to a high post in the New York State Administration.

Another straw in the wind showing attempts to whittle down the militancy of Negro women was the State Department's invitation to a representative of the National Council of Negro Women—the only Negro organization so designated to witness the signing of the Atlantic Pact.

Key Issues of Struggle

There are many key issues facing Negro women around which struggles can and must be waged.

But none so dramatizes the oppressed status of Negro womanhood as does the case of Rosa Lee Ingram, widowed Negro mother of fourteen children—two of them dead—who faces life imprisonment in a Georgia jail for the "crime" of defending herself from the indecent advances of a "white supremacist." The Ingram case illustrates the landless, Jim Crow, oppressed status of the Negro family in America. It illumines particularly the degradation of Negro women today under American bourgeois democracy moving to fascism and war. It reflects the daily insults to which Negro women are subjected in public places, no matter what their class, status, or position. It exposes the hypocritical alibi of the lynchers of Negro manhood who have historically hidden behind the skirts of white women when they try to cover up their foul crimes with the "chivalry" of "protecting white womanhood." But white women, today, no less than their sisters in the abolitionist and suffrage movements, must rise to challenge this lie and the whole system of Negro oppression.

American history is rich in examples of the cost—to the democratic rights of both women and men of failure to wage this fight.

The suffragists, during their first jailings, were purposely placed on cots next to Negro prostitutes to "humiliate" them. They had the wisdom to understand that the intent was to make it so painful that no woman would dare to fight for her rights if she had to face such consequences. But it was the historic shortcoming of the women's suffrage leaders, predominantly drawn as they were from the bourgeoisie and the petty-bourgeoisie, that they failed to link their own struggles to the struggles for the full democratic rights of the Negro people following emancipation.

A developing consciousness on the woman question today, therefore, must not fail to recognize that the Negro question in the United States is *prior* to, and not equal to, the woman question; that only to the extent that we fight all chauvinist expressions and actions as regards the Negro people and fight for the full equality of the Negro people, can women as a whole advance their struggle for equal rights. For the progressive women's movement, the Negro woman, who combines in her status the worker, the Negro, and the woman, is the vital link to this heightened political consciousness. To the extent, further, that the cause of the Negro woman worker is promoted, she will be enabled to take her rightful place in the Negro proletarian leadership of the national liberation movement, and by her active participation contribute to the entire American working class, whose historic mission is the achievement of a Socialist America—the final and full guarantee of woman's emancipation.

The fight for Rosa Lee Ingram's freedom is a challenge to all white women and to all progressive forces, who must begin to ask themselves: How long shall we allow this dastardly crime against all womenhood, against the Negro people, to go unchallenged! Rosa Lee Ingram's plight and that of her sisters also carries with it a challenge to progressive cultural workers to write and sing of the Negro woman in her full courage and dignity.

The recent establishment of the National Committee to Free the Ingram Family fulfills a need long felt since the early movement which forced commutation to life imprisonment of Mrs. Ingram's original sentence of execution. This National Committee, headed by Mary Church Terrell, a founder of the National Association of Colored Women, includes among its leaders such prominent women, Negro and white, as Therese Robinson, National Grand Directoress of the Civil Liberties Committee of the Elks, Ada B. Jackson, and Dr. Gene Weltfish.

One of the first steps of the Committee was the visit of a delegation of Negro and white citizens to this courageous, militant Negro mother imprisoned in a Georgia cell. The measure of support was so great that the Georgia authorities allowed the delegation to see her unimpeded. Since that time, however, in retaliation against the developing mass movement, the Georgia officials have moved Mrs. Ingram, who is suffering from a severe heart condition, to a worse penitentiary, at Reedsville.

Support to the work of this committee becomes a prime necessity for all progressives, particularly women. President Truman must be stripped of his pretense of "know-nothing" about the Ingram case. To free the Ingrams, support must be rallied for the success of the million-signatures campaign, and for UN action on the Ingram brief soon to be filed.

The struggle for jobs for Negro women is a prime issue. The growing economic crisis, with its mounting unemployment and wage cuts, and increasing evictions, is making its impact felt most heavily on the Negro masses. In one Negro community after another, Negro women, the last to be hired and the first to be fired, are the greatest sufferers from unemployment. Struggles must be developed to win jobs for Negro women in basic industry, in the white-collar occupations, in the communities, and in private utilities.

The successful campaign of the Communist Party in New York's East Side to win jobs for Negro women in the five-and-dime stores has led to the hiring of Negro women throughout the city, even in predominantly white communities. This campaign has extended to New England and must be waged elsewhere.

Close to fifteen government agencies do not hire Negroes at all. This policy gives official sanction to, and at the same time further encourages, the pervasive Jim Crow policies of the capitalist exploiters. A campaign to win jobs for Negro women here would thus greatly advance the whole struggle for jobs for Negro men and women. In addition, it would have a telling effect in exposing the hypocrisy of the Truman Administration's "Civil Rights" program.

A strong fight will also have to be made against the growing practice of the USES to shunt Negro women, despite their qualifications for other jobs, only into domestic and personal service work.

Where consciousness of the special role of Negro women exists, successful struggle can be initiated which will win the support of white workers. A recent example was the initiative taken by white Communist garment workers in a shop employing twenty-five Negro women where three machines were idle. The issue of upgrading Negro women workers became a vital one. A boycott movement has been initiated and the machines stand unused as of this writing, the white workers refusing to adhere to strict seniority at the expense of Negro workers. Meanwhile, negotiations are continuing on this issue. Similarly, in a Packard UAW local in Detroit, a fight for the maintenance of women in industry and for the upgrading of 750 women, the large majority of whom were Negro, was recently won.

The Struggle for Peace

Winning the Negro women for the struggle for peace is decisive for all other struggles. Even during the anti-Axis war, Negro women had to weep for their soldier-sons, lynched while serving in a Jim Crow army. Are they, therefore, not interested in the struggle for peace?

The efforts of the bipartisan warmakers to gain the support of the women's organizations in general, have influenced many Negro women's organizations, which, at their last annual conventions, adopted foreign-policy stands favoring the Marshall Plan and Truman Doctrine. Many of these organizations have worked with groups having outspoken anti-imperialist positions.

That there is profound peace sentiment among Negro women which can be mobilized for effective action is shown, not only in the magnificent response to the meetings of Eslanda Goode Robeson, but also in the position announced last year by the oldest Negro women's organization, under the leadership of Mrs. Christine C. Smith, in urging a national mobilization of American Negro women in support of the United Nations. In this connection, it will be very fruitful to bring to our country a consciousness of the magnificent struggles of women in North Africa, who, though lacking in the most elementary material needs, have organized a strong movement for peace and thus stand united against a Third World War, with eighty-one million women in fifty-seven nations, in the Women's International Democratic Federation, exploited and oppressed sections of the working class and its allies.

Our Party, based on its Marxist-Leninist principles, stands four-square on a program of full economic, political, and social equality for the Negro people and of equal rights for women. Who, more than the Negro woman, the most exploited and oppressed, belongs in our Party? Negro women can and must make an enormous contribution to the daily life and work of the Party. Concretely, this means prime responsibility lies with white men and women comrades. Negro men comrades, however, must participate in this task. Negro Communist women must everywhere now take their rightful place in Party leadership on all levels.

The strong capacities, militancy, and organizational talents of Negro women, can, if well utilized by our Party, be a powerful lever for bringing forward Negro workers—men and women—as the leading forces of the Negro people's liberation movement, for cementing Negro and white unity in the struggle against Wall Street imperialism, and for rooting the Party among the most exploited and oppressed sections of the working class and its allies.

In our Party clubs, we must conduct an intensive discussion of the role of the Negro women, so as to equip our Party membership with clear understanding for undertaking the necessary struggles in the shops and communities. We must end the practice, in which many Negro women who join our Party, and who, in their churches, communities, and fraternal groups are leaders of the masses, with an invaluable mass experience to give to our Party, suddenly find themselves viewed in our clubs, not as leaders, but as peoples who have "to get their feet wet" organizationally. We must end this failure to create an atmosphere in our clubs in which new recruits—in this case Negro women—are confronted with the "silent treatment" or with attempts to "blueprint" them into a pattern. In addition to the white chauvinist implications in such approaches, these practices confuse the basic need for Marxist-Leninist understanding which our Party gives to all the workers, and which enhances their political understanding, with chauvinist disdain for the organizational talents of new Negro members, or for the necessity to promote them into leadership.

To win the Negro women for full participation in the anti-fascist, anti-imperialist coalition, to bring her militancy and participation to even greater heights in the current and future struggles against Wall

Street imperialism, progressives must acquire political consciousness as regards her special oppressed status.

It is this consciousness, accelerated by struggles, that will convince increasing thousands that only the Communist Party, as the vanguard of the working class, with its ultimate perspective of socialism, can achieve for the Negro women—for the entire Negro people—the full equality and dignity of their stature in a socialist society in which contributions to society are measured, not by national origin, or by color, but a society in which men and women contribute according to ability, and ultimately under Communism receive according to their needs.

HEROINES OF PEEKSKILL MADE STIRRING HISTORY

DAILY WORKER
SEPTEMBER 15, 1949

The thousands of women who formed part of the magnificent labor progressive audience at the Peekskill Robeson concert on Sept. 5, at Peekskill, again testify to the determination of American women to fight against the war and fascist danger. It testifies also to a truth which reaction fears, namely, that the participation of women brings strength and numbers to the emerging anti-fascist, anti-imperialist war coalition in our country.

The working-class and progressive women went to Peekskill, some with their teenage children and husbands. In so doing, they showed that side by side with their men—with their families, they will fight for peace and democratic rights, which the great Negro leader and people's artist Paul Robeson symbolizes. They showed, by their participation, that they are ready to stand up and be counted against all attempts of officially inspired "spontaneous" attacks that prevented, for example, the original Robeson concert from taking place.

Real heroines arose in the buses, when police anti-state troopers unconcernedly allowed the mob to ambush and stone the passengers.

Women manned buses and helped to bring the children and other passengers to safety. With Paul Robeson at both concerts were such artists as Sylvia Kahn (brutally assaulted by the mob at the first Peekskill concert) and Hope Foye; the women were part of the magnificent defense of the people's forces, which sponsored the concert, and arranged to help guarantee the safety and protection of the people who attended the concert. That women weren't part of the magnificent young guard of veterans and trade unionists who stood on the hill doesn't mean that women didn't play a large and heroic role, or that their role was identical with that of the men.

One of the victims, Miriam Langbert, for example, received her eye injuries at the hands of the mob, backed by police collusion, because she alone stood in the bus urging the wavering driver to stay at his post and to speed the people through Strawberry Road to safety.

A nineteen-year-old girl, Nina Phillips, whose finger was amputated, was the one in her bus who calmed the victims, holding close to her own heart the fact that she was injured until all passengers were brought to safety.

Frances Smith, Negro woman trade unionist of Local 6, Hotel and Club Employee Union, who sustained a head injury from a huge stone, gave leadership in helping to guarantee the safety and protection of the people in her bus, when the attack came following the concert by a frenzied mob which desperately and unsuccessfully sought to cancel out the great anti-fascist victory for free speech demonstrated in the unprecedented response of twenty-five thousand people to this concert.

A granddaughter of the nation's suffrage leader (Elizabeth Cady Stanton, whose statue stands in Washington, DC), Mrs. Nora Stanton Barney, who virtually fought the police-backed mob with her own hands on her way to her car, was assaulted by the mob, who jeered her, even as they jeered the brave women who militantly fought for the right to vote.

These and numerous other heroic examples testify to something else. It shows that here in America, as in Nazi Germany when fascism was on the rise, part of the ideological mentality which stamped the mobs, from which the fascists recruited man and woman power, was their racist bias. This racist bias, directed in the US first against the Negro people, included as its target the Jewish people, the youth and women.

We saw here, on the side of the mob, the callous contempt of women and children. We saw here, on the side of the mob, women too, their faces revealing political backwardness, anti-Negro, anti-Semitic, religious prejudices, and downright ignorance, hurling stones with sadistic glee at busloads of children, elderly women, and men. We saw the face of fascism stamped on the face of one bourgeois woman who drove by our bus marked as target by its shattered glass, miles away from Strawberry Road, coldly saying: "I'm glad it happened."

Many felt, for the first time, even as do Rosa Lee Ingram and the widow of the lynched Negro Robert Mallard, Mrs. Amy Mallard, what it is to feel the cold terror from lynchers who cry for blood of defenseless Negro women, children, and men because of their determination to fight for freedom, and to associate themselves with ideas that stand for peace, security, and equality, as symbolized by Paul Robeson.

Many see more clearly today that those who resort to violence are "the people in glass houses who shouldn't throw stones"—they, who are responsible for the unpunished lynchings, police brutality, the loyalty oaths, the persecution of Communists and progressives—the ruling class itself.

Many see that only if the people themselves defend the Bill of Rights and the Constitution is it possible to smash fascist terror and the threat of war.

Not fear then, but courageous determination was the result of this baptism of struggle for thousands of women, men, and children. In the communities, as in Kings County, women who never spoke before, never before participated in political activity, are speaking on street corners, bringing the Peekskill events to the community. In the established organizations of Jewish and Negro women, calls for greater unity of Negro and Jewish women are being voiced.

This unity of Negro and Jewish women can and should be enhanced. It can help to lay the basis for the unity of women of all nationalities.

In all of these protests, progressive forces, and particularly women, will not fail to draw proper conclusions, that the breakdown of law and order in Peekskill occurred because lynch terror, anti-Semitic attacks, brutal assaults are sanctioned by the Truman Administration, in which Democrats and Republicans are joined to hasten the American people onto the disastrous path of war with all its attendant anti-Communist hysteria, witchhunts, loyalty oaths, and persecution of Communists, and the drive to outlaw the Communist Party.

Let the events of Peekskill be a clarion call to the masses of women who love democracy and civil rights to unite and act now for peace, civil rights, and democracy. Let them, as they act in support of demands for punishment for the guilty, of the arrest of all county and state officials guilty, of the prosecution of KKK revival, understand and protest also against attempts to outlaw the Communist Party, whose leadership reaction fears, even as it fears the democratic exercise of civil rights by the masses of people.

THE LEOPARD HASN'T CHANGED ITS SPOTS

DAILY WORKER
SEPTEMBER 20–21, 1950

The recent appointment of Mrs. Edith Sampson, Chicago Negro woman attorney, as the first American Negro to serve as alternate delegate to the United Nations is undoubtedly an unprecedented step. Since her appointment also represents the highest post ever held by a Negro woman in the United States, it is fitting to inquire, whether, as is being widely interpreted, this is a step "offering liberation" to America's fifteen million Negroes.

In a Chicago interview, Mrs. Sampson rushed into print expressing joy at being named, stating that she was "thrilled" at reports of her appointment. What occasioned Mrs. Sampson's "thrill" at being named to this high international post? Was she "thrilled" at the opportunity to raise the innumerable pitfalls faced by the thriced-oppressed Negro working women, whose sons, victims of Jim Crow on Tokyo's beaches, are today expendable in Wall Street's Korean war against the heroic colored peoples of the Far East? Was she "thrilled" perhaps, at the opportunity through the UN to raise the case of Mrs. Rosa Lee Ingram, mother of fourteen children, falsely imprisoned for over three years in a foul Georgia jail for defending her dignity against the assault to her person by a KKK landlord?

It appears that Mrs. Sampson's source of pleasure stemmed from quite another source. Hastening to guarantee herself, and aligning herself with the tenor of press reports that appointment of a Negro would "counteract Soviet propaganda" regarding racial discrimination in the US, she declared:

> I would be glad to refute such propaganda. There are pit-
> falls for our race, in this country, of course, but they are
> not as the Kremlin would like to picture them. (*New York
> Times*, Aug. 20.)

As the record will later show, the true "pitfalls for our race" which
she claims as her concern, have nowhere been really pictured by Edith
Sampson. Perhaps this explains why she rushed with such haste to
jump on the now lucrative anti-Soviet bandwagon. It is in this context
the question as to the real reason for her appointment as to whether
her appointment is a "step towards integration of Negroes in American life" undoubtedly can be answered.

In the candid assertion of Wall Street's bipartisan press, then, slav-
ishly mouthed by bought sections of the Negro press, a Negro woman
is appointed to the United Nations as alternate delegate—not by virtue
of constitutional right and ability, but "to counteract Russian propaganda." Who else but a racist-minded imperialist crew could brazenly
couch as the basis for a Negro appointee to a world body such a justification—on racial grounds, "to counteract Russian propaganda?"

It is the essence of imperialist contempt to assume that Negroes
can be fooled so easily. That a Negro may lend herself to this assump-
tion does not make it any less contemptuous. One is known by
the company he keeps. That Mrs. Sampson's "colleagues" will be
John Foster Dulles and John Sparkman, white supremacist poll-tax
Alabama Senator, on the General Assembly of the UN, only further
exposes the questionable motives of her "integration."

But there is still another side to Mrs. Sampson's appointment. It
is acknowledgment that American propaganda of "equality," "opportunity," and "free enterprise" is suffering from serious setbacks
despite the "Niagara" of Voice of America broadcasts—to Africa,
India, China—and Korea too, where wanton murderous bombings
of Korean women and children take place by B-29's. For here the
peoples have heard of Rose Lee Ingram, the Martinsville Seven, Willie
McGee, and the Trenton Six. They heard of the killing of FEPC the
day after the unjust Korean war was launched on Truman's unilateral
order which is bringing death to millions of colonial colored peoples.

They laugh in their cups at the State Department's assertion, in
denial of a passport to Paul Robeson, that racial discrimination is

a "family affair." The very assertion, therefore, that Mrs. Sampson's appointment is to "counteract Russian propaganda" is unwitting admission that racial discrimination in the US never was, is not and cannot be a "family affair!"

Millions of darker peoples know that the touchstone of America's sincerity in world affairs is the status of its Negro citizens. They will know, as will millions of Negro men and women, that this Truman appointment in no ways "offers liberation" to Negro citizens. They will know that the leopard has not changed its spots.

No appointment, even of a Negro woman, can erase from the consciousness of darker peoples, including millions of Negro working women, the ever-present status of lynching, poll taxes, segregation, and third-class citizenship. Do not myriads of Negro women still weep for their lynched sons and those cut down in the prime of their manhood by trigger happy cops? And what of the Negro war widows whose sons and husbands are expendable in Korea, where correspondents "nail their exploits" but cannot censor news of the foul insult by a Georgia Senator to a Negro leader on the floor of Congress?

What of the millions of our sisters in the fields and on the job, whose lot is still the most menial of tasks? All these are molding a militant Negro womanhood, cut in the cloth of Harriet Tubman and Sojourner Truth. They do not run or crawl but stand and fight like Rosa Lee Ingram, Bessie Mitchell, Amy Mallard, and Rosalee MeGee, who hurl lie for lie into the teeth of reaction!

It is the people's struggle for Negro rights which compels partial concessions to the indignant—yet unmet—demands for full equality for America's fifteen million second-class citizens. Hence the appointment of a Negro woman to stay this rising cry of militant Negro womanhood who are everywhere demanding peace and equality now for their families; hence the effort to win Negro support for anti-Soviet pro-imperialist intervention and an atomic world war of conquest. To do this it is necessary to make partial concessions. But these partial concessions are marked by complete indifference to the real fate of the masses of Negro people, who suffer unemployment, intensified national oppression, despite demagogic assertions of "equality," "integration," which issue forth as a regular crop yearly by the American two-party system. There is no other framework in which American imperialism can, of its own volition, advance Negroes to higher posts today.

Negro reformists seek to obscure this truth by talk of "integration," the advance of Negroes to higher public posts, etc., as they
bargain under the table of American intervention against the embattled colonial peoples of the earth, for better positions, from which
vantage point they seek to play their lucrative role of craven apologists
for American imperialism.

American imperialism must, nevertheless, meet the ever-widening
criticisms, resentments, and counterattacks of colored peoples all over
the earth who, like a tidal wave, are indicating that they are done with
imperialist subjugation—and their own reformists! And, due to the
extreme pro-racist vulnerability of American imperialism, which is
in the woof and warp of their every declaration and deed, this same
imperialism must meet the truthfully well-aimed criticism, in relation
to the champion, looked to by ever increasing oppressed millions in
Asia and Africa—the socialist Soviet Union.

Not least of all, of the criticisms they must meet, is the unflagging
championship in struggle on behalf of the full economic, political,
and social equality of the Negro people, of Negro-white unity, based
on the firm rock of the Negro-labor alliance, fought for over thirty
years, by the vanguard Party of the American working class—the
Party of Foster, Dennis, Hall, Winston, and Davis—the American
Communist Party.

What an exposure is this imperialist admission that they must
appoint Negroes to higher posts to counter this struggle! To put it in
other words, it is an exposure of the oft-used lying imperialist charge
that we Communists "use the Negro question" to advance our own
aims. There can be no question that a clear distinction exists between
forces who fight to advance the Negro people to full citizenship, by recognizing the special nature of their national oppression, in Jim Crow
America, and those who hide Negro national oppression by obscuring
the fight for special recognition of the Wall Street roots of their oppression under the guise of "cosmopolitanism, "integrationism," etc.

To be sure, this is not the first appointment made relative to
Negroes by American imperialism. Many bipartisan "token" appointments form a growing pattern.

Inherent here, of course, is crafty imperialist discernment of
the powerful and growing militancy of the Negro people of Negro
working women—a key part of the Negro liberation movement—the

most oppressed in the strata of American capitalist society, and hence one of the most potentially powerful sectors for the growing anti-fascist, anti-imperialist coalition.

But these appointments, in contrast to the Roosevelt New Deal, of necessity must be doubly guaranteed. After all, the "safety" of certain appointees is an old stock-in-trade of every ruling class. All the more so, of course, by American imperialism, long practiced at this art, since the days of Negro chattel enslavement. All the more necessary to be employed when a decadent system cannot rule as of old, but must utilize as puppets the reformists among the very oppressed peoples they are contemptuous of, to do their dirty work. And, if it is done "graciously"—well, the mask fits a little less wobbly.

If not alone by her own admission, Mrs. Sampson's record speaks for itself in this regard. For she is a "safe" choice, as safe as the specially privileged predecessors who worked in the homes of the plantation owners more than three hundred years ago. Not safe enough, to be sure, to be a full fledged UN delegate. Even this distinction, slight though it appears, corresponds to the exact status of Negro citizens in the United States, which actually is a second-class status.

A look at Mrs. Sampson's record reveals that she has practiced law for twenty-five years on Chicago's South Side. Chairman of the Executive Committee of the prominent National Council of Negro Women and reputed to be active in civic affairs, she, together with Walter White of NAACP, was named to a group of thirty-one representatives from numerous organizations to take a "round the world tour" under sponsorship of "America's Town Hall of The Air."

Whatever may be the attributes of Mrs. Sampson's legal talents, her concern to quote her statement, for the "pitfalls for our race," was amply shown in an international broadcast when, in Calcutta, world-minded Indian students gave her a rough time of it. It is not quite accurate to say that Mrs. Sampson never pictured the "pitfalls for our race." It must be recorded that it was Mrs. Sampson who fell into the "pitfall" by evasive, nay, apologetic alibis for American racial discrimination, which Indian students brilliantly exposed for her.

If, then, we may ask, the "pitfalls for our race" are not as the "Kremlin would like to picture them" why didn't Mrs. Sampson expose them before an audience of aware Indian students? Could it be that long established contact has smeared on Mrs. Sampson some of the contemptuous imperialist veneer towards the masses of oppressed peoples, including her own, from which she stems?

It is obvious then that the appointment of Mrs. Edith Sampson is in no way a "victory" for integration of Negro women in public life. Nor is it a step "offering liberation" to the Negro people.

But it is still necessary to pose the question: Can there be in this period of growing war danger and fascist reaction, integration of Negroes into posts of public leadership that would represent an advance for the Negro liberation movement? Assuredly there can be such appointments. But the pre-conditions for such a victory must be the active democratic intervention of the Negro people and their advanced labor-progressive white allies to shape the character of such appointments, which today can be important partial concessions wrung from the incumbent pro-war, pro-imperialist administration.

Such integration can only be won, not in spite of, but as part of the growing people's struggle against imperialist war and fascism in our country to reverse the present pro-fascist, pro-war, bipartisan foreign policies of government.

The test for the candidates is a simple one, within such a context— it is simply that once they achieve such posts, there must be no betrayal of Negro rights.

Let us ask of Mrs. Sampson: Will she fight for peaceful mediation in the present Korean conflict in the General Assembly, for inviting both sides in Korea to the UN meeting? Will she fight for genuine human rights, the basis of which is self-determination in the first place for the oppressed colonial peoples of the earth? Will she allow the Dixiecrat John Sparkman to speak for American "equality and opportunity" without challenge? Does she know, for instance, that between V-J Day and today, American imperialism has provided arms and succeeded in killing over two million colored peoples in the dirty wars in Malaya, Vietnam, and Indo-China, to say nothing of Greece and Korea?

Nor does such struggle to guarantee integration of Negro women into all phases of life begin and end with top public posts. Such integration should ever more militantly be fought for by all sections of the Negro people and their white allies to guarantee integration of Negro women into trade-union posts on all levels, into mass organizations of men and women, and in community elective posts of all kinds.

A second pre-condition likewise is the leadership and support given in Negro communities to the programs of mass organizations of Negro women.

Only thus can the Negro people and their advanced labor-progressive white allies raise Negro women from their degraded level of third-class citizenship achieve victories for the Negro liberation struggle today, and save their sons from the degradation of imperialist war and fascism.

JIM CROW CRUELTY IN FEDERAL JAILS

DAILY WORKER
JUNE 29, 1954

I'm going to keep on stinging—'til I awake the conscience of America.
—Harriet Tubman

Almost three long years have passed since that bleak July morning when Ben Davis and his colleagues began serving their savage sentences.

Terre Haute Prison, where Ben Davis has been for all this time, is like all federal prisons in the United States—a Jim Crow prison. In these jails there are not only Jim Crow cells for Negro prisoners, but even a Jim Crow Honor Privilege system: meritorious conduct lists, like some employers' lists and some seniority lists, are established on the basis of the infamous time-dishonored "separate but equal" rule for Negro Americans.

Terre Haute Penitentiary is one of the six institutions of its class operated by the Bureau of Prisons of the Department of Justice. It contains approximately 2,500 prisoners of whom about 250 are Negroes. They are segregated in the dormitories, in mess halls, and in recreational facilities.

Such segregation and discrimination not only violates the rights of Negro prisoners guaranteed by the Fifth Amendment to the Constitution, and the right to be free from cruel and unusual punishment as guaranteed in the Eighth Amendment, but also the laws and statutes pertaining to the government of the United States prisons.

Accordingly, though Ben Davis has met the standard of "meritorious" conduct and his work is classified as "exemplary," he is denied special valuable benefits enjoyed by white prisoners: for example, the door to his cell remains locked during waking hours; he is denied the freedom of a recreation room where there are ping-pong tables and other facilities; access to a library; daily showers after work; the right to engage in conversation with prisoners meeting like standards.

Even in prison, then, the "separate but equal" rule for Negro Americans exists! And this is not a criminal but a political prisoner jailed for his beliefs!

Is it any wonder that Ben Davis, who has struggled against Jim Crow all his life, contemplates a suit against this hateful racist policy? The *Afro-American*, outstanding Negro journal, declared in an editorial entitled "Job for Mr. Brownell:" "We hold no brief for Mr. Davis' political conviction. But we cannot help but admire his courageous outcry against this denial of elementary justice for men in federal custody."

"With every ounce of my strength I shall continue to fight for the people!"

In these words Ben Davis opened his farewell speech to the people of his community and all his former constituents the night he spoke for the last time before his jailing, in Harlem's famed Dewey Square.

The square was jammed with people and placards urging "Repeal the Smith Act!," "Free the Eleven Communist Leaders," "Stop Thought Control," and homemade signs scrawled "Ben, We Love You."

Some people had clenched fists, and tears of anger were in their eyes.

But Ben Davis continued to speak: "The son of liberty is rising all over the world . . . " He talked of the unbreakable fraternity which we have with the peoples of Africa, Asia, the West Indies, Europe, Latin and South America, who are achieving national independence and freedom, as well as with the peoples of the Soviet Union whose nation has wiped out racial discrimination and made it a crime. Ben spoke of our bonds with the people in the wide world who fight for peace, equality, national independence, and security against atomic wars, and for friendship between nations.

And Ben said: "I'll be back on these Harlem streets someday; I know I will . . . "

. . . Spring, and the early harbingers of the Summer season reach Lenox Avenue. Sun bathes the Harlem streets people stroll, and forums sprout in the sidewalks.

Here is a woman who remembers how, when evicted, it was Ben Davis and his party, the Communist Party, who were among the first to fight against her eviction, helped put her furniture back in her house. Here is a bartender who asks, as you open a paper, the *Daily Worker*, of which Ben Davis was publisher before he was jailed, "How is Ben?"

Here is a Negro woman, whose sad eyes contrast strangely with the strong lines in her stern face. I recognize her as the mother of one of the five bereaved families from whom death claimed five victims, three of whom were children, and who lived in a firetrap in Harlem. That was January 1947, when there were forty-five deaths in one month from slum housing in the Harlem–Puerto-Rican–Washington Heights area. "How is Mr. Davis?" She presses your hand meaningfully.

Here is a Negro minister who, when you talk to him, quotes the scripture: "Smite Down the Shepherd and the Sheep Will Be Scattered!" to show his understanding of Ben's jailing.

Here is a white couple who knew Ben and who ask: "What can we do to help free Ben Davis?"

Two youths, Negro and white, striding arm in arm—they seem like students—come up and say in the bright tones of youth: "We Must Free Ben Davis!"

Yes, we can hear his voice! Even from behind the prison bars, Davis' fearless voice scathes racist Jim Crow!

And because it is the supreme evidence and continuation of his entire fight for his people, for all the oppressed, it is all the more resounding.

It is resounding, because it is one with the Negro leaders of the South who rallied in fifteen states against the McCarthy tactics of the Jenner Committee, condemning them as a blow against the entire Negro community of the nation.

It is one with those who fought to save Ethel and Julius Rosenberg.

It is one with the millions here and abroad who kept Wesley Wells from execution in the California gas chamber and who fight to free Mrs. Rosa Lee Ingram.

It is one with all our people who fight in these crucial 1954 elections for an anti-McCarthy, pro-labor, pro-democratic Congress, for extended Negro representation, for peace, security, and democracy!

It is one with our brothers and sisters in the South, in Atlanta itself, in Ben's birthplace, in Dawson, Ga., who asked: "What are you doing to get Ben Davis out of prison?"

Ben Davis' voice and his fight for freedom is one with the Jomo Kenyatta of Africa; Cheddi Jagan and Burnham of British Guiana; with Gabriel D'Arboussier of French Equatorial Africa; with all the valiant men and women fighters of all creeds and national independence of all people throughout the world.

They've jailed Ben Davis. But his ideas are still abroad. It is Ben Davis himself who can best express his ideas from the ladders on the streets of Harlem, in the broad arena of political and legislative struggle, in unity meetings with his people, Negro and white, and with white allies, and in the councils of his own Party. Until Ben Davis can do so, the McCarthyites and the racists will have a strong weapon with which to spread fear and subversion.

Will you answer Ben's confidence that he will be back on the streets of Harlem—and all the broad highways of the nation—someday soon?

The one answer—the one response to Davis' fight against prison Jim Crow and his jailing for his ideas is contained in the word—AMNESTY!

To sing the hallelujah of the famed Negro spiritual: We must free him for he "bears our burden in the heat of the day!"

(Reprinted from *Masses & Mainstream*)

AUTOBIOGRAPHICAL LETTER TO WILLIAM FOSTER

DECEMBER 6, 1955

Ed. note—The following text was pulled from a typewritten letter with annotations by Claudia Jones and transcribed to the best of our ability. Her handwritten annotations are in italics, and missing or illegible words are denoted with ——.

To Comrade Foster

Dear Comrade Foster: The following is the autobiographical (personal, political, medical) history that I promised to forward to you.

Personal: As a child of eight, I came to the United States from Port-of-Spain, Trinidad, British West Indies. My mother and father had come to this country two years earlier in 1922, when their economic status (which were middle-class landowners on my mother's side and hotel owners on my father's side) had been worsened as a result of the drop in the cocoa trade *in the world market* from the West Indies, which had impoverished the West Indies and the entire Caribbean. Like thousands of West Indian immigrants, they hoped to find their fortunes in America where "gold was to be found on the streets" and they dreamed of rearing their children in a "free America."

This dream was soon disabused. Together with my three sisters, our family suffered not only the impoverished lot of working-class native families and its multinational populace, but early learned the special scourge of indignity stemming from Jim Crow national oppression.

My formal academic education on American soil began when I entered Public School, entering 4A. I have early recollections of being hurt by youngsters of my own age who mouthed anti-West Indian propaganda against me and my sisters. But by the time I reached Junior High School, I had formed friendships and become integrated in the student body, and was nominated in *Harriet Beecher Stowe Junior H*[igh] for the highest office in the school and was subsequently elected Mayor. (The form of student administration of this particular junior high was patterned after the then-established pattern of the NYC City Administration). One incident I recall with some pride today, namely that running with me then as President of the Board of Alderman was a young Chinese girl. Numerous teachers tried to pressure me to refuse her as a running mate, on the grounds that she was Chinese, and that had the situation been reversed, this would not happen in China of that day. I refused to be drawn in or to accede to any such narrow concept—choosing instead to have her as my running mate. (To use the phrase I exercised my "peremptory challenge!") We were elected by an overwhelming majority of the students, proving the teachers wrong and showing the internationalist approach of the student body.

My mother had died two years earlier of spinal meningitis suddenly at her machine in a garment shop. The conditions of non-union organization, of that day, of speed-up, plus the lot of working women, who are mothers and undoubtedly the weight of immigration to a new land where conditions were far *from* as promised or anticipated, contributed to her early death at the age of thirty-seven. My father, who together with her had come earlier to America, was left to rear four young girls, the oldest of whom was fourteen. I am the second child of my parents. This was during the days of the Great Depression. Because of my pride, I didn't ask friendly teachers to help provide me with a graduation outfit, at which I was to receive high honors *including the Theodore Roosevelt Award for Good Citizenship* and officiate as Mayor of the school, choosing instead to stay away, sending them some lame excuse while I bawled my eyes out in humiliation and self-pity.

I was later to learn that this lot was not just an individual matter, but that millions of working-class people and Negro people suffered this lot under capitalism if not identical, in one degree or another.

Following my graduation from Junior High School I entered Wadleigh High School. Here I was confronted with Jim Crow in the classrooms and in the social life of the school, and then on leaving the school would turn their faces the other way under pressure of the Jim Crow society. Teachers with audacity would hold Negro students after school, asking if we wanted to make an extra dollar by doing domestic work for them or as they not-so-quaintly put it, whether I wished to "wear a pretty white apron" at their own social affairs. Or they would select poems in dialect and ask Negro kids to read these pointedly. While I even then had, as do other Negro youth, a searing indignation about these things, I didn't know that they were part of a conscious plan designed to perpetuate the national oppression of the Negro people in the US, of which these incidents were reflections of the badge of inferiority perpetrated on the Negro people in the North, with the more hideous features of lynching, poll taxes, crop lien laws, and economic strangulation devolving on the Negro people in the heartland of their oppression, in the Black Belt of the South.

I began to wonder why there was wealth and poverty; why there was discrimination and segregation, why there was a contradiction between the ideas contained in the Constitution and the Bill of Rights which contained its precepts of the pursuit for all of "life, liberty, and happiness."

My formal academic education in a bourgeois sense ended with my graduation from Wadleigh High School. One year before my graduation however, in the midst of the great depression, where I was one of the so-called "lost generation" of American youth, I contracted tuberculosis of the lung. My family's economic condition had worsened as had millions of American families, native and foreign born, and second generation, etc. My dad, who was an editor of an American–West Indian newspaper, lost his job; as later also when he became a furrier and had to guarantee our support, became a superintendent of an apartment in Harlem where I lived all my life in the US. In the room where I slept, it was later discovered that open sewerage flowed, and undoubtedly it was this dampness that contributed to my contraction of TB. I was sent to Sea View Sanitorium from Harlem Hospital at the age of seventeen, where with pneumothorax treatment for my condition I fully recovered, since fortunately my sputum was never positive. I was there for one full year. There too, I had an opportunity to read avidly, to think deeply about the social ideas instilled in me by my mother and father. My mother had left the Catholic church, in which faith we were baptized from early childhood, choosing to become a Bible student, since her alert mind rejected early the hierarchical teachings of Catholicism. My father's social ideas instilled in us were that of a pride and consciousness of our people, of our relation to Africa, from which my antecedents sprang, to our interrelationship to Caribbean independence the dream of San Simeon, great Caribbean patriot; to the new recognition of the struggle for Negro equality in the US, linked indissolubly as I later learned with the freedom and equality of the American trade unions and working class as the future class of society. One incident, I remember, while in Sea View—namely when I gave a blood transfusion voluntarily (since I was her blood type) to a young Italian woman patient. This created quite a stir in the hospital on the question of "black blood" and "white blood." Many of the white patients looked for days to see if the young Italian woman, who was eternally grateful (to the point of my embarrassment!) to me, would turn "black." One of the first hospital speeches I ever heard was from a young Jewish doctor who in the midst of this scientific ignorance stood in the middle of the ward and gave a lecture to the interracial patients asserting the inviolability of blood types as the antithesis of any false teachings on "race."

Upon recovery, I completed the last term of High School at Wedleigh. Upon graduation, I went to work in a factory, since college was out for me and I had to help support myself and contribute to the family larder.

My first job was in a laundry, where I observed, under the incredible (to me then) conditions of overwork, speed-up, etc., in the heat of summer young Negro women fainting regularly because of the unbearable conditions. I didn't want to become like them, so I went to work in a factory. But being unskilled, my job was setting nailheads— with a toothpick, a small jar of paste and placing these in the nailhead setting. Boredom and ennui set in and I quit this job. Besides, the pay was about $14 a week. Next, I got a job in a Harlem millinery story and lingerie shop as a salesgirl. This continued for quite a while— about two years or so.

These were the years of the Ethiopian war and the invasion of Mongolia. During this period, I worked on a Negro Nationalist newspaper, where I wrote a column (circulation about four to five thousand copies) and had a weekly column called "Claudia's Comments." My job consisted there also of writing précis of the main editorial comments on Ethiopia from general commercial press, Negro press, trade union press, etc. To my amazement, on attending one of their meetings (of the nationalists) I saw my boss reading my précis to the applause and response of thousands of community people in Harlem, men and women. When the next day, he would come in and tell me what a "Big Negro" he was, I would challenge his facts. What he did was to read books on Ethiopia all day and fuse his accumulated knowledge with my précis, which were listened to by thousands of people in the mass rallies held by nationalists in Harlem. I spent a lot of time coming from work listening also to the street corner meetings of the various political parties and movements in Harlem. This was the days of the famed Scottsboro Boys Frame-up. I was like millions of Negro people, and white progressives and people stirred by this heinous frameup. I was impressed by the Communist speakers who explained the reasons for this brutal crime against young Negro boys; and who related the Scottsboro case to the struggle of the Ethiopian people against fascism, and Mussolini's invasion. Friends of mine who were Communists, although I didn't know it then, seeing my interest, began to have frequent discussions with me. I joined the Party in February 1936 and was assigned to work in the YCL shortly thereafter. My first assignment was secretary of the YCL executive committee in Harlem and it was about this time, I got a job in the Business Dept of the *DW*. This job coincided with my application for $150 a week job in the field of dramatics with the Federal Theatre Project under WPA. I took the job at the *Worker* for $12–25 a week instead.

The National Negro Congress first organizing conference had been held in Chicago. It was when I met James Ashford, outstanding Young Communist Leader who died at the age of twenty-seven, that I was oriented to work in the youth movement, in the YCL.

During the next ten years from 1936–1946–7, I was active in the YCL and the youth movement. Served as organizer of the YCL in Harlem for a year. [In] 1937 was sent to a six-month National Training School of the CP. On my return was elected to National Council YCL and became associate editor of the *Weekly Review*. I was active in the work of the great American Congress, the organization of the

National Council of Negro Youth, the Southern Negro Congress (where I attended many conferences in Alabama, Atanta, Richmond VA), and also in the National Negro Congress.

During my teens I was active in numerous social clubs in the community, in the junior NAACP and tennis clubs and also studied dramatics at the Urban League. I performed in this capacity with a troupe in many churches in the Harlem community and in Brooklyn.

Later I became editor of the *Weekly Review, 1938–40.* During 1943–45, became editor of *Spotlight,* national publication of American Youth For Democracy. This publication, many of whose articles were entered into the Congressional Record and for whom Admirals and Senators wrote, inspired the victory in the anti-fascist war among youth and was widely read by GI subscribers throughout the war fronts.

Worked from 1945–46 as editor of Negro Affairs, *Daily Worker.*

Elected full member National Committee 1945 Convention CP.

Assigned on "graduation" from youth movement to be Executive Secretary National Negro Commission CPUSA 1945–46.

Arrested Jan. 28, 1948 under ancient statute or warrant for deportation to my native Trinidad, BWI. Sent to Ellis Island. Bailed out overnight. Arrested June 29, 1951 with seventeen working-class Communist leaders, including Elizabeth Gurley Flynn under the infamous Smith Act for writing an article which described the forward movement of Negro and white women in opposition to the fascist bent world domination US foreign policy.

Rearrested under Walter–McCarran Law, October 1951. Held with eighteen working-class and Communist leaders on Ellis Island in special "Walter–McCarran" wing for eighteen days until bail was won $5,000.

From 194——[7/8]–52—active in national women's movements and united front movements such as Congress of American Women: National Council of Negro Women toured nation—forty-three states—in connection with main Party assignment of work among women, organizing Party Conferences of work among women, helping to implement this arm of our National Committee's work among the masses of women, particularly working-class and Negro women in struggle against the Korean war, for peaceful coexistence between nations, for peace, national dignity, full equality for women, and the equal rights of women.

This was the basis of my "overt act," an article I wrote, printed in *Political Affairs* which urged American women, Negro and white, to unite lest their children, like those in Korea, suffer the fate of Hiroshima's atomic destruction.

From '52–53—worked on National Peace Commission on CP giving leadership actively to peace centers, to peace struggle, namely around Korean war for the program registered at Geneva for peaceful coexistence among nations for East–West trade, cultural exchange between nations, international friendship in a world of peace.

July 4, 1953, at the end of trial seventeen, suffered heart failure diagnosed as hypertensive cardiovascular disease. Hospitalized at Mt. Sinai for twenty-one days. Took five months leave of absence. Placed on digitalis and drugs for control of hypertension. Hospitalized again for coronary heart disease in December 1953. Two months leave. Returned to work again served as editor of *Negro Affairs Quarterly*, and special fields of work among Negro people, participated as member of NAC, throughout this period.

Jan. 11, 1955 entered prison serving a year and a day sentence at the Federal Reformatory for Women at Alerrson [Alderson], W. Va. Got seventy-two days off, serving nine months and eighteen days for so-called "good behavior." *Won first prize, Blue Ribbon in August State Fair of W. Va for women —— —— —— skill learned there.* Was to be summarily deported straight to the Caribbean from prison on October 23 day of release of this year—but for protests here and abroad and in event of British authorities. Brought suit for first time in challenge to the Walter–McCarran Act which declares it a "crime" to be a noncitizen, even a permanent resident alien. I was forced to withdraw my suit due to my health status, which is precarious and must be guarded.

December 9—scheduled to leave the US after residing here for thirty-two years in the United States.

I think this sort of summarizes it. I should add (happily) due to digitalis poisoning while imprisoned I was taken off digitalis August 3, 1955 and have not had to use other than occasionally nitroglycerine for heart pain—which I have used not for two months and only used on two occasions during the last year when imprisoned. Now on drugs (supercil) for control of hypertension. If you summarize the medical status you should know that at the time of my imprisonment admitted by a court-appointed physician—contrary to the attitude of the first women prison physicians I was diagnosed as suffering from essential hypertension, cardiac disease, and coronary arteriosclerosis—with my background of arrested tuberculosis, the exact diagnosis of my personal physician.

I wrote this quite fully in the full knowledge, dear Comrade Foster, that your extracts would contain only what you consider pertinent, but I gave it as fully as I can to facilitate that end.

Best personal regards
to you and Comrade Esther.

Comradely yours,
Claudia Jones

P.S. I was married to Abraham Scholnik in September 1940 in NYC. I was divorced Feb. 27, 1947. My plans are to remarry in England within the next four months.

P.P.S. At the age of twenty-three I applied and received my certificate for finishing papers for American citizenship—but this was denied me by the US government since I was politically active from the age of eighteen.

LETTER TO GEORGE MATTHEWS, EDITOR OF *DAILY WORKER*

MAY 7, 1963

Editor, *Daily Worker*
75 Farringdon Road
London, EC 1

Dear George Matthews:

I thought it best to follow up our telephone discussion of this morning on the matter I raised with you re: the current news story entitled "Economic Ban—Not Color—Sir Learie" in this morning's issue of the *Daily Worker*.

I hope you'll find it possible to print my letter in your columns, except of course, the first and last paragraphs.

✳✳✳✳✳

The news article captioned "Economic Ban—Not Color—Sir Learie" appearing in the May 7 issue of the *Daily Worker* was most unfortunate. Coming as it did in the midst of a widespread protest by West Indians in Bristol and their Labour-Progressive and student allies, following the refusal of the Bristol Omnibus Company to hire an eighteen-year-old West Indian, Guy Bailey, on the clear-cut ground that the company refused to hire colored workers, it can only have the effect of mitigating the struggle and confusing the issue. If this was not a clear-cut case of color bar, I do not know what is.

Yet the *DW* story was captioned "Economic Ban—Not Color Says Sir Learie."

The essence of Sir Learie's remarks as quoted by you gave the impression that the issue of color bar no longer exists, and in fact, was not the issue at all in this case. The lead paragraph of the story ran: "The non-employment of West Indian crews on the Bristol buses is not a color-bar issue at all, Sir Learie Constantine High Commissioner for Trinidad and Tobago said in Bristol last night."

But actually, in the context of your story, Sir Learie, after being quoted as denying the existence of a color bar, went on to say: "It is something more fundamental. It is due to fear generated by the small wage paid to the people employed by the bus company, who augment it with overtime.

"The service is certainly not properly staffed, and everybody is afraid that if it is properly staffed overtime will be lost."

If the burden of Sir Learie's remarks on Bristol television was to emphasize that underlying color-bar practices and actions, there is an economic basis, that's one thing, and is a useful point. Color bar is profitable to capitalism, to the employers and serves as a divisive tactic to the unity of the workers.

But it is quite another thing to counterpose the existence of color bar to the economic fears of the workers, whether on buses or elsewhere in this country. The economic fears of all workers is what is always played on when the issue of color bar comes to the fore. The white worker is encouraged in his fears to fight not the bosses, but the colored man who "threatens" his job. The color worker is told to "understand " that the economic recession means he can't take away other men's jobs etc. Hence, to counterpose the economic issue (or economic fears) to the fight against the color bar or to deny its existence as a factor, only accelerates the disunity of the workers which only benefits the employers, the racialists, and the Tories whose policies brought about the situation in the first place. To stress one without the other, in an instance where there is clear evidence of the existence of both factors, is to renege on our responsibility of exposing color-bar practices and manifestations.

What other implication can be drawn when one reads in the text of the same story "it was easy to talk about a 'color bar' to hide the real issue which was an economic one"??? This surely was not Sir Learie's quotation.

In the story's context this should have been made clear. Otherwise, it appears what we have is a counterposing of the economic issue to the fight against the color bar, which, of course, could provide a handy excuse to those who do not wish to fight it, or who use the real question of the workers' economic fears as an excuse to justify their actions. But this would only result in making West Indians or other colored workers additional "scapegoats" to be last hired, first fired in an economic recession, or as in this case not to be hired at all. (How often have we heard similar excuses in the field of housing from prejudiced landladies: "We would, of course, take West Indians in our homes, but our neighbours would object"; or from prejudiced employers, "The workers object to the hiring of colored workers," hence the maintenance of a color bar in its employment policy, etc.)

We should be mindful of the fact that often when color-bar issues exist, the retort is that it is economic. But such an approach could well mean the delay, postponement (or failure to expose) the fight against the color bar, when clearly, in the context of British economic life (and political considerations of Commonwealth colored workers among the British working class today) the question of discrimination of colored workers must be squarely faced and fought as inimical to the unity of the workers.

The implications of the phrase "it is easy to talk about 'color bar'" is to dangerously minimize this issue. Assuredly, it is far from "easy" to talk about color bar—far more experience this indignity, and most colored workers would prefer forthright struggle for its elimination rather than "talk" about it.

It is this element that was witnessed in Bristol when the community (or a section of it) took action to end it, which deserves the wholehearted support of all progressives.

Completely eliminated from the story, i.e. the earlier statement of discrimination in the refusal of the company to hire an eighteen-year-old Jamaican who applied for a job. Instead, your article quoted Mr. Ian Fatey, general manager of the Bristol company as saying, "There are no vacancies for bus crews anyway. We have a waiting list for jobs, so that when these are available, there are local men to fill them."

"Local"—meaning <u>native</u>? Is this not another manifestation of a color bar that they will hire no outsiders only those native to Bristol? And if this was the situation in the first place, how explain the earlier statement of the company that it will not hire colored workers?

The statement of the Bristol Communist municipal candidates condemning the bus color bar and other political forces, the action of Bristol University students in their swift support, and the original protest of West Indians themselves, should be highly commended. It is our job to expose these incidents to fight and support all efforts that will bring to the fore instances of color bar not recognised yet by many British workers and even progressives, to speed its elimination from British life.

❖❖❖❖❖

All in all, I'm afraid I must agree with you as you indicated on the telephone, that I read this in a different context than you say did the *Daily Worker* staff. This does not, as you imputed, however, mean that I expect you to fight "color bar" <u>only</u>. I quite naturally expect that the *Daily Worker* as a Communist journal will be foremost in fighting color bar, and I would hope that it will increasingly recognize the subtleties in the struggle against it must likewise be fought, lest we fall into an opportunist position unwittingly. It behooves us to be alert to these trends, even if these views obscuring them are mouthed by certain West Indian leaders. (You should also know that I am awaiting results from my calls to the Trinidad office and it is not yet clear whether he was quoted out of context or not. I shall keep you posted.)

With all good wishes, yours fraternally,
Claudia Jones

'THIS SMOKESCREEN OF HYSTERIA:' ANTI-COMMUNISM AND REPRESSION

This section addresses Claudia Jones's response to the persecution she and her party faced, and to her eventual detention, trial, and deportation by the US government. Jones argued that McCarthyite anti-communism reflected a hysterically racist reaction to struggles against Jim Crow, the socialist movement, and the peace movement in the years immediately after World War II.

Anti-communism, Jones argued, reflected a bipartisan "fear of the peoples' rule at home and abroad." In a series of *Daily Worker* articles written during the opening years of the Cold War, Jones contended that McCarthyism was a broader attack on the Black struggle for freedom, condemning the "pro-fascist, social-democratic lie" that the Communist movement in the US had "'used the Negro Question' for our own ends!" Jones later described the conditions of her detention in a letter from Ellis Island, observing how detainees suffered through solitary confinement, constant surveillance, and deteriorating health. In the face of such treatment, she insisted on the necessity of mass public action to enforce their citizenship rights. Further, in a 1952 essay for *Political Affairs*, Jones analyzed the US peace movement amidst a renewed drive for war, highlighting how Black people saw "the struggle for their rights impaled on the blade of Wall Street's greed," while the working class at large withstood declining wages and rising unemployment.

In this moment of anti-communist hysteria, Jones pushed forth the idea that the primary goal was to build and consolidate "united front peace organizations" rooted in working-class and Black communities. Throughout her writing, she discusses how her participation in the movements against lynching, and for peace, served as the immediate triggers for her subjection to McCarthyite hysteria. Speaking in her own defense at her hearing, Jones denounced "the obscenity of this trial of ideas," namely, her beliefs in racial equality, peace, and the abolition of exploitation under socialism.

UN-AMERICAN COMMITTEE AND THE NEGRO PEOPLE

DAILY WORKER
AUGUST 1–3, 1949

First of Three Articles (August 1, 1949)

The procedure of the House Un-American Committee in bringing before it spokesmen of the Negro people to impugn and place under suspicion the loyalty of the Negro people is something new. Never before in the history of the nation has the loyalty of a whole people been so attacked. It is not enough that the Negro people are subjected to lynch violence, terror, and police brutality, and numerous other indignities under the second-class Jim Crow lynch system which is our lot in the United States. But the very citizenship of fourteen million Negro Americans was put under suspicion in these hearings in which Negroes were treated as wards or field hands of an imperialist state.

Unwittingly, of course, these hearings were a reverse admission of the nationhood of the Negro people, who, as a people, are nationally oppressed in the Black Belt of the South. That is their condition of life, regardless of their class position throughout the land. The hearings confirmed the proof of their special oppression and the warning that the drive to fascism overnight can wipe out the progress made by a people enslaved in a hundred different ways despite the abolition of chattel slavery.

Under Hitler Germany many Jewish citizens integrated into German life and society.

But, despite this integration, the poison of "Aryan" supremacy, and the cultivation of anti-Semitism and other chauvinist practices led to the wiping out of six million Jews and laid the basis for the

151

murder of millions of non-Jews in Germany and throughout Europe as well. How much more so is this true of the United States, where the historic use of racism and "white supremacy" is a virtual springboard for fascism.

Assuredly, to haul citizens before a witch-hunting Congressional committee is to lay the basis for a continuing pro-fascist strategy of big business and its mouthpieces in Congress, which demand adherence to the "ideals" of the committee. Those ideals can best be gauged by the "loyalty" and "patriotism" of the committee members, including its poll-tax chairman, and the members' silent acquiescence to the KKK murders of Negro citizens. Those ideals are nurtured and sustained by an Administration and Department of Justice, who wink at lynching, poll taxes, denial of bail to deportation victims and Communist defendants while they shout their pious concern for civil rights in America—and push forward police-state rule.

A day after the hearings, the homes of three Negro citizens were burned by the KKK in Stuckey's Hill—the Negro community of Groveland, Fla. A week later bombs destroyed the suburban home of Chicago Negro residents. Not a peep has yet been heard from this committee who demands loyalty to the Jim Crow lynch system. Not a hearing has been scheduled to question the loyalty of the KKK white supremacist mobs who do violence to the Constitution and the Bill of Rights. Nor will any be called.

This pattern of commanding loyalty by "thought control" (in these days of reactionary offensive in which Communist leaders are jailed without bail for their political beliefs in a biased trial before a biased judge) is a smokescreen to obscure the issues of peace, security, and equality for the Negro people, labor, and other oppressed minorities.

American imperialism has increasing need for this smokescreen of hysteria as the people become more aware of the danger, as they feel the burdens of the economic crisis. Thus, imperialism accelerates national chauvinism and racial chauvinism, the better to facilitate its drive towards world conquest, fascism and war. Thus, on all issues, the Hitler lie of Communist-baiting and war hysteria. Like robbers, the imperialists do not hesitate to utilize the oppressed themselves, if necessary, to achieve their foul ends.

The hearings were timed at a strategic moment for American imperialist reaction. To begin with, and primarily, they coincided with the pivotal attack on civil liberties at Foley Square where twelve Communist leaders face a heresy trial for their political ideas because of indictments by the Department of Justice and the Truman Administration.

Three of the defendants were jailed for protesting the obvious bias of a judge, who serves monopoly capital, and who sought to put in jeopardy the names of thousands of working-class men and women by demanding that the defendants become stool pigeons. Among those protesting this infamy was Henry Winston, outstanding Negro leader, national administrative secretary of the Communist Party, a Negro veteran who was remanded to jail for the duration of the trial with two white defendants for the statement that "over five thousand Negroes had been lynched and not a single lyncher brought to justice!"—and, for his protest against the stool pigeon edict of a judge which would result in the lynching and terrorizing of Negro workers.

The trial reached a significant highlight in the testimony of Benjamin J. Davis, Communist leader and Councilman from the City of New York. Davis had indicted the Jim Crow lynch system. His powerful indictment of the varied forms of capitalist class violence against the working class, the Negro people and other democratic minded people could not be refuted by the government's prosecutor. Vulnerable as it always is on the Negro question, the prosecution did not dare to jail Davis. It is still burning somersaults in an effort to explain away his testimony, which was all the more powerful, because as part of the Negro liberation movement, the Communist leader utilized the weapon of Marxism-Leninism to throw light on the forces responsible for the national oppression of the Negro people—the capitalist class itself.

The same capitalist class that stupidly calls Ben Davis a "dupe" or insultingly a "good boy" is the same capitalist class that rushes to editorialize on Jackie Robinson—*Daily News* style—as "a credit to his people and nation" while it imprisons Henry Winston for protesting unpunished lynchings.

And it is the same capitalist class that seeks to throw its dwarf-like shafts against Paul Robeson—a man who strides on five continents with anti-fascist, anti-imperialist truth as a weapon, for which he is beloved. The capitalists simply show their fear of the democratic forces with which Robeson is aligned in his profound identity with his own people, the Negro people, the nationally and colonially oppressed peoples of the world.

Their aim in these hearings was to black out the impact of Davis' testimony, the jailing of Winston—in short, to obscure the truth of what Robinson himself declared, namely "the fact that a Communist denounces injustice in the courts, police brutality, and lynching when it happens doesn't change the truth of his charges."

It is necessary, therefore, to further examine why the House Un-Americans selected Jackie Robinson as the star witness among the Negro leaders that they hauled before their committee.

Second of Three Articles (August 2, 1949)

It is more than a passing coincidence that at the Un-American Committee loyalty hearings on "Communism and the Negro" the Negro reformist leaders—such as Lester Granger, Charles S. Johnson (to say nothing of the miserable stool pigeons such as Manning Johnson)— were not powerful enough, or convincing enough in their views on this subject. This, despite the American bourgeoisie's all-out efforts to control the Negro press through ads, or to meagerly give crumbs from its profit-laden tables for the support of such institutions as the reformists may lead.

The ever-present virus of "white supremacy," intensified national oppression, and second-class citizenship, plus intellectual integrity compelled Rev. Sandy Ray, one of the leading Negro religious leaders, the chairman of the Social Service Commission of the National Baptist Convention, to boldly declare, without apology, of the Jim Crow lynch system in the United States:

> We do, however, seek to overthrow an intangible empire which exists within our government and many of our institutions throughout the land. It is that empire which shelters injustice, oppressions, exploitation, segregation, discrimination, ill will, and all of the inconsistencies which make for separation, tension, and strife. It is against that empire that we wage our war. It is that empire that must be subdued if we are to have domestic peace and give effective leadership in world chaos.

Indeed, the House Un-Americans, American monopoly capital, and the Southern landlords needed still a fresh voice to do their dirty work of disunity among the Negro people, whose just grievances they fear and whose Jim Crow status haunts their every hypocritical declaration of civil rights at home and around the globe.

Thus, they selected Robinson, a man who has become a symbol of fair play and sportsmanship in the nation's national pastime—baseball—a man who broke Jim Crow's chains with the full weight of the Left in American politics—led by the Communist Party, which pioneered in the fight and who has not ceased to fight Jim Crow in baseball and every phase of American life.

The "grand designs" of the Un-Americans was to wheedle Jackie Robinson, the Dodger baseball star, into a position of appearing as a disunity force among the Negro people themselves. What was old in the tactic was the imperialist "divide-and-rule" adage. What was new was the further development of the Truman policy on the domestic and international scene, to use Negroes to help rescue the ever-growing vulnerable position of the American imperialist policy, that it is "saving the world for democracy," while, in its own backyard, millions of citizens of darker hue are enslaved, lynched, terrorized as daily occurrences in ghettos throughout North and South.

Truman's "bold new program for Africa" must necessarily have a "bold new approach" among certain Negro leaders at home for its success. Reliance then, on the old type Negro reformists, who are under inceasing criticism among the Negro people themselves, must be bolstered by new fresh young voices, who are all the more to be selected if their own lives represent a "typical" American success story—that is, of course, for Negro Americans!

That Jackie Robinson allowed himself to become such a tool is more than regrettable. In an interview in a metropolitan paper, he declared, after testifying, that he had the help of Lester Granger, Dan Dodson (of the Mayor's Committee on Unity), and Branch Rickey, in making his decision. He ignored numerous plain people—fans—and organizations such as the NAACP and the *Baltimore Afro-American*, which asked him to spurn with contempt the Un-Americans.

He played ball with the Un-Americans whose poll-tax chairman, Wood, conveniently absented himself from the hearing, after the task was accomplished of getting a Negro to attempt to refute another. Thus they obscured the real responsibility of government for the failure to pass legislation for FEPC, anti-lynching and anti-poll-tax, etc.

It was hardly befitting one, who is not, by his own claim, "an expert on world affairs," to dismiss as "silly" views (which were misquoted in the first place). But the real views of Robeson are heard from the lips of Negro veterans, who like the Negro people as a whole, fought in the anti-fascist war for a "double victory" against fascism abroad and Jim Crow white supremacy at home. These masses, the flower of the Negro people, its young men and women, certainly will want an accounting of those who deny equality at home, but who ask them—and all white Americans—to serve in a Jim Crow army to help establish a Jim Crow world in an imperialist war! Clearly then, the net effect of Robinson's playing ball with the Ku Kluxers of the Un-American Committee was to help them against his own people, the Negro people, his country—and himself.

It is important to register that, despite his falling into the trap set for him, Jackie Robinson did not completely satisfy the Un-Americans or their Big Business bosses. Even the "peons of praise" from reactionary columnists cannot hide their chagrin that Robinson came short of meeting the old adage they sing to "successful Negroes" namely: "Why worry about the plight of the mass of the Negro people?"

These reactionaries, don't, of course, know that the basic tie of leaders to the masses from Douglass to Robeson is that the Negro people revere those who never forget whence they spring!

As a Negro, a veteran, then, one whose rise to prominence was born out of the struggle against Jim Crow, Robinson reminded the Committee that any Negro worth his salt is against Jim Crow and discrimination of all sorts.

It is not at all surprising that Robinson holds different views of the ultimate perspectives for Negro liberation with which he is undoubtedly concerned. Such views are part of the many class outlooks and influences at work among various strata of the Negro people. Here, as among all peoples, one's social consciousness is determined by one's condition of life, and not the other way around.

The most advanced views on Negro liberation are those held by the Communist Party and by the Negro communist leaders in the Negro liberation movement. The Marxist-Leninist leadership and views of

Benjamin Davis and Henry Winston have influenced all strata of the Negro people.

The leadership of Paul Robeson and his views represent and reflect the growing ferment of advanced thought and militancy among all sections of the Negro people. Robeson's years of experience and leadership, has, as a result, earned for him, a place not only among the Left, but among wide sections of the people—labor, the Negro people, all nationalities, in this country and throughout the globe.

How then, could Jackie Robinson air the truth (which even anti-Communists are forced to admit), namely the Communist Party's contribution to the economic, political, and social equality of the Negro people—and yet fall into the trap of red-baiting and slander—the net result of which was to repeat the social-democratic lie that Communists use the Negro question for their own ends?

Last of Three Articles (August 3, 1949)

Among all sections of the Negro people (except for renegades and bought-out reformists), their oppressed status makes for an ideological unity against the Jim Crow lynch system to which all Negroes are subjected. From Ralph Bunche to Rosa Lee Ingram, the virus of white supremacy and Jim Crow haunts our tracks. Hence, the ideological unity against Jim Crow, second-class citizenship, demands for equal rights now, among all strata of the Negro liberation movement. This fundamental concept is undoubtedly what led Jackie Robinson to air the profound truth that "the fact that a Communist denounces injustice the in the courts, police brutality, and lynching when it happens, does not change the truth of his charges."

It is precisely this truth that the Communist leaders—Foster, Dennis, Winston, Davis, and our Party—have symbolized all along, throughout the existence of the Communist Party! It is a pro-fascist, social-democratic lie that our Party has "used the Negro Question" for our own ends! This is a white chauvinist insult, in the first place to the Negro people themselves!

Our "use of the Negro Question" has been to throw the clear light of day on the lynchers lair; our "use of the Negro question" has been only to give proper Marxist-Leninist analysis to the unique national oppression of the Negro people in the United States; our "use of the

Negro question" has been to match our words with active deeds from Scottsboro to the Trenton Six, to Rosa Lee Ingram to the fight for Negroes in the Big Leagues; to upgrading of Negro workers in industry; against the white supremacist violation of Negro womanhood; to expose lynch terror, police brutality, restrictive covenants, and other vile evils of Jim Crow. Our "use of the Negro question" has been to show white Americans, particularly the workers, that the struggle for the full equality of the Negro people is in their basic self-interest, especially today in the fight against imperialist war and fascism.

Moreover, without the Communist Party (notwithstanding Robinson's statement "that we can get along without the Communists") there could be no progress in the last twenty years on any of these issues for equality for the Negro people or for the advancement of American democracy!

No less a paper than the *New York Age*, editorializing on July 30 on "The Core of the Red Issue Concerning the Negro," declared:

> The fact is that the Communists, right or wrong, have gotten the jump on everybody else by putting into the record something concrete to prove what they teach . . . The Communists have simply walked through the wide loopholes of the democratic system and reached the people the other side has ignored. Were Communism a lily-white philosophy it would likely fall into a category resembling the Democrats, the Republicans, the American Federation of Labor, Dixiecrats or the Ku Klux Klan, which the South, represented by Wood, and others like Thurmond of South Carolina, regards more or less as an "American institution."

It is not in spite of, but because we cannot get along without Communist leadership on the fundamental issue of Negro oppression that the American bourgeoisie fears the Communists and seek to outlaw the Party.

Outlawing of our Party by legislation, or court procedure, or persecution, is one of the ways they count on to silence the protests of the Negro people themselves, and the most advanced forces who fight for labor, Negro liberation, against white supremacy and lynch justice.

It is this same reactionary capitalist class that seeks to make Jackie Robinson the scapegoat of their hypocritical preachments of democracy which they deny to fourteen million Negro people and which must yet be fully won in organized baseball.

Without fundamental understanding of the Negro question, one cannot effectively fight against oppression, or for peace, the right of labor, or against fascism and war! It is because Un-Americans fear this truth that they sought to use leaders of the oppressed Negro people to impugn the loyalty of an entire people.

But the hearings boomeranged.

They boomeranged, first, because the Negro question is itself "the Achilles heel of American imperialism" in the words of the national chairman of the Communist Party, William Z. Foster. And because, the more they touch it, the more the imperialists are exposed for what they are: the oppressors of the Negro people, of the working class, the organizers of force and violence against the Negro people, the financiers of exploitation of six million Negroes and four million whites in the South, from which exploitation they wring the profits to stuff their coffers for the financing of an imperialist atomic war and domestic fascism!

The hearings boomeranged for a second reason. And that is because, even as they utilized the old "divide-and-rule" tactic, the eyes of fourteen million Negro Americans; the eyes of countless white Americans; the eyes of nationally and colonially oppressed peoples in Africa, the West Indies, and in Liberated China; the eyes of the New European Democracies; the eyes of the leader of the world democratic forces, the Soviet Union; were upon them.

And thirdly, these hearings boomeranged because even among reformist Negro leaders, intellectual integrity and intensified national oppression pushes many of them to a clearer realization of the profound truth spoken by Frederick Douglass: "Power concedes nothing without struggle."

That is why from their newspapers and columns they hastily cleaned up comment about the praise for Jackie Robinson as a "closed incident"; that is why they editorialize, as did one Scripps-Howard columnist, that a Paul Robeson, "the automatic success story," is "hard to understand"; that is why they are still editorializing about

Davis' testimony in magazines, which they cannot refute except impotently to say of this Communist leader that "he" is "misled."

The Negro press comment in the main didn't satisfy them either. For many utilized the anti–Jim Crow statements of Robinson as a take-off for an even more strenuous demand for Negro unity and for a demand to the Truman Administration that it make good its election promises of civil rights legislation now. The mass of the Negro people, as reflected in the man-of-the-street talks, in letters to the editors, are discussing even a deeper question—namely comparing the statement of Paul Robeson to their own ideas, their anti-war, anti-imperialism, as they question as did Robeson: Why should we fight an imperialist war—a war against the Soviet Union, which has wiped out discrimination and prejudice within its borders?

And all this is why labor, and the Negro people, and all progressive women and men, must by drawing the proper conclusions, accelerate unity of the Negro people, unity of Negro and white and wrest from the foul stable of a jail, by renewed and popular protest, Henry Winston whose life and time is a symbol of the courageous contribution of the Communist Party to the Negro Question in the United States. Free the Three!

CLAUDIA JONES WRITES FROM ELLIS ISLAND

DAILY WORKER
NOVEMBER 8, 1950

"We can and will win this round against the ruling circles who seek to bring fascism at home and atomic war abroad," writes Claudia Jones, in a letter to John Gates, editor of the *Daily Worker*, from her prison cell on Ellis Island. Miss Jones, national secretary of the Women's Commission of the Communist Party, was arrested in the recent McCarran raids. Her letter follows:

ELLIS ISLAND,
Saturday afternoon.

Dear Johnny:

In thinking about the collusion of the "free press" with the ruling circles' attack on American democratic liberties, I decided to write to you. Of course, if I attempt to write descriptively, it will only be because, while I know you (and I) hold brevity to be the soul of wit, description should not be the second-class citizen. So here goes my letter:

Homing pigeons gather aimlessly in the large yard on an island which lies in New York's great harbor. Occasionally, a homing pigeon flies in from the bay dotted with whitecaps and the pigeons scatter.

They either gather in a solid mass and noiselessly fly away together, or, with loud grace, flap their wings and soar away . . . One flapped his wings thirty-one times before he ascended to fly over the massed brownstone building with numerous windows.

If one looks closely, it is obvious this is not just a haunt of homing pigeons or seagulls. The windows on all buildings are all wired with criss-cross light iron bars. Others are heavier . . . Around the huge yard, barbed-wire, way beyond the height of a man, towers and outdoor lights, as on a baseball diamond, are spaced with regular frequency . . .

Look even closer . . . Men in shirtsleeves or rough lumber jackets peer out from occasional windows on the right end of the yard, looking out on the bay, where, now and then, on this foggy, rain-swept day, foghorns cry their warning to approaching vessels . . . Some of the ships are more beautiful than others. There are lugs and passenger ships . . . . Coast guard cutters and barges are anchored to the pier on the left end of the island, which barely commands our view.

It is not too foggy to see the towering skyscrapers which beckon beyond the bay, on the other shore, on the mainland.

One cannot imagine the mainland without its wealth of men, women, and children of many lands who for centuries—and likewise today—toiled in mine, mill, factory, and the endless plain—all the stretch of these great green states to make America.

From this view, another famous island, that so many ships and their passengers from five continents have eagerly nodded to, throughout the last three hundred centuries, cannot be seen. Bedloe's Island, home of the Statue of Liberty, gift of the descendents of Joan of Arc, lies on the left of this shore . . . And well it does—for this woman, with liberty's torch, still stands proudly aloft her earthy home . . . And literally stands with her back to Ellis Island.

Here, on Ellis Island, it would not be well for her shadow to grace the newly established wing of the Attorney General of the US—or, as the seventeen imprisoned inmates of this wing call it— the "McCarran Wing." In this wing are seventeen men and women—a virtual United Nations composition. O yes, and the guards—one woman guard and two men guards.

Among our company of seventeen is a Slavic American, the brawn and brain of whose people are forever merged with the great industrial achievements of America's working people—the miners of Pittsburgh, the auto workers of Detroit, the anthracite and copper miners on the Mesable range of the Minnesotas.

Here is a Finnish American, who sat four years in a similar detention jail, when another attorney general, Palmer by name, sought to
impose Alien and Sedition raids and laws, defeated by the mass protests of Americans of an earlier day.

Trade Unionists

Here are the trade unionists from fur, electrical, and maritime industries, who smile from their firm greetings of approval when, from
shops and locals, wires or letters come, telling of actions taken on
behalf of American liberty. Here is a Negro man from the British
West Indies, whose people's blood mixed with Crispus Attucks, on
that early day on Boston Commons when West Indian warriors, of the
strain of Toussaint L'Ouverture, fought in the American Revolution.
Second-class citizens, like fifteen million Negro Americans whose
sons serve in Jim Crow units in Korea, they are not strangers to the
second-class, Jim Crow justice likewise meted out to West Indians of
foreign birth.

Here are women, Negro and white, whose lives, like those of
Emma Lazarus and Harriet Tubman, are a refutation of women's
inequality in any field of endeavor; women, whose lives from early
youth was pursuit of truth learned in American homes and schools to
help guarantee life, liberty, and the pursuit of happiness in devotion
to the American people and to future generations of children by participating in the struggles of the people.

Here too, are leading representatives of the vanguard party of all
of the toiling people—Communist leaders.

One of the women, as you know, was confined for over a week to
solitary confinement and was under constant surveillance.

Devotion to Struggle

All seventeen here are examples of devotion to the struggles of the
labor movement, in the fight for Negro rights, against discrimination
and lynching, in the fight for democracy, in our efforts on behalf of
the peace and security of the people. And some hold beliefs that only
under a socialist society can these rights be finally secured!

There is a Spanish American, a Ukrainian American, an Italian
American, a Greek American, and Jewish Americans. Descendants of

Haym Solomon and Guiseppe Garibaldi, and of the people of Simon Bolivar and La Pasionaria, San Martin, they are proud and honored descendants of these heroes and heroines.

Why are we here—on this notorious "Island of Tears"—so close to Liberty's statue, where we have always been in mind, spirit, and action?

The majority of newspapers tell you that we are here because we are awaiting deportation hearings. That is a foul lie. Like many others now incarcerated, we have been out on bail for various periods of time pending disposition of deportation proceedings launched against us.

Many of us have had no hearings or legal examinations of any kind. We have never been confronted with any evidence or made familiar with any crime alleged or charged against us. Nor have any of us been informed or charged with the slightest infraction of the terms of our release on bail . . . Nevertheless the government has rearrested us without due process of law and seeks to assign us to a virtual life-long imprisonment on Ellis Island.

Government's Threat

We are threatened by the government with becoming the first inmates of America's concentration camps, the direct victims of the mad drive of the ruling circles to fascism at home and atomic war abroad.

Others, like US Attorney Irving H. Saypol, who fought our plea for a restraining order against illegal rearrest and who argued against the writ of the eleven, already here nearly two weeks, for bail (which has already been substantially placed on all our heads), claim that the US Attorney General used his discretionary power under the unconstitutional McCarran Act to deny us bail. This too, is a foul lie. The ridiculous part of it is that the American people are supposedly asked to believe that we are "awaiting deportation hearings"—a "normal procedure," and hence, the Attorney General so uses his discretionary powers that he first illegally rearrests people, already out on bail, then asks the court to give him time to ascertain whether he was discreet about the use of his discretionary powers. But Lincoln once spoke of the basis on which people can be fooled.

The truth, of course, is that this is a clear violation of the American Constitution, the Bill of Rights, both of which guarantee the right of bail and the right of habeas corpus. That Judge F. McGohey ruled on the government motion on postponement, first, and not on the right of bail is a clear violation of this time-honored right.

Mass Struggle

I feel, and I'm sure all the rest do likewise, that legal struggles, important as they are (and we feel our attorneys and the American Committee for Protection of Foreign Born are doing a heroic job), are incidental to the mass struggle to free us. We can and must win the right to remain free on bail. We must and can win the right to our citizenship—the onus of which legal lack is on the Department of Justice and its Immigration Service, who denied us naturalization, purely on the grounds of our conscience, our beliefs, and our ideas.

But no law or decree can whittle away or pierce by one iota our convictions and loyalty to America's democratic and revolutionary traditions. We are Americans, each and everyone of us, similarly persecuted, not by accident of birth, but by choice. We yield to no one in laying claim to being true patriots.

Everyone asks in letters which have begun to come in what they can do for us. Of course it is welcome to receive mail here. We look forward to it. We are being sent packages of food, candy, papers, including my favorite, the *Daily Worker*, fruit, and books. Our conditions are the conditions of imprisonment, of being denied absolute liberty. We won the right after protest for the women to move from the hotbox of a room and to be together during the days with the men.

The heat was unbearable for Rose Nelson Lightcap, longest confined of the women, and what with Betty Gannett's sinus and fear for a flaring up of my bronchitis, the change was necessary, hazardous as it was to our health. What we want is out—freedom! What we want is aid—aid morally, financially, and above all by mass protests and action, to the mass campaign of the American Committee for Protection of the Foreign Born, by the trade unions, the Negro people.

THE STRUGGLE FOR PEACE IN THE UNITED STATES

POLITICAL AFFAIRS
FEBRUARY 1952

President Truman, in his capacity as chief political servitor of US imperialism, once again proposed, in his recent State of the Union Message to Congress, a criminal crusade of force and violence against the vast majority of the human race. Truman, though demagogically prating about peace, glorified Wall Street's aggressive expansionism which is now flagrantly directed against the colored peoples of Asia and Africa, and proposed an unrestrained armaments race.

Mr. Truman cynically boasted of the colossal size of US imperialism's armed strength and its pile of A-bombs. By way of perspective for peace, he urged even more intensive arming to be accompanied by further cuts in consumer goods output and in real wages. While he lectured the people about the need for "sacrifice," in a year marked by the largest total profits in the history of American capitalism, he proposed an additional $5 billion in new taxes.

Truman used hundreds of words in an effort to justify further burdens upon the people, but not a mumbling word did he voice about the terrible repression of civil rights in our country, the political persecution led by his Administration of Communist and other working-class leaders. The genocidal oppression of the Negro people, as highlighted just before his message by the killing of Mr. and Mrs. Harry T. Moore, was ignored and not a phrase fell from his lips about FEPC, or anti-lynching and anti-poll-tax measures. Dropped was all talk of the repeal of the Taft–Hartley Law, but instead he indulged in a concern for a "fair" version of that slave statute.

Nor could the farming masses derive any satisfaction from the Truman message. A recent Federal report signed by James Patton,

President of the National Farmers Union, indicated that two million farmers (in a total of five to six million farms) will be forced off the land and into industry to meet the "defense" requirements. When one adds the already heavy drainage of farmers' sons for the armed forces, it is clear that further impoverishment awaits the already greatly harassed lower-income farmers.

Of course, Truman's sabre-rattling message had its "peace-loving" interludes, confirming the accumulating peace sentiment in our country, to which hats must be tipped in accordance with the demands of good campaign strategy. Thus, Truman declared: " . . . day in and day out we see a long procession of timid and fearful men who wring their hands and cry out that we have lost the way—that we don't know what we are doing—that we are bound to fail. Some say that we should give up the struggle for peace and others say we should have a war and get it over with." Mr. Truman "struggles for peace" by putting aside a total of 11 percent of his budget to meet all the needs of all social services!

In his pose as "savior" of the "American way of life," Truman invokes the divine right to impose war's "blessings" on the Korean people and on the rising national liberation movements of the colonial and dependent countries. Moreover, Truman seeks to convince the American people of the "necessity" to rally behind Wall Street on the basis of a "peril" which he dares term "internal aggression." But Truman perpetrates a gigantic and vicious hoax when he asserts that our nation is in "peril" because the Chinese people do not want Chiang Kai-shek, and the Korean people do not want Syngman Rhee; because the peoples of Egypt and Iran want to control their own natural resources, and because the peoples of Indo-China, Burma, Spain, and Greece want a free, democratic existence. The Truman war program, unless routed, dooms our nation to endless war in which the rich become richer and the poor poorer; it consigns the nation's youth to death for the glory of Wall Street profiteers. The Truman perspective is that of looting the national wealth, of crushing the national aspirations of the freedom-seeking peoples, of extending the Korean adventure into a World War. Stripped of its demagogy, Truman's message confirmed our Party's estimate that the war danger has heightened, albeit its defensive tone reflects the growing counter-struggle for peace of the masses of workers and the people generally. It likewise reflected growing contradictions of an inter-imperialist character as well as within the US bipartisan war coalition, and in effect acknowledged the decisive and ever-increasing strength of the world camp of peace, democracy, and socialism.

The utter futility of the twenty-month war in Korea and Ridgway's seven-month stalling of the truce talks have increased the sharp uneasiness of the American people, with whom the Korean war was never popular and who have long seen it as a threat to world peace.

The startling significance of the Truman–Churchill "secret agreements" to A-bomb Manchuria and to take the war to China, to "save" Southeast Asia from its own peoples with the help of hired Chiang mercenaries armed with American weapons, must be viewed in the light of Truman's fundamental adherence to the criminal bipartisan war policy, ruinous to our nation and to all humanity. And it is in this light that we must view the current Senate hearings for ratification of the so-called Japanese Peace Treaty signed without the consent of the major Asian powers and without the Soviet Union, the Dulles call for "hardening" of US policy to "overthrow" the Chinese People's Republic, and the new wave of incendiary war talk.

Setbacks for Wall Street in the UN Assembly

The recently concluded Paris UN Assembly meeting graphically revealed the real reason for Truman warning to his NATO allies against "faltering" since the road is "long and hard." For there the exceedingly shaky nature of the coalition forming the US imperialist bloc in the UN became clear. It was evident that the satellite delegates could not be held securely by the US imperialist leash of economic sanctions.

Wall Street dollars could not eliminate the justified fear that these representatives have of their impoverished and insulted peoples. Those peoples of Western Europe, Latin America, Africa, Australia, Asia, and the Near and Middle East do not want any part of a war on China. This is shown by the extreme difficulty the US had in forcing a UN vote denouncing the Soviet Union for "violating" its 1945 treaty with the Chiang regime, on the "theory" that it is "Soviet aggression" for the Chinese people to sweep out the butcher-regime of Chiang Kai-shek and to inaugurate a self-determined, independent, and democratic People's Republic.

It is in this light that the now-tempered bulldog bark of Churchill is to be understood in his speech to Commons, following his US tour. Nor was this the only moral defeat suffered by the US imperialist bloc at the Assembly meeting. There was, too, the vote on UN admission of Greece from which the entire Latin-American bloc initially abstained; and not to be forgotten is the significant presentation of the Civil Rights Congress petition, "We Charge Genocide," by William Patterson, precisely at a time when the Wall Street delegation was boasting of "human rights" and at a moment when the eyes of the world were on Florida, scene of the genocide bombing of Mr. and Mrs. Harry T. Moore.

New Moods for Peace

Over a year ago, Gus Hall, in his main Report to the Fifteenth National Convention of the Communist Party, said, truly and profoundly:

> The clearer the war danger becomes, the more people move in defense of peace. This new upsurge is based on a new appreciation of the war danger, on a growing realization that the present course of the bipartisans has led to a dead end. It is based on a growing confidence that peace can be won. The new turn of events in Korea packed a double wallop because millions of Americans were never enthusiastic about this reckless adventure and were never sold on the idea that this was a war for which they should willingly make sacrifices .... We must be confident that we are going to win the working class as a class, the Negro people as a people. And that the poor farmers, church groups, and large sections of the middle class are going to participate in the organized peace movement. A powerful American peace front is clearly emerging from these developments. This peace front will be based on the working class, the Negro people, poor and middle farmers, and yes, sections of the capitalist class. This is especially true of the capitalist elements who see their imperialist aims best fulfilled on the "continent" and those closely tied to agriculture. (*Peace Can Be Won!* by Gus Hall, New Century Publishers, 1951, p. 24.)

The subsequent months have vindicated Comrade Hall's analysis. There has been and there is a maturing peace sentiment among the

American people, heightened during the US imperialist deliberately stalled Korean truce talks. A striving is evident amongst broader and broader masses for an overall negotiated settlement of all outstanding differences among nations. Even the Gallup Poll reported 70 percent of the American people desired a Truman–Stalin meeting devoted to resolving US-USSR differences. The growing peace sentiment stems not only from new sections of the population as a whole, but primarily from new sections of the working class and Negro people. More and more the inequality of "sacrifice" and the genocidal policy towards the colored peoples abroad and at home serve to expose the sickening hypocrisy in the Truman bipartisan foreign policy. These peace moods are reflected not only in growing queries and doubts, but in an insistent note that our country take a new path—that it reverse its present bipartisan war policy for a path of negotiation of outstanding differences between nations and for a Big Five-Power Peace Pact. This note has a real grassroots quality and is being sounded more and more frequently and openly by mothers, wives, veterans, youth, and GI's themselves. Despite continued and sharpened governmental harassment of the advanced defenders of peace, a "second look" is being taken as increasingly masses weigh the real alternative to the bipartisan dead-end—the principle of negotiation between nations, which, premised on the concept of peaceful coexistence of states with different social systems, can lead to the conclusion of a Five-Power Peace Pact.

These masses, faced by declining real wages and mounting unemployment, demonstrate a growing awareness that it is the war economy which is responsible for this suffering and are moving to challenge more boldly the monstrous bipartisan "alternative" of an "all-out war" to "get it over with quick" or a huge armaments race and "more Koreas."

The development of these peace sentiments is not the result of a sudden awakening but rather stems from a process of long duration. Among the many forces stimulating the growth of these desires have been the 110,000 reported US battle casualties, the cynical seven-month long delay in the truce talks, the open alliance of the US rulers with Japanese and Nazi militarists and fascists, and the immense rise of the worldwide peace struggle exemplified by the liberation efforts in Asia, the Near East, and Africa, the mounting hatred of US imperialism throughout Europe, and the signing of the demand for a Five-Power Peace Pact by over six hundred million of world humanity.

What is taking place is the beginning of a basic reevaluation of the suicidal anti-Soviet premise of the Truman bipartisan policy. And this applies to large masses who have not yet broken with monopoly capital's two-party system and are still attracted by the "peace" demagogy of one or another bipartisan spokesman.

While trade-union leaders in ever increasing numbers cry out for an end to the Korean war and the anti-imperialist sentiments of the Negro people reach an all-time high level; while Truman's "holy war" propaganda is delivered a blow by the defeat of his proposal to appoint General Mark Clark as Ambassador to the Vatican; while the whole State Department effort to make peace "subversive" suffers a blow in the great victory of the acquittal of Dr. Du Bois and his associates of the Peace Information Center—at such a time Truman still waves the threat of atom-bomb superiority and projects new proposals for extending hostilities.

And Truman does not repudiate the hideous statement of his field commander in Korea, Gen. Van Fleet, who felt the war in Korea was a "blessing in disguise," and that "there had to be a Korea either here or somewhere else in the world." (*New York Times,* Jan. 20, 1952.)

A "blessing"—the annihilation and maiming of literally millions of men, women, and children! A "blessing" which has brought the horrified condemnation of world opinion from a leading French Catholic intellectual like Charles Favril to the Women's International Democratic Federation! US peace forces must dissociate themselves from these "blessings," not only in the interest of common decency, but also of true patriotism and internationalism. History will not excuse the American people any more than it did the German people, if we fail effectively to dissociate ourselves from our "own" racist imperialists in their drive for world conquest and domination. This makes it necessary to deepen the understanding of all peace forces of the special white chauvinist content of the Truman bipartisan war-policy against the colored peoples of the world.

The sharpening crisis in Wall Street's foreign policy, and particularly in the solidity of its bipartisan coalition, is seen in the blunt "admissions" of failure from monopolists like Henry Ford II and Charles Wilson, accompanied by the attacks against "Truman's war" by a Senator Taft or a Herbert Hoover.

Reflecting the crisis amongst their masters are the lamentations of such bourgeois ideologists as Demaree Bess of the *Saturday Evening Post* and Walter Lippmann. More and more, these "confessions" take the form of admitting that the danger of "Russian aggression" was a maliciously conceived Big Lie. Such expressions, causing the "free enterprise" racketeers no little worry, mainly show that the peace movement at home and abroad is making it difficult for Wall Street to choose, as of today, the "all-out war" alternative. It does not mean that the imperialists have lost their urge to war.

In this connection, it is useful to refer to Comrade Hall's summary address at our Party's Fifteenth National Convention:

> The speeches of Hoover and Taft do reflect the crisis in Wall Street's foreign policy. They are admissions of the bankruptcy of the bipartisan war policy. They are attempts to capitalize on the growing peace sentiments of the American people. Speeches of this kind open new doors for the peace movement But these men belong to the war camp. We can have no illusions about Herbert Hoover, Kennedy, or any one else in the war camp! *(Political Affairs, February, 1951, p. 15)*

It would be wrong, of course, not to pay close heed to these monopolist "admissions." Some of the force in the emerging people's peace coalition hold that the Left does not accurately appraise these trends and that the real choice is between Hoover and Truman. Thus, I. F. Stone, starting from the correct premise that "the world can be saved by coexistence," finds Hoover to be "much closer to Henry Wallace's old position, which was also FDR's, than to Truman." "The Roosevelt–Wallace position," writes Mr. Stone "had sufficient faith in America and to be afraid of Communism. Hoover has faith enough in capitalism to feel that Communism, as he said 'will decay of its own poisons.' *Pravda* is not afraid of that challenge but the Truman–Acheson Democrats and the Dulles–Dewey Republicans are." *(Daily Compass, Feb. 5, 1952)*.

We agree, of course, with Mr. Stone's basic premise of the possibility of peaceful coexistence. Is this, however, as Stone holds, only a question of "faith" in one or another society? No, in part the concept is influenced by "good business" reasons of trade. But this still is not the core of the matter. The core of the matter is the mass will for peace and the people's power to impose this will on the war-makers. This must be sealed in a Five-Power Peace Pact. Then, and only then would it be possible to conclude that the war danger had lessened. A key to Mr. Stone's error may be found in his conclusion that "the Hoover–Taft policies might easily lead in the same direction [as Truman's] if and as new Communist victories abroad frightened the propertied classes here into support of fascism."

But fear is at the heart of the present bipartisan policy—a fear of the peoples' rule at home and abroad. History teaches that it is not the peoples' victories that lead to fascism, but their immobilization and disunity in the face of reaction's assaults. The finance capitalists move towards fascism when they become convinced that they can no longer rule in the old way; they adopt fascist methods of terror and rule rather than adhere to the most elementary democratic process at home and abroad. In resorting to this policy of external and internal aggression, they raise the hysterical cry of "aggression" against all who resist that very aggression. Thus, they howl "Soviet imperialism" and slander all movements of peoples anywhere for national liberation and national reconstruction upon democratic foundations as "internal aggression."

This policy of imperialist onslaught and fascism at home is the policy of the Truman–Dulles camp as it is of the Hoover–Taft camp. The differences between them are not of a strategic, but of a tactical, nature. Their strife is a "family quarrel" of finance-capitalist groupings, which fear and resist the peoples' victories here and abroad, and some of whom, like the Midwestern industrialists, want at this time to concentrate upon the American and Asian continents for their "spheres of interest." They are fearful of losing all in "all-out" war on the European continent.

But it is a "family quarrel" which can ripen into a crisis for the entire strategy of the bipartisan war policy. An alert peace move-ment can and should enter into debate on such questions, in order to strengthen their growing advantage, to press for realization of the real alternative—the alternative of lasting peace, based on coexistence of the USA and the USSR, on the basis of peaceful competition, honor-ing of commitments, negotiation of all outstanding differences, and recognition of the basic democratic right of all peoples to choose their own form of government. It is this deeper ideological meaning, underlying the real concern of certain top monopolists with the "reckless pace" with which the bipartisan camp moves to the twin disaster of war and depression, that a people's peace movement must grasp hold of, in order to curb the warmongers.

Main New Demagogic Arguments

The real essence of US foreign policy is pro-imperialist, anti-Soviet, anti-democratic—and anti-American. This bipartisan foreign policy seeks to destroy every "Communist State" and to annihilate every "Communist." It seeks to "overthrow internal aggression," and build "situations of strength." It poses as a "holy" crusade in order to cover its chauvinist and racist ideology as it adopts the *Mein Kampf* concept that "nationalism is the enemy of liberty."

What of the Acheson-formulated anti-Soviet "situations of strength" argument? This formula not only means continued unemployment and hastening economic crisis, but it means perpetual arming-to-the-teeth, perpetual warmongering and forcible efforts to destroy existing governments not to the liking of US imperialism. Small wonder that the "situation of strength" policy moves the high brass to express alarm that "peace may break out" in Korea, and to issue "warnings" that the flame in Korea "threatens" to end. This policy engenders, not strength, but hatred, so that the peoples of the world already compare our youth to the youth of Hitler. It is the policy of the Rommels and Mussolinis who wrote sonnets to the "beauty" of bursting shells and who gleefully watched the torture of Communists and non-Communists in concentration camps—a policy which is unfolding in the actual present building by the bipartisans of concentration camps for "Communists first" and then for all who dare to oppose this ruinous war policy.

The more brutal "internal aggression" argument is nothing but a Truman version of the racist *Mein Kampf* aim of domination over "inferior peoples" who need the benign "blessings" of Anglo-American imperialism to lead them to "salvation." It represents a naked "white man's burden" imperialist approach of bloodily—and vainly—trying to reverse the triumphant worldwide colonial and national liberation movements highlighted by the historic victory of the People's Democratic Republic of China, and inspired by the establishment of the Union of Soviet Socialist Republics.

US imperialism, faced with ever-rising and growing struggles from the oppressed Negro people within it own borders, must attempt to hide from world view its own genocidal practices, fearful lest exposure further pulverize its shibboleth of a free nation in a free world. Consequently, the fable that "nationalism is the enemy of liberty" is designed not to whittle away the concept of an arrogant boastful nation, who can "take on the world" and "get it over with quick," but in typical white supremacist manner, to heighten chauvinist nationalism and white chauvinism through the program of "imposing salvation" on "childlike" peoples to whom self-government has been ruthlessly denied in century-long suppression.

One and all, these demagogic arguments of the bipartisans hide a policy of betrayal of the true national interests of the United States and its people. It is the Hitler dream to destroy every "Communist" state, but in the context of today it could culminate not only in world war, but in a world atomic holocaust, from which the imperialists will not and cannot emerge victorious, but in which tremendous suffering will result to our people and all the world's peace-loving peoples. What is in peril, therefore, is not the "American way of life" but the wages of workers who are asked to rob themselves of billions of dollars so that Truman and the Wall Street monopolists can roam over the earth trying to crush freedom-seeking peoples who want independence and peace and to advance socially on the basis of their choice. The peoples of the world will never yield to these Wall Street terms. The vital interests of our own country demand that a mighty peace front be built through which can emerge a people's peace coalition capable of curbing the Wall Street monopolists' drive for a third world war and fascism. Such a peace front, based on the working class and the inherently anti-imperialist growing Negro people's movement, will include broad sections of the farmers and millions of people in intellectual and professional pursuits.

State of Progress Towards a People's Peace Coalition

The question arises: How can we help to "build and expand" on this perspective of a people's peace coalition in the context of a day-by-day peace struggle which, in the first place, must be rooted among the workers? It must be frankly said in evaluation of the present organized peace movement in the US that the growing sentiment for peace among the workers does not yet find expression in adequate peace organization of this decisive class. Necessary for this orientation and for advancing the peace movement in the US by deepening its anti-fascist and anti-imperialist content, is rooting the peace movement among workers and organizing peace activities on union and shop levels. Any tendency to liquidate labor peace centers under the guise of real difficulties, means only abandoning this perspective. There is no doubt that right opportunist tendencies are camouflaged in the advocacy of such "left" sectarian practices, while little enough is done to seek the precise forms of peace organization to which the workers do readily respond. The struggle to win the working class is fought, not in the realm of abstract theories of the Right or the "Left," but around specific issues, around policies as regards wages, speed-up, equal rights for the Negro people, foreign affairs, inner union democracy, etc. In the words of Comrade Hall:

> We must have confidence that we can win the entire working class to the policies and programs based on class struggle. We can do this, not in isolation, but by organizing and leading in struggle the rank and file in the existing unions, in the departments, shops, locals, and internationals. (*Political Affairs*, December, 1949, p. 37.)

Every index shows an increasingly anti-war feeling among the workers. More and more trade-union expressions as those emanating from figures like Carl Stellato, William R. Hood, Frank Rosenblum, etc., call for a Five-Power Peace Pact. Clearly, this higher anti-war militancy of the workers emphasizes the interlocking of the fight for peace with the fight for a decent standard of living, unshackled unionism, collective bargaining, an end to discrimination, and other clementary demands. Numerous shop stewards' peace conferences and peace ballot campaigns confirm the ready response to the peace issue among the workers. Growing mass unemployment and high taxes are undoubtedly the reason for the gloomy complaints even of Social-Democratic leaders like Walter Reuther.

What bothers class collaborationist labor leaders like Reuther, of course, is the growing rank-and-file pressure of the auto workers who face mass unemployment, and who are questioning the bipartisan foreign policy which has brought them, not the promised prosperity, but worsening economic conditions. The workers see wages frozen, higher prices and taxes and the growth of repression against the people's liberties, heightened chauvinist oppression of the Negro people, and enhanced corruption in government. Even Reuther's complaints can serve to tear the mask from the eyes of many workers, who may well wonder why Reuther and the class collaborationist labor leaders persist in trying to hold the workers within the framework of the two rotten old parties of capitalism.

In this connection it is useful a refer once again to the advice of Gus Hall:

> It was in Korea that the masses saw the greatest danger of a world war and a war with China. The Republicans very cleverly identified the Truman Administration with this central danger point, and thus were able to capitalize on the peace feelings of the masses. We must conclude that, yes, large sections were misled. But they are for peace. They will follow the correct road in the struggle for peace if they get the right leadership. We must be able to offer the masses a practical alternative, one which they see provides a real chance to win outside the two old parties. This alternative must correspond to their present level of understanding in the arena of political action . . . Large sections of the working class are beginning to draw some very important lessons from the last election campaign. The big lesson is not that the trade-union leaders took a licking. The lesson is that there must be some road that does not lead into the blind alley to which the workers have been brought by the labor officialdom. This is the outlook on which we must build, and which we must help to expand. (*Peace Can Be Won!*, p. 54.)

The Present Organized Peace Centers

A basic ideological weakness underlies the tendency of failing to concentrate the peace struggles and organization among the workers and the Negro people. How is this to be observed in practice? Here is an actual example: an organized peace coalition exists in a particular city. This coalition in its present state experiences difficulty in getting a hall for a certain project. A fight is carried through unsuccessfully—and privately. Certain advanced forces in the coalition suggest that the peace issue is so urgent and the need so great that "broader forces" be sought out for this project. So far so good. Even the "private" negotiation, which should be criticized, is not the main point. Broader forces *are* secured and the existing peace coalition, which supports parallel peace actions, supports this one. Lo and behold! However, there are certain forces in the coalition who do not understand the Negro question or the decisive role of the working class. Where is the emphasis of the left forces in the coalition? They rightly express concern that this state of affairs jeopardizes the new coalition which is emerging and some of the forces in it. They themselves certainly appreciate that not all the components of the coalition will fully understand all these questions, but it is expected that they will come into the coalition on the basis of its minimum program. But its minimum program is premised on the fact that there is a great ferment for peace especially among the masses of workers and the Negro people; it is premised on the fight for labor's rights and on the effects of the war drive on the Negro people. Do the left-progressives battle on these issues? Yes, they battle, but unfortunately oft-times incorrectly. They usually "battle" by arguing that to struggle ideologically on these issues, would "create a problem." What they fail to recognize and oft-times fail to do, is to examine their own weaknesses which, having their source in right opportunism and "left" sectarianism, usually boil down to a retreat in meeting these arguments. Experience confirms, however, that many of these broader forces respond to and learn from a struggle for the correct ideological and practical position on these questions.

Errors such as this isolate the peace coalition from decisive working-class forces and the Negro people. Now, no section of a united front coalition can be ignored or "asked" to accept second-class citizenship status. How much more serious this becomes when it affects the decisive core of the coalition, the labor-Negro people's alliance! Of course, where the Negro people are concerned, this reflects white chauvinism as well. Yet serious strains, affecting relations with top labor and Negro peace leaders, having a mass base on national and state levels, exist because of this most costly error in peace activity.

A key reason for such serious errors lies in the lack of a common estimate of the character and role of the present organized peace centers among labor, women, youth, and in overall peace coordination. To be concrete: Can it be said that full clarity exists among progressive forces, including Communists, relative to the programmatic character of the American Peace Crusade, the American Women for Peace, the National Labor Conference for Peace, the Youth Division of the Peace Crusade? No, it cannot! The American Peace Crusade and the above-mentioned independent organized peace centers, themselves coalitions, emerged as a result of the need for an organized peace center of a special kind, shown particularly in the powerful, grassroots response evoked by the Stockholm Peace Petition campaign. This response came from leading forces among intellectuals and professionals, as well as among the working class and the Negro people. Thus, the American Peace Crusade (APC) came into being and dedicated itself to advancing a principled program. Key elements of the APC program are the principle of peaceful coexistence and the negotiation of outstanding differences between the Big Five Powers. The program, based also on a recognition of the war drive's ravaging effects on the working class and the Negro people, spurs the struggle for Negro-white unity. This peace coalition includes left-progressive forces, and, in line with its principled advocacy of peace, programmatically rejects red-baiting and all other divisive ideologies. Many of the forces in the APC—and in varying degrees the other peace centers— express unclarities and disagreement on several phases of basic policy, including the whole question of the working class and its relation to the peace coalition, the role of the Soviet Union, etc. This is as we should expect in a genuine united front peace coalition.

But a grave persistent weakness is the lack of a working-class base and real roots among the Negro people. The point is not only that these weaknesses exist, but that many of the advanced left-progressive forces fail to accept their special ideological role and, on numerous issues in and out of the present organized peace coalitions, this weakness seriously jeopardizes the continued growth of the coalition. Consequently, entirely too much time is consumed in necessarily resolving these problems, on top levels, while the task of rooting and organizing a united front working-class base goes by the board.

Experience teaches that where these questions have been frankly subjected to friendly discussion, the progressive forces in the coalition, together with the left-progressives, resolve the matter satisfactorily.

All peace forces, and left-progressives in particular, must be keen to cooperate with every progressive tendency that may manifest itself, under the strong pressure of the masses, in the trade-union leadership—on all levels—and within the Negro people's movement. All peace forces must learn to cultivate such trends and utilize them for the building of a broad peace coalition.

This is all the more decisive, since the new and increasing difficulties of the warmongers do not imply the cessation or necessarily a lessening of the war danger. On the contrary, the masses must be alerted as never before to combat the machinations of the war incendiaries.

The task demands mastery of the united front and the bold grappling with special ideological questions on all issues confronting the peace movement. Some left-progressive forces, including some Communists, argue that the present coalition peace centers are "too left." "We must build broader ones and scrap the old," they say. Frequently this argument hides a tendency of capitulation to so-called "broad forces" which, in fact, reject the peace coalition's minimum program. Others demonstrate in practice that to fail to build and expand present organized peace centers is to fail to take advantage of the current mass peace upsurge. Thus, the development of "broader centers" is wrongly counterposed to the strengthening of the present organized peace centers. Some left-progressives, including some Communists, even take the initiative in dissuading groups who come into activity as a result of the stimulus of these peace centers, from coming closer to them, in day-to-day working relationship.

The "great debate" goes on and on, while at a standstill is the heart and core of the real issue, that of not only moving with the stream, but of building and consolidating united front peace organizations among the workers and the Negro people, and of organizing united front activity from below on the key peace issue and primarily on the economic and social consequences of the war drive.

The right opportunist danger, reflected in a neglect to come to grips with basic ideological problems relative to the peace struggle, is mainly expressed in the failure of many left-progressives, including some Communists, to play their special ideological role of convincing people of the correctness of the previously agreed on minimum program. Nor should left-progressives fail to note the effect that such wrong approaches have on non-left Negro and white forces in the coalition who see their own roles being reduced and who quite correctly resent being "written off." No argument that such discussions will isolate "broader forces" holds water. The existence of an organized peace center, or even of parallel peace movements on special issues, does not excuse lack of ideological struggle in *all* coalition peace movements.

Conversely, the "left" sectarian danger reflects a narrow approach to the peace movement and is based on a defeatist attitude that world war really is inevitable.

The necessity for broader forms of peace struggle complements, it does not contradict, the necessity of strengthening the present organized peace centers, particularly in terms of developing their working-class base. To pose these efforts as mutually exclusive is to endanger not only existing organized peace centers, but the whole concept of the united front, of an anti-fascist, anti-imperialist people's peace coalition based on the working class and Negro people.

Just as there is no contradiction between a mass united front coalition policy and the special responsibilities of the left-progressives in the fight against white chauvinism, so is there no contradiction between the development of broader movements around specific peace issues and the building and strengthening of the existing organized peace centers based on the working class and the deepening of their ideological leadership.

The Negro People and the Fight for Peace and Freedom

If it is true that the Truman war crusade, brutally exemplified in the atrocious war against the colored peoples of Asia, develops in an atmosphere of rising counter-struggle for peace, it is also certainly true that even greater counter-struggle by the Negro people is developing as they resist the Wall Street bipartisan attempt to destroy their liberation movement, and their leaders—Paul Robeson, W. E. B. Du Bois, William L. Patterson, Benjamin J. Davis, Henry Winston, James Jackson, Ben Careathers, Pettis Perry, Roosevelt Ward, Mrs. Charlotta Bass, and many, many others. But against this white supremacist, chauvinist war drive upon the peace-loving peoples of the earth, there also develops in our epoch, the liberation movement of the peoples in colonial and dependent countries. It is clear then, that this liberation movement "is inseparably connected with the movement for peace. Therefore any forcible attempts by the imperialists to keep these peoples in a state of dependence and colonial subjection is a threat to the cause of peace." (I. A. Seleznev, in *Political Affairs*, December, 1951.)

Faced with rising anti-imperialist counter-struggle of the colonial peoples and nations and at home with the growing, and ever-more conscious anti-imperialist Negro liberation movement, American imperialism multiplies its hourly crimes against the Negro people.

At the same time there is taking place a sharpening in the whole Negro liberation movement, and a dissociation from the Truman bipartisan war policy by increasing sections of the Negro people as expressed by more and more Negro spokesmen. Thus, many State Department Negro spokesmen are competing widely in the Negro press in "warnings" to Truman that his Point Four Program, which accompanies Wall Street's imposed "blessings," is being rejected by the independence-minded peoples of Asia, Latin America, the West Indies, and Africa. Thus, it is not only the forthright Dr. Mordecai Johnson, president of Howard University, who raises this issue, but even the State Department representative, Dr. Dailey, on return from a tour of the Far East and Africa "warns" US imperialism to reject this anti-national liberation path. Further, Negro spokesmen such as P. L. Prattis, editor of the *Pittsburgh Courier*, Dr. Benjamin Mays, and numerous Negro journalists, commenting on recent Truman messages, warned that "Negro voters still have to be convinced." In the words of the influential Negro historian and publicist, J. A. Rogers:

> Colored voters are convinced that they have been ruthlessly carried for a ride and exploited on the civil rights appeal. Now they are face to face with the cold facts that not a single civil rights measure has been passed in Congress. They also know that these measures have been checked on all turns by the Southern Democratic bloc. President Truman admitted in his recent State of the Union message that these issues had not been effectuated (*New York Amsterdam News*, February 2, 1952).

Nothing so points up the basic *new* element in the relationship between the struggle for peace and the Negro liberation and people's movements than this increasingly sharp criticism by the Negro people of the Truman bipartisan policy. The Negro people as a whole see the struggle for their rights impaled on the blade of Wall Street's greed, in a war against the colored peoples of Korea which threatens to spread into a war against the oppressed colored people of the entire world.

As decisively placed by Comrade Benjamin J. Davis in his Report to the Party's Fifteenth National Convention:

> The new element in the relationship between the struggle for peace and for Negro liberation is the growing acuteness of the contradiction between American imperialism in its war program, on the one hand, and, on the other, the struggle of the Negro people and their supporters to defend their elementary liberties and to advance the cause of full citizenship. This is by far the most important single new factor to be noted in connection with the struggle for national liberation of the Negro people.

It is exactly the "new element" basically analyzed in Comrade Davis' Report that must yet be grasped by left-progressive forces and the Party cadres. The further significance of this fundamental relationship between the struggle for peace and for freedom was documented and analyzed by Comrade Pettis Perry. These profound contributions require study and mastery by all left-progressives and Party cadres without delay.

An appreciation of the great contributions of Comrade Davis and Perry will do much to heighten the ideological level in the struggle against white chauvinism, which still plagues the whole peace movement. We cannot speak of the new militant features of the Negro people's movement without recognizing that this very fact places new and tremendous responsibilities on our ideological and practical work. We must sharpen the understanding of the national question, particularly as this applies to the Negro people, in order to advance the leading role of the workers in the Negro liberation movement. This is of basic importance in the specific context of the struggle for peace in order to guarantee strengthening the alliance of the working class and Negro people. Such an alliance must form the solid core of the emerging people's peace coalition, which will reverse the present ruinous direction the imperialists are traveling.

We must put an end to the false conception that "broader forces" cannot understand the Negro question. While it would be incorrect to demand that the full program of the Negro liberation movement be part of the program of struggle of the existing organized peace movement, it is necessary to demand—and certainly to expect of left-progressives and Communists in the peace movement—an all-out battle against the white chauvinist poison which permeates many of these movements. To assert the impossibility of spreading an understanding of the Negro question is to excuse inactivity in the fight against white chauvinism and to insult the broad masses eager for peace and democracy. We must convince our allies in the anti-war struggle of the correctness of the minimum program in terms of the rights of the Negro people and Negro-white unity, which they are duty bound to fight for. The struggle for peace requires a struggle against colonialism and rejection of racist warmongering. We must labor to deepen the understanding of the masses as regards the inherent relationship between the attacks on the Negro people and the attacks on the peace movement and dem-ocratic liberties, as regards the synthesis between the fight against a robber war in Asia and the imperialist attempt to thwart the Negro liberation movement and keep its leaders from exposing US imperialism claims that it is a "free nation" in a "free world."

The superb people's victories in the Du Bois case, in Stuyvesant Town, and in the development of the National Negro Labor Council Movement, fused with past struggles around Trenton, Martinsville, McGee, etc., show how the struggle for Negro rights and Negro-white unity advances and heightens political consciousness on the part of participating Negro and white masses.

Merely to master the full significance of the State Department's "reason" for the denial of a passport to Paul Robeson on the grounds that "racial discrimination" is a "family matter," the public exposure of which is inimical to the interests of the security of the United States Government, is to pose the question: Why have not the peace forces fully mounted a mass campaign that can lead to victory around this prime issue involving the revered people's artist and world peace leader—Paul Robeson? All over the world, especially among the hun-dreds of millions of darker peoples in Asia, Africa, Latin America, and the West Indies, the US imperialists are finding the Jim Crow system in this country a most serious obstacle in their path of aggression. And it is the Communists everywhere who, together with the left-progressives, are the leaders of the masses in this sharp condemnation of the Jim Crow outrage in the United States.

Hence, ideological struggle on this front assumes urgent significance, particularly in view of the leadership assumed in all peace centers by outstanding Negro men and women. Their contributions cannot and should not be concentrated on "doing battle" on these issues. Their white coworkers must assume greater responsibility and initiative in this regard, not only because this is proper in the struggle for Negro rights, but also in order that these capable Negro men, women, and youth fighters may be freed to give fullest leadership, in their authoritative positions, to building a broad peace base among the Negro people; to developing relationships with the emerging peace expressions from very broad sections of the Negro and white forces, coming from churches, fraternal organizations, Negro women's organizations, etc.

This is of prime importance, since as things are today there persists a serious lack of an organized peace movement and organization in the decisive Negro communities, particularly in the South. This lack exists in the midst of rising intensity of mass actions of the Negro people against the growing lynch murders and intimidation, as in Cairo and Cicero, Illinois, Mims and Groveland, Florida, etc.

The warmakers, trying to offset this powerful anti-Jim Crow sentiment at home and abroad, have put forward a number of prominent Negro figures to belittle and deny the existence of Negro persecution in the United States. These shameful figures include Channing Tobias, Mrs. Edith Sampson, Ray Robinson, and the like. These sorry apologists for white supremacy must be exposed far more vigorously than heretofore. This can best be done by the Negro people themselves, and a peace base among the Negro people on the foundation of alliance with the Negro people's movements would help greatly in exposing such misleaders. This is particularly true among Negro women, who in their significant and developing Sojourners for Truth and Justice movement, will have to deal with the burning problems of the war and its effects on the Negro children and the family, on Negro mothers and wives, among whom a fiercely powerful peace sentiment exists. All this will strengthen the growing mass independent women's peace movement in our country and its present independent peace center, American Women for Peace. Coming to grips with the consequences of the war effort opens up new and rewarding avenues of broad mass contact with the overwhelming majority of working-class Negro women, whose militant desires for freedom and peace are the most outstanding in the nation.

Five-Power Peace Pact

The campaign for a Five-Power Peace Pact offers a magnificent opportunity to strengthen the whole organized peace movement in our country.

Barely five months old, the organized Pact campaign is receiving unprecedented response among masses who thus again show the error in hesitations on this question within the organized peace movement and among left-progressive forces, including the Party. There is no doubt that influencing this vacillation was a certain amount of disorientation among the organized peace forces following the significant Chicago Peace Congress. Such moods, as that of "hanging on hopes" that the military would effect cease-fire following the "ebbs and flows" of the truce talks, had to be quickly discarded, in the course of self-critical examination, for the plain truth that peace can only be won through mass struggle. Basically influencing the hesitancy was not only this factor but the underestimation of the decisive character of this Five-Power Pact effort which will not end until peace is assured by the signing of such a pact. Underlying all these factors, was a fundamental ideological weakness in comprehending the full implications of the possibility of peaceful coexistence between states of different social systems, in addition to a tendency to shy away from vigorous struggle, particularly among the working class and the Negro people, against vile anti-Soviet lies and fables about "Soviet imperialism."

The American Peace Crusade leadership in the Five-Power Peace Pact effort has been outstanding. It has stressed the many-sided approaches to this campaign and has served to stimulate trade-union, farm, Negro, women, cultural, and youth peace forces into similar activity. Numerous APC conferences on a state level and peace workshops have been held. Many petitions carrying special appeals, such as Peace Prayers, union resolutions, etc., have been issued. Scheduled for March, in Washington, is a National Delegates Assembly involving the Crusade and many other forces who do not adhere to the entire

Peace Crusade program. Here delegates from the entire country will convene to exchange experiences in the signature campaign for a Five-Power Peace Pact, with the purpose of stimulating the campaign.

Great initiative behind the Five-Power Peace Pact effort has come from the American Women for Peace which has, in many cases, boldly canvassed existing women's organizations and urged them to participate, jointly or separately, in the campaign. Supporting the work, too, is the World Youth and Friendship Book Campaign, where signatures for a Five-Power Peace Pact are gathered by young people for eventual presentation to the United Nations.

Expressions of support have come from additional varied sources, notably from trade-union leaders such as William Hood and Hugo Ernst, and from many leading intellectual, professional, and cultural figures, such as Professor Anton Carlson, Dr. W. E. B. Du Bois, Dr. Robert Morss Lovett, Paul Robeson, Dr. Alice Hamilton, and Professor Philip Morrison. Again, groups such as the Committee on Peaceful Alternatives and the American Friends Service Committee (Quakers) have reiterated their support of peaceful negotiations among the great powers. Significant leaders in the religious life of the country such as the Rev. Dr. Jemison, of the National (Negro) Baptist Alliance, Bishop Bromley Oxnam, and Rabbi B. Benedict Glazer have also spoken out for agreement amongst the great powers.

These, and many similar facts, not only confirm the growing pro-peace upsurge, but show that where the initiative is seized boldly around particular issues, broader forces do come forward, unity is achieved, and wider and wider segments of the population are reached.

Two forthcoming international events offer further excellent opportunities for broadening and deepening the anti-war struggle. The first is the American Inter-Continenttal Peace Conference, scheduled for March. The prime responsibility of US imperialism for the terrible exploitation of the peoples of the West Indies, and of Central and South America, makes active participation by peace lovers of the United States in this Congress all the more significant.

In April, an International Conference in Defense of Children will be held in Vienna. "To save the children, the most precious wealth of all mankind," declares the International Sponsoring Committee, "we appeal to all men and women of goodwill, to all organizations which are interested in the problems of children, to participate . . . . This

Conference will study what can be done in order to defend the right to life, to health, and education of all children in the world." Surely, profound interest of all peace forces in the United States will be manifested towards this great international event.

The Party and the Peace Struggle

The Communist Party, whose leaders are victims of Smith Act repression, can be proud of its modest contribution to the struggle for peace. What would our nation have been, had we not had the inspiring leadership of the Party led by William Z. Foster and Eugene Dennis? The whole activity of the Party has been devoted to reversing the present ruinous path of our nation, resulting from the Wall Street bipartisan policy. The membership, in and out of the organized peace movement, have been selfless in their work for peace, and have experienced and are experiencing many reprisals as the Communist Party fights for its legal rights as an American political party, a fight which is itself, of course, of the essence of the struggle against war. Communists must and do bring to the peace movement the selflessness, enthusiasm, and confidence in victory characteristic of Marxist-Leninists, not because they are self-righteous, but because the Party is correct, because its path is the path of the development of human society.

As Communists, we struggle for peace, equality, freedom, and socialism—we struggle for the best interests of the working class, the Negro people, the farming masses, the vast majority of the American people. To fulfill these high Communist principles, we must learn from the people and we must shed all moods of "spontaneity" in the peace struggle. The mastery of the united front tactic, the deepening of our ideological weapons, must be strengthened.

To work to unite all people who understand that our country is in danger of war and fascism; to work so that our nation is not viewed with fear and loathing by the people of the world; to root our peace struggle basically among the working class and Negro people—this is the path to the achievement of the correct main line of our Party in this period. That main line seeks the emergence of an anti-fascist, anti-monopoly people's peace coalition, that will lead to a people's front against war and fascism strong enough to curb the warmongers in 1952 and thus open to all the American people a vista of happiness, security, equality, and *peace*.

CLAUDIA JONES' DEFENSE*

1953

Your Honor, there are a few things I wish to say. For if what I say here serves even one whit to further dedicate growing millions of Americans to fight for peace, and to repel the fascist drive on free speech and thought in our country, I shall consider my rising to speak worthwhile indeed.

Quite candidly, your Honor, I say these things not with any idea that what I say will influence your sentence of me. For, even with all the power your Honor holds, how can you decide to mete out justice for the only act to which I proudly plead guilty, and one, moreover, which by your own prior rulings constitutes no crime—that of holding Communist ideas; of being a member and officer of the Communist Party of the United States?

Will you measure, for example, as worthy of one year's sentence, my passionate adherence to the idea of fighting for full unequivocal equality for my people, the Negro people, which as a Communist I believe can only be achieved allied to the cause of the working class?

A year for another vital Communist belief, that the bestial Korean war is an unjust war? Or my belief that peaceful coexistence of nations can be achieved and peace won and struggled for?

Another year for my belief that only under socialism will exploitation of man by man be finally abolished and the great human and

---

*   Claudia Jones, "Claudia Jones," in *13 Communists Speak to the Court* (New York: New Century Publishers, 1953), 19–26.

industrial resources of the nation be harnessed for the well-being of the people?

Still another year's sentence for my belief that the denial of the exercise of free speech and thought to Communist only precedes, as history confirms, the denial of the exercise of these rights to all Americans?

Et cetera, Honorable Judge?

Of course, your Honor might choose still another path for sentence. You will no doubt choose as the basis for sentence the concocted lies which flowed so smoothly from the well-paid tongues of stool pigeons and informers who paraded before you here and gave so-called evidence which the Court has asserted was "amply justified."

"Amply justified," your Honor? What has been amply justified? The lies of degenerate witnesses like Younglove who can only be compared to Van Der Lubbe, of the famous Reichstag Trial? The despicable forced admission of the Negro witness Cummings who laughed at the thought of his $10,000 Judas gold jingling in his pocket when he said he would turn informer on his own mother for a mess of the prosecutor's pottage?

The ill-practiced and unspeakable dronings of the other Negro informer Rosser, who blurted out his well-memorized script, and even, on your Honor's prodding, would drift off into half-intelligible intonations, "I don't know what you are talking about," to name but a few examples!

"Amply justified!" Indeed! This "evidence!"

There was no official stamp powerful enough, your Honor, to dignify the obscenity of this trial of ideas. Hence, for me to accept the verdict of guilty would only mean that I considered myself less than worthy of the dignity of truth which I cherish as a Communist and as a human being, and also unsuitable to the utter contempt with which I hold such sordid performances.

That is why I find now, as throughout this trial of the ideas of Marxism-Leninism, that it is we, the defendants, who are morally free, and conversely it is the prosecutors and the Court itself that stands naked before the Bill of Rights and the Constitution and the people of our country.

It is this, your Honor, that explains the not-so-strange reason that you yourself observed that we feel no guilt. For true though it is that the prosecutor has its framed-up verdict on a framed-up indictment and trial, it is not we Communist defendants who tremble at this final stage of these trial court proceedings, but the very prosecutors of our ideas.

Truly, the prosecution's victory sits shakily. For our ideas were confirmed in the course of this trial itself.

It was the world-renowned Karl Marx, founder of the Marxist-Leninist science, for which application to American and world historical conditions we were so fearfully convicted, who long ago predicted that *"The time would come when the powers that be would no longer live by the very laws they themselves have fashioned."*

In the libraries and great institutions of learning, and, yes, your Honor, particularly in the homes of Negro and white workers, will not such reading—which will not stop with this or any other Smith Act trial—will not men, women, and youth think and ponder that such a time is here?

The thinking process, as your Honor well knows, is a process that defies jailing. When it is all boiled down, what shows is not the strength of the policies and practices of our prosecutors—which are akin to police-state practices— but their desperate fear of the people. Nothing shows this more, your Honor, than our exposure of the biased jury drawn from a system which virtually excludes Negro, Puerto Rican, and manual workers. This virtual exclusion exists not because of lack of qualifications or even financial hardship, but because of deliberate discrimination based on consciously cultivated white supremacist ruling-class prejudice which sullies our boasted Western culture.

This conscious white supremacist prejudice, which Mr. Perry so well pointed out, was shown in the gingerly handling by the prosecutors and ofttimes the Court of the Achilles heel of this alleged "force and violence" charge against us in relation to the Negro question.

Introduce a title page to show Claudia Jones wrote an article during the indictment period, but you dare not read even a line of it, even to a biased jury, on which sat a lone Negro juror, there by mere accident, since he was an alternate well through most of the trial. You dare not, gentle men of the prosecution, assert that Negro women can think and speak and write!

Moreover, you dare not read it because the article not only refutes the assertion that the ruling class will ever grant equality to fifteen million Negro Americans, but shows that what we are granted is unrequited force and violence, not only in the unpunished barbaric crime of lynching, but in eating, in everyday existence, in living, in the armed forces, in jails, in the denial of land, in recreation—yes, even in the nation's cemeteries.

The prosecution also cancelled out the overt act which accompanied the original indictment of the defendant Jones entitled "Women in the Struggle for Peace and Security."

And why, your Honor? It cannot be read, your Honor—it urges American mothers, Negro women and white, to write, to emulate the peace struggles of their anti-fascist sisters in Latin America, in the new European democracies, in the Soviet Union, in Asia, and Africa to end the bestial Korean war, to stop "operation killer," to bring our boys home, to reject the militarist threat to embroil us in a war with China, so that their children should not suffer the fate of the Korean babies murdered by napalm bombs of B-29s, nor the fate of Hiroshima.

Is all this not further proof that what we were also tried for was our oppositon to racist ideas, so integral a part of the desperate drive by the men of Wall Street to war and fascism?

One thought pervaded me throughout this trial and pervades me still, and it is this: In the nine and one-half months of this trial, millions of children have been born. I speak only of those who live. Will the future of those children, including those of our defendants, and even your Honor's grandchildren, be made more secure by the jailing of thirteen men and women Communists whose crimes are not criminal acts but advocacy of ideas? Is this not a tyrannical violation of the American dream of "life, liberty, and the pursuit of happiness"?

It was in an American junior high school where I first learned of the great traditions of popular liberty of American History, for which I then received the Theodore Roosevelt Award for good citizenship. That I have learned to interpret that history and to work; to influence its change for the betterment of the people with the indispensable weapon of Marxist-Leninist ideas, that is the real crime against me.

Of all other charges I am innocent.

It was here on this soil (and not as Mr. Lane would depict to this Court, as a young child of eight years of age waving revolutionary slogans), that I early experienced experiences which are shared by millions of native-born Negroes—the bitter indignity and humiliation of second-class citizenship, the special status which makes a mockery of our Government's prated claims of a "free America" in a "free world" for fifteen million Negro Americans. It was out of my Jim Crow experiences as a young Negro woman, experiences likewise born of working-class poverty that led me in my search of why these things had to be that led me to join the young Communist League and to choose at the age of eighteen the philosophy of my life, the science of Marxism-Leninism—that philosophy that not only rejects racist ideas, but is the antithesis of them.

In this courtroom there has often flashed before me the dozens of meetings of Negro and white workers in the great auto plants at the Rouge, of New England textile workers, of students, and of women active in the peace struggle which I have addressed on behalf of my Party. Just as now, there flashes in my mind's eye those young Negro women I have seen at the Women's House of Detention, almost children, of whom, but for my early discovery of Marxism-Leninism I might have had to say now, "There might I have been."

For what crimes? Petty crimes born of poverty, of the ghetto, of Jim Crow living, the crime of being born black on American soil, of resisting treatment, rebellion against which, unchannelized, became lawless against the very Jim Crow society that perpetrates their lawlessness.

One need only be a Negro in America to know that for the crime of being a Negro we are daily convicted by a government which denies us elementary democratic rights, the right to vote, to hold office, to hold judgeships, to serve on juries, rights forcibly denied in the South and also in the North. And I want to concur with Mr. Perry's proposal to Mr. Lane that he recommend to the Department of Justice that they show more zeal, since they have not ever prosecuted a single anti-Semite or a Ku Kluxer in these United States with its total of five thousand lynched Negro men, women, and children since the 1860s.

I am aware that these things are not to the liking of the prosecution or even of this Court, but that cannot be helped, for one of the historical truths of all history is that the oppressed never revere their oppressors.

Now I come to a close. The probation official who interrogated me was a Negro official. Your Honor undoubtedly has his reports before you. One of the questions that he asked me was "Did I ever believe in any religion?" I told him then that this was a personal, private matter, and was guaranteed under the First Amendment of the Constitution. I wonder now, your Honor, if he somehow falsely reckoned, as many officials falsely reckon, that a change of belief or conviction in one's mature life is like putting on a new dress or a new hat? I could have quoted scripture to him, the scripture applied by a leading Negro religious figure in tribute and in observation of the Smith Act jailing of one of the outstanding sons of the Negro people, Ben Davis, now incarcerated in the Jim Crow Federal Penitentiary of Terre Haute, Indiana. The scripture runs: *"Smite down the shepherd and the sheep will be scattered!"*

And this, Honorable Judge, is exactly what is the purpose of all Smith Act trials, this one in particular. I share the faith of Elizabeth Gurley Flynn and Pettis Perry and all my codefendants that America's working people, Negro and white, will surely rise, not like sheep, but with vigilance towards their liberty, to assure that peace will win and that the decadent Smith Act, which contravenes the Bill of Rights, will be swept from the scene of history.

It was the great Frederick Douglass, who had a price on his head, who said, "Without struggle, there is no progress." And echoing his words was the answer of the great abolitionist poet, James Russell Lowell: "The limits of tyranny is proscribed by the measure of our resistance to it."

If, out of this struggle, history assesses that I and my codefendants have made some small contribution, I shall consider my role small indeed. The glorious exploits of anti-fascist heroes and heroines, honored today in all lands for their contribution to social progress, will, just like the role of our prosecutors, also be measured by the people of the United States in that coming day.

I have concluded, your Honor.

THE PRECIOUS CHARTERS OF LIBERTY

PARTY VOICE
FEBRUARY 1954

To stamp out the imperishable achievements of the abolitionists and the anti-slavery movement; to erase the heroic history of the Negro people; to intensify white supremacy in every facet of American life; to revive the lying policy of imperialist colonialism and slaughter of darker peoples; to abort the present struggles for Negro rights and Negro-white unity—such are some of the key and ominous aims of fascist McCarthyism in the United States.

McCarthyism, McCarthy, and his backers are patently anti-Negro, because they are anti-democratic and anti-peace, and because they are anti-democratic and pro-war, they are anti-Negro.

Unfailing mark of the anti-Negro and anti-Semitic racist essence of McCarthyism is the nature of his backers, grouped around powerfully wealthy Texas monopoly oil interests, well known for their openly admitted racist, anti-Negro, and Ku Klux Klan connections. What's more, the character and conduct of his inquisitions are increasingly designed to create *"the impression that authors (or other spokesmen attacked) who dare expose or protest American racial shortcomings are 'following the Communist line' and therefore must be subversive."* (*Afro-American*, July 18). Also adhering to this anti-Negro premise are the Velde and Jenner committees, and, of course, the enabling acts of fascist McCarthyism—the Taft–Hartley, Smith, McCarran, and Walter–McCarran Acts.

If, in the frame-up in Foley Square, the eleven heroic Communist leaders made as one of their major exposes, the rigged and biased jury system in the South (as did the case of the thirteen) it was because we had long recognized and fought against the racist prism of the courts of law of this land. Our Party was the first to challenge the vicious lily-white jury system in the South. In the vicious provisions of the McCarran–Walter act are embedded the racist restrictions on West Indian immigration (once sixty thousand a year) to one hundred annually from all the West Indies. In similar disproportion are other national group (non-Anglo–Saxons) immigration quotas affected.

Increasingly, among victims of the witch hunt are professors and teachers who declare that discrimination based on color is undemocratic. Suspect also are those who assert that scientific inquiry supports the thesis of the basic equality of peoples regardless of race or color.

Today, "loyalty" is tested in these United States on the basis of whether one believes in the equality of black and white peoples; if one is for an FEPC, or jobs for Negro workers; or entertains Negroes socially in their homes, or advocates nonsegregated housing or low-cost public housing. The oldest racist movement in this country, the old Ku Klux Klan, is dressed up in a new garb—the garb of fascism!

Now, an old aphorism of the Negro people goes: *"It pesters a man dreadful when he gets mad and don't know who to cuss."*

It fortunately can be said that the Negro people not only *know who to be angered at*; they are applying this saying because they have discerned the enemy and are speaking up!

Universal condemnation of McCarthyism cuts across class lines in Negro life, affording great possibilities of unity among the Negro people themselves, on this issue, and in relation to their white allies. Everyone remembers how the magnificent Mrs. Eslanda Goode Robeson set McCarthy back on his heels. The Rt. Rev. William J. Walls, of the African Methodist Church of Zion, on the occasion of the attacks on Mrs. Robeson and Doxey Wilkerson dryly observed that he disbelieved McCarthy feared ministers and Communism; what they were against was *"religion and righteousness."*

The Forty-Fourth NAACP Convention warned against the *"discernable . . . pattern which tends to link the advocacy of full equality for Negroes and other minorities to subversion or 'Un-Americanism.'"* Urging defense of *"the precious charters of liberty,"* the resolution called *"in these days of pilloring . . . browbeating . . . branding and cunning indictments . . . to stoutly defend"* the Constitution and the Bill of Rights.

McCarthy intends to squash any anti-racist thought. When hundreds of authors were banned from the US Overseas Library last year, the works of two well-known anti-Communists, Walter White and Gunnar Myrdal *(A Rising Wind* and *An American Dilemma*), were included. Among the books banned were books about Negro folk tales—even laughter, like Hughes, *Laughing to Keep From Crying*—books exploding the myth of racist propaganda like *The Races of Mankind* by Dr. Gene Weltfish and Hugh Benedict; *The Souls of Black Folk* by Dr. W. E. B. Du Bois; *Special Problems of Negro Education* by Doxey Wilkerson; *African Journey* and *Paul Robeson, Negro,* by Eslanda Goode Robeson; Fast's *Freedom Road* and Aptheker's *American Slave Revolts* and *A Documentary History of the Negro People in the United States,* etc.; even a book by Dr. Bernhard J. Stern, revealing that for every white baby born ten Negro babies die, was considered "unduly stressing Negro medical statistics."

These and other trenchant facts were recently correlated by Charles R. Allen Jr., former assistant editor of *The Nation* in an excellent article entitled *"McCarthy—Enemy of the Negro People* (published Nov. 1953, *Jewish Life*).

Walter White and other Negro reformists have not yet drawn the full conclusions from the McCarthyite menace. As observed by Hugh Bradley in his report to the National Party Conference, White still calls for complete confidence in and support of the Eisenhower Administration, an administration whose policies are generating still further anti-Negro measures in the country. But the growing anger of the Negro masses is reflected in the twenty-one Negro organizations who recently condemned both GOP and Democrats for failure to do anything in Congress on civil rights legislation.

McCarthyism, Comrade Bill Foster has correctly pointed out, is fascism. And, in Germany, Italy, Franco Spain, and elsewhere, historically as the great Dimitroff also teaches us: *"Fascism not only inflames prejudices that are deeply engrained in the masses, but also plays on the better sentiments of the masses, on their sense of justice and sometimes even on their revolutionary traditions"* (G. Dimitroff, *The United Front Against Fascism,* p. 7–8).

In his State of the Union message, Eisenhower blandly proposed, to raucous rebel yells, that the American Communists be stripped of their citizenship, if convicted under the Smith Act. In the same breath he stole one of our foremost slogans—the slogan *"old enough to fight, old enough to vote."* And in the same speech, Eisenhower placed the Negro question as one of *"interracial difficulty,"* seemingly placing equal responsibility on Negro and white.

We know as Communists that this is a patent untruth. We know that it is the Communist Party which basically clarified the Negro question in the United States. By placing the Negro question as a national question, as one of special oppression, we emphasized why the white workers must fight for full economic, politcal, and social equality of Negro workers in their own self-interest. And we know, as Gus Hall once observed, our influence, the influence of Marxism-Leninism has contributed to influencing the course of struggle of the Negro liberation movement in this country.

It is for holding these ideas—the ideas of peace, security, and Negro equality, the warmongers have convicted our comrades, Dennis, Hall, Davis, Thorppson, Winston, Potash, Williamson, Gates, Stachel, Green, and Winter. In the inspiring words of Bob Thompson's speech before the court that sentenced him to seven savage years, they and the over one hundred under indictment and sentence behaved *"in a spirit of calm confidence in the future of my country, my class and my Party."*

Can it be otherwise then, that one of the tasks to which we dedicate ourselves this Negro History Week is that we will not rest until we set them free?

I WAS DEPORTED BECAUSE I FOUGHT COLOR BAR

GEORGE BOWRIN
CARIBBEAN NEWS
JUNE 1, 1956

Trinidad-born Claudia Jones has lived in the United States since she was eight years old, but was imprisoned and finally deported last year.

In this interview, Miss Jones answers some questions put to her by our reporter, George Bowrin.

Why were you deported from the United States Miss Jones?
I was a victim of the McCarthyite hysteria against independent political ideas in the USA—a hysteria which penalizes anyone who holds ideas contrary to the official pro-war, pro-reactionary, pro-fascist line of the white ruling class of that country.

I was deported from the USA because as a Negro woman, Communist of West Indian descent, I was a thorn in their side in my opposition to Jim Crow racist discrimination against sixteen million Negro Americans in the United States, in my work for redress of these grievances, for unity of Negro and white workers, for women's rights and my general political activity urging the American people to help by their struggles to change the present foreign and domestic policy of the United States.

I was deported and refused an opportunity to complete my American citizenship because I fought for peace, against the huge arms budget which funds should be directed to improving the social needs of the people.

I was deported because I urged prosecution of the lynchers rather than prosecution of Communists and other democratic Americans

201

who oppose the lynchers and big financiers and war mongers, the real advocates of force and violence in the USA.

Racist Bias

Is there any special significance to the fact that you are a West Indian and, as such, were deported from the United States?

Yes, I definitely think so. The very law under which I was deported, the reactionary Walter–McCarran law widely known for its special racist bias towards West Indians and peoples of Asiatic descent. This law, which came into being as a result of the whole reactionary drive against progressive ideas in the United States, encourages immigration of fascist scum from Europe but restricts West Indian immigration, once in their thousands annually to the United States, to one hundred persons per year, from *all* the Caribbean islands.

This works special hardships among West Indians who have family ties and who are permanent residents and citizens of the USA.

You are a Communist, are you not Miss Jones? Would you tell us what led you to become a Communist?

Gladly. From an early age, like most native Negro Americans and with the additional penalty of being foreign-born and a Negro in the United States, I experienced the indignity of second-class citizenship in the US. My parents emigrated from the West Indies in 1924 in the hope of finding greater economic opportunity and freedom to rear their children. But what we found instead in the US was not only economic poverty for the working class, but the special brand of American racism—Jim Crow.

No Escape

In the USA, no matter what the social class status, no Negro escapes the scourge of Jim Crow.

I learned that those who fought most consistently for the interests of the workers, for their trade union organization and social needs were the Communists.

My daily experiences as a Negro youth in the USA led me to search out political forces that were doing something about these things; political forces who not only fought on a day to day basis to alleviate these conditions but who had a perspective as to a radical solution to these conditions.

I learned through study and participation in the Communist movement that the Communist Party, based on its political science, the science of Marxism-Leninism, that these conditions were man-made and therefore could be changed by mankind through understanding of their origin, and to eliminate these practices and conditions.

Dangerous Ideas

So that it is as a result of these struggles that you were indicted, convicted, and jailed in the United States?

Yes, for these struggles, I was indicted, convicted, and served a year and a day sentence, despite a heart condition and related illnesses, under the infamous Smith Act—a reactionary statute under which progressive fighters are convicted and jailed not for committing any overt act, but merely for their ideas.

Did you ever meet West Indians in the US? Could you tell us something about their conditions?

Yes. There are over one hundred thousand West Indians in New York City alone. The West Indian community in the States plays an active political, economic, and social role in the life of the nation, and particularly lends its strength to advancing the struggles of the Negro people in the USA for full equality and freedom. Numerous West Indians are among the most active trade unionists in industry.

Then there are numerous West Indian professionals associated with various political and social welfare organizations in the community. As a whole, West Indians in the USA constantly express concern and support for the liberation struggles of the people in the West Indies, for freedom from colonial exploitation and slavery, for dignity and self-government.

Would you say something about your view of the role of women in the West Indies?

I have been quite impressed with the activities of the women of the West Indies and their growing participation in the liberation movement as well as the international movement for peace, security, and the rights of children. There is no question but that West Indian women represent an indispensable ally in the fight for colonial freedom, because women are triply exploited in the colonies, as women, as mothers, and as colonials, subjected to indignities and great suffering because of the status of their countries.

Participation of increasing numbers of West Indian women, side-by-side with their men in struggle for national independence and self-government, will grow because women, above all, want a better life, dignity, and equality, and a better world in which their children will live.

Is there anything else you would like to add?

Yes. I would like to thank West Indians in the Caribbean, in Britain and America, as well as all other democratic and progressive forces who interceded on my behalf while jailed for my ideas in an American prison.

TOWARD A
PEOPLE'S CULTURE

This section represents examples of Claudia Jones's engagements with culture, as a revolutionary journalist, critic, and writer. In a review of James Baldwin's now-classic *The Fire Next Time*, Jones draws out the implications of his critique of "American imperialism-racialism," careful to note his "lack of differentiation of either the white or black masses to whom he addresses his works." Remarking that this must reflect Baldwin's choices as a writer, Jones explained that "society, like people, is made up of classes, entrenched interests, not just power or conscience." An earlier interview with Paul Robeson, "whose voice and heart the little people of the world claim as their own," sets the terms of a popular culture emanating from and unifying the working people of the world.

As a poet herself, Jones strove to reflect that popular culture. A series of included poems give small glimpses into how Jones lived her politics as she moved through the world. In "Paean to the Atlantic," written aboard a ship that carried her to Great Britain after her deportation, Jones takes inspiration from the "ceaseless motion" of the Atlantic to renew her commitment to the struggle through which "millions move towards ascension." In a 1962 poem from the "Russia" sanitorium where she sought treatment for her chronic heart disease, exacerbated by the conditions of her imprisonment at Ellis Island, Jones reflected on the specificity of the Soviet process of socialist construction, so deeply rooted in the particularities of the land where it was being built. In a 1955 "Lament for Emmett Till," Jones renewed her call for a united front against racism and fascism, and in "For Consuela—Anti-Fascista," Jones proclaimed her anti-fascist sisterhood with the Puerto Rican nationalist Blanca Consuela Toressola.

PAUL ROBESON—MAN AND ARTIST

WEEKLY REVIEW
JUNE 22, 1943

"... Learn more about the Soviet youth," says Robeson in interview with Review *Editor*

Interviewing Paul Robeson impresses you anew with the greatness of this man, not only as a people's artist but as one of the world's outstanding men. You sense in his every expression his rare grasp of the relationship of the minutest issue to the struggle for victory over fascism.

Mr. Robeson was busily conferring with Dr. Max Yergan at the Council for African Affairs offices when I met him to get his views on what youth could do to weld friendship ties with Soviet youth. With a characteristic smile and a nod of his massive head, he told me that he would be right out for the interview.

Although he had just returned from a strenuous concert tour, and even more recently from Morehouse College in Atlanta, Ga., where he had been awarded a Doctorate of Humane Letters, he gladly consented to the interview, since, he said, he believed the subject to be "very important."

"My old boy," Mr. Robeson proudly told me, "was educated in the Soviet Union. Only the other day, Paul spoke to Soviet exchange students—a development which is of tremendous value. This should set the pattern of participation not only for youth, but for all peoples."

Paul Robeson, who spent many years in the Soviet Union, is not unlike the warm booming "hello everybody" with which he greets his receptive and nationwide audiences. He spoke from personal testimony when he said intently:

"The deepest social and political reasons for friendship with the Soviet Union are winning of the war and the needs of the post-war world. These things are clear to all anti-fascist Americans. The struggle of the United Nations; the complete winning of the war requires the participation and friendship of these same nations in a post-war world."

"Meaning in our own interest?" I cut in.

"Absolutely," he emphasized. "The Soviet Union must be linked in closest bonds with us, not only for their own good, but for our own good."

Lesson for World

In this connection he discussed with me the relationship of the all-out stake which such peoples as the Negro, Indian, African, and Latin Americans have in this war against fascism. "The entire progressive democratic world can learn much from the Soviet Union which is the foremost champion of the common people," he said.

Mr. Robeson paused as I rapidly took down notes. Then, as though sensing my thoughts, he plunged into a discussion of Soviet youth.

"I know that no youth has seen more clearly what the democratic spirit against fascism means," he began. "We know that no youth in any nation has had the benefits of so deep a training and conviction that all youth are equal. The development and capacities of their society is shown in their epic struggles of today. The complete necessity for the maturing of American youth's understanding is bound up with learning more about the culture and experience of Soviet youth."

Mr. Robeson expressed his conviction that the Soviet Union "will influence and give out of the wealth of its different peoples; out of its culture, profound sources not only of enjoyment but of cultural enlightenment and cultural education."

As to what could be done to spur this "cultural enlightenment," he emphasized visits of American students to the Soviet Union would be of great value, and that "in the curriculum of every university, the achievements of Soviet science, art, and the languages should be taught."

No better guide to spur Soviet-American youth friendship could be mentioned than the example of Robeson's seventeen-year-old son, Paul Jr.

It was right after Mr. Robeson had been called by the Office of War Information. Two appointments, one with Russian War Relief, were demanding his attention. He was leaving to catch a cab uptown, but he paused to tell me this story.

I learned that when Paul Jr. spoke to the Soviet students he had to make a choice. Paul, who is studying engineering, follows in his dad's footsteps: he is a high-jump, broad-jump, and quarter-mile track champ. On that very day he was scheduled to appear at the statewide track meet in Massachusetts as well as on his own campus.

Son Made Own Choice

"These three events presented a personal choice for Paul," Mr. Robeson told me. He laughed indulgently as he went on . . . "But he made his own decision though, he wrote his own speech. He chose speaking to the Soviet exchange students because he felt that although personal advantage was involved, nothing was more important than speaking to those students for friendship with the Soviet Union."

After his warm handclasp, he was gone. I felt that I had had a rare experience. And I thought then as now—with men like Paul Robeson, whose voice and heart the little people of the world claim as their own, the youth of America have a mighty example to follow as they weld unbreakable bonds of friendship in battle and in victory with the great heroic youth of our Soviet ally.

PAEAN TO THE ATLANTIC

Ship Log   *December 10, 1955*
  Written aboard the Queen Elizabeth 10:45 p.m. ship time
  (I write my poem to the sea—it burst from me after churning inside
  all day . . .) I call it . . . .

Paean to the Atlantic

To watch your ceaseless motion
Your foam and tideful billows view
Is but to gleam your beauty
Of immemorial hue

Oh, rest wide Atlantic
Path of nations old and new
Asylum path of peoples
Bound to social progress true

I stand awe-struck before you
As swiftly league on league
You cradle us to lands—accrue
Of mankind's search for freedom's clue

To understand your motion
Is to reason why like you
Millions move towards ascension
Nurtured by your ancient daw.

REVIEW: *THE FIRE NEXT TIME*

WEST INDIAN GAZETTE
OCTOBER 1962

The Fire Next Time
by James Baldwin,
Michael Joseph, 13s. 6d.
By Claudia Jones

Sitting in a cafe not far from the United States London Embassy, I first directly witnessed the impact of James Baldwin's writings on some white Americans. The day was August 28. I had—with other African, Asian, and Caribbean representatives and English supporters—just come from presenting our own solidarity protest with the American Negro people's struggle for equality and human dignity marked in their unprecedentedly demonstrative March for Freedom and Jobs in the US capital.

There, around a table and coffee, we engaged in discussion with a young Southern writer, a white Virginian, who had asked for an interview to do several freelance articles. He had been, he told us, termed a "Yankee" by his own family for his sympathies with Negro youth with whom he grew up.

But in the course of our talks when reference was made to James Baldwin's writings, he sharply disagreed with what Baldwin had to say. Essence of his disagreement, and, he admitted—his resentment—was Baldwin's assertion that white Americans must search their consciences as to why they need an object of hate—the Negro—to vent their dislike of themselves and each other.

In *The Fire Next Time,* James Baldwin enlarges on this very theme. He deals with American imperialism-racialism in two essays; [in] one to his nephew, he piercingly describes what it is like to grow up in the dungeon of "Jim Crow" color-bar Harlem. Rejecting caricatures of inferiority imaged against twenty million American Negroes, his plea is for all to *commit* themselves to erase this state of things.

All men are brothers. Here too, is revealed the key to what Julian Mayfield, the American Negro writer has so well assessed: that Baldwin, above all other Negro American writers, has *kept the dialogue* open with white America.

Baldwin advises: "Try to imagine how you would feel if you woke up one morning to find the sun shining and all the stars aflame. You would be frightened because it is out of the order of nature. Any upheaval in the universe is terrifying because it so profoundly attacks one's sense of one's own reality. Well the Black man has functioned in the white man's world as a fixed star, as an immovable pillar, and as he moves out of his place, heaven and earth are shaken to its foundations . . . " and further, he concludes "And if the word *integration* means anything, this is what it means: that we, with love, shall force our brothers to see themselves as they are, to cease fleeing from reality and begin to change it."

The same Baldwin poses the inner thoughts of Negro Americans as the Negro grasps the significance of his contemporary struggle for his country's future: "Do I really *want* to be integrated in a burning house?"

Where the first essay deals with the reality and the need for change both as regards the Negro status, and by implication, the society which spurns this oppressed status, the second deals with its extreme counteraction with the Black Muslims who advance the idea of rejection of everything in white American civilisation in favor of Black integrity and Mohemmedanism.

Baldwin's virtue lies in that while associating himself with the categoric indictment of American racialism, which in common underlies the Black Muslims' motivation, he also scathingly rejects the essence of the Black Muslims ideology of Black racialism, i.e., the theory: "All Black men belong to Islam. They have been chosen. And Islam shall rule the world." With consummate skill, Baldwin explains: "The dream, the sentiment is old, only the color is new. And it is this dream, this sweet possibility, that thousands of oppressed Black men and women in this country now carry away with them after the Muslim minister has spoken, through the noisome, ghetto streets, into the hovels where so many have perished. The white God has not delivered them, perhaps the Black God will."

For his refusal to wholly condemn the Black Muslims who have been persecuted by police and other official agencies for fighting Jim Crow, he has earned the approbation of some of his friends. Some call him Baldwin X.

Baldwin, however, stands on the sound premise, *"Whoever debases others, debases himself."* He frankly criticized the Black Muslim's ideology as he sees it. Querying the source of their wealth, he shows that rumor has it that the Birchites (the American fascist group) and certain Texas oil millionaires look with favor on the Black Muslim Movement." George Lincoln Rockwell, Chief of the American Nazi Party, recently contributed twenty pounds to the Muslim cause, and he and Malcolm X decided that racially speaking, at any rate, they were in complete agreement.

Baldwin's second virtue consists of tracing the seeming rise of the Black Muslims (Elijah Muhammed's movement has existed in America for thirty years) not so much to its ideology but to the continuing hostility to American Negro equality in the land of their birth. Decades of unpunished lynchings, police brutality, bomb-murders, color-bar housing, second-class jobs, "separate but equal" education, in short, second-class citizenship—all of which were consistently protested—stand behind the heightened struggle. During and following World War II against Hitler fascism, when the Negro people emblazoned on their banners: Double "V" victory at home and victory abroad. The catalyst is the liberation wind of change blowing from Africa, Asia, Latin America, and other democratic and socialist nations and peoples for peace, equality, and security.

A writer, with a growing mindfulness of the world's relationship of forces, Baldwin notes that progress must be measured by certain yardsticks. Whatever concessions have been made to Negro advancement, it undoubtedly has resulted not as a matter of love and justice, but due to the competition in the Cold War and the fact that "Africa was clearly liberating itself, and therefore, for political reasons, to be wooed by the descendents of her former masters."

He Cannot 'Go Home'

Baldwin insists: the American Negro cannot "go home." Neither to Africa and certainly not to Islam. Home for him is America, the land by which he has been formed.

The great strength of Baldwin's essays and writing is that they make people *think*—even if some are made uncomfortable. There are, to be sure, naturally, weaknesses, notably his lack of differentiation of either the white or black masses to whom he addresses his works. Society, like people, is made up of classes, entrenched interests, not just power or conscience. If Baldwin set his own limitations on spelling this out, I cannot believe it is because he lacks awareness but rather the prism he has, so far, chosen to make his mark of ideas.

'Read Wisely'

And one should read Baldwin in the discerning spirit voiced by the American Negro writer, Augusta Strong, who wrote "with acuteness of vision and profound hatred of injustice, he has told us what no other writer has, what it means to be a Negro in America today, in prose that sings and thunders. I hope Baldwin is being as widely read as he has been widely published. Far from offering any palliative to the conscience of white America, he has illuminated the background against which, as he says 'The myth of white supremacy is exploding from the Congo to New Orleans'" (*Freedomways*, Vol. 2, No. 2, Spring 1962).

Indeed, Baldwin's warning is there for all to see and hear if they but listen:

"God Gave Noah the Rainbow Sign
No More Water, the Fire Next Time!"

PAEAN TO THE CRIMEA

1962

In what great century did your mountains rise,
To tower near level with your skies,
And in what age did stately trees,
Begin to sprout their roots and seize
The warm, moist earth to multiply
Their species in a thousand leaves,
That now lend beauty to the eye.

In which earth's crust were your depths
                probed,
To fill your breasts with blue-green seas

That touch the shores of ancient lands
And is milieu for echoing chants,
Of paeans of praise to you, Crimea.
And to your people's system-rare.

My heart will fill with thoughts of you
My brain and mind will fashion, too,
Memories, long to inspire me,
In climes and lands so unlike thee!

October 11, 1962
Salta, Crimea
"Russia" Sanitorium

LAMENT FOR EMMETT TILL

1955

Cry lynch—
Cry murder!
   —Sear the land
        Raise fists—in more than anger bands.

Mother, mother—you who bore
Son from womb of sorrow know
White washed justice sure will reap
More than it can ever sow. . . .

Uncle, uncle you who stood
Firm-head-in jim crow dock of wood
Facing lynchers eye for eye
Meeting sadism of parading child.

People, people you who surge
Vengeance for this brutal hour
Make your unity soar above strife
To swiftly avenge young Emmett Till's life!

FOR CONSUELA—ANTI-FASCISTA*

JANUARY 1, 1955

It seems I knew you long before our common ties—of
          conscious choice
Threw under single skies those like us
Who, fused by our mold
Became their targets as of old

I knew you in Jarama's hills
Through men and women drilled
In majesty, whose dignity
Rejected shirts and skirts of dimity.

I heard you in Guernica's songs
Proud melodies that burst from tongues
As yet unknown to me—full thronged
With Liberty

Anti-anti-fascistas!
That was your name
I sang your fame
Long fore my witness of your bane of pain

---

*   Dedicated to Blanca Consuela Toressola, now serving four years in the Federal
Reformatory for Women in Alderson, W. Va, USA, and who, upon completion of this
sentence faces a 140-year jail term in her native Puerto Rico for her heroic participation
in the struggle for Puerto Rican independence.

I saw you in the passion-flower
In roses full of flame
Pure valley lily, whose bower
Marks resemblance to your name.

Oh wondrous Spanish sister
Long-locked from all you care
Listen—while I tell you what you strain
        to hear
And beckon all from far and near.

We swear that we will never rest
Until they hear not plea
But sainted sacrifice to set
A small proud nation free

O anti-fascist sister—you whose eyes
        turn to stars still
I've learned your wondrous secret—source
        of spirit and of will
I've learned that what sustains your heart, mind
        and peace of soul
Is knowledge that their justice—can never reach
        its goal!

INTERNATIONALISM

The final theme of this reader details Claudia Jones' involvement, writing, and meditations on the vitality of internationalism, which she considers to be essential to our understanding of Marxism and participation in global struggles for liberation. Beginning with her speech to the Twenty-Fifth Congress of the Communist Party of Britain—taking place two years after being exiled to the United Kingdom by the United States—Jones underlines the importance of the colonized person's position within Marxist thought and political organizing, emphasizing that the conditions of our collective freedom becomes more clear when we view the colonized as bearers of the seeds that will sow our the future. She affirms that we have much to learn from the Third World, and the paternalism of the Global North must be shed. Jones asks her comrades in the Congress to turn towards the Global South, for it is the colonized who are at the very center of social struggle.

From this foundational speech, the following sections weave in essays, articles, and letters penned by Jones on American imperialism, her visits to the USSR—where she experienced the "growth of [Soviet] society, its culture, its technological and scientific advance"—travels to China and Japan, thoughts on Cuba's victorious story as an "island aflame," musings on the Caribbean diaspora and future of the West Indies, reflections on the anti-war movement in Asia, and notes on the state of racial discrimination in the US and UK, among other critical subjects. Sweeping and pointed, these pieces provide a powerful account of Jones' writing and activity at the height of the mid-twentieth century. Her words and observations continue to reverberate into the present, as the necessity of internationalism is urgent and relevant as ever.

SPEECH TO THE TWENTY-FIFTH CONGRESS OF THE COMMUNIST PARTY OF BRITAIN

1957

Sunday morning, Twenty-Fifth Congress, 1957

Comrades, it is a great honor to be present as a delegate to this Congress of the Communist Party of Britain. I deem it an honor because I share with all delegates the responsibility for arriving at correct decisions which can help to put our Party in Britain on the broad highway to working-class unity and socialist consciousness. Also because it provides the long-awaited opportunity to thank the British Communist Party through you for the international solidarity shown to me when, as one of the many victims of American imperialist reaction, your protests and support were invaluable in fighting to secure my entry into Britain, as is the right of all British subjects.

If, therefore, in my first Party Congress, I, in turn address you on the theme of greater solidarity with the struggles of colonial peoples, and with the colored workers and peoples in Britain, you will understand that it stems from the firsthand experience and confidence that this Party of ours, the British Communist Party, has it within its capacity to make this turn—a needed turn which is in the interest not only of the colonial people but also in the present and future self-interest of the British working class and people.

No other section of our programme adopted at this special Twenty-Fifth Congress will be as widely discussed among colonial and ex-colonial people as the section which defines our attitude towards colonial liberation now, and in the future.

Colonial, and particularly colored peoples in Britain will also want to know what policy the Party Congress advances to meet the special problems facing them in the present economic situation—problems which stem from a common origin—the same monopoly capitalists in Britain who exploit the British working class, but who super-exploit the colonies—thereby requiring a joint struggle against the common evil of imperialism.

Why is this so?

This is so, because the imperialist-oppressed peoples consider it a prime test of Communist sincerity, particularly of white Communists from the oldest and biggest imperialist power, as to how clearly they differentiate themselves from other social forces on the key question of colonial liberation.

There is still another reason for their interest. The colonially oppressed people have come to understand, even if not wholly, that Communist principles, the science of Marxism-Leninism, is the antithesis of exploitation in any manner, of racism, and of chauvinist ideology.

Now, unfortunately—or perhaps fortunately in the long run—to the degree that we remain ever vigilant, being members of the Communist Party, does not automatically absolve white Communists from suspicion by colonials as to whether one is completely free from infection of imperialist ideology. We should not find this strange, or regard it as an accident, when as we have already observed in our discussion, ideologies alien to Marxism-Leninism, such as revisionism, sectarianism, bourgeois nationalism, do creep into our ranks.

Nor is an eternal immunity from distrust by colonial peoples won merely by constant reference to our past record, no matter how glorious that record may be! One should learn to be modest and learn something from the experience of the CPSU that big-nation chauvinism does not automatically die even after the achievement of socialism. I would agree that such distrust must be combatted, but how this is done makes all the difference!

No, comrades, we must more fundamentally grasp the reason for this distrust, which is, I say, justified from their experience of long years of heinous imperialist exploitation and indignities, and by false promises by Western advocates of individual freedom and liberty.

Hence, to win the confidence of the oppressed people, a Marxist party, as Lenin taught us, has to fulfill its responsibilities in its fight against great-nation chauvinism and petty-bourgeois nationalism, and has to go out of its way to allay these suspicions and fears.

It is not a very wise tactic to seek to allay disquiet, uneasiness, and dissatisfaction, by telling those whose experience has taught them otherwise, that they are foolish, or to dub them as backward. For in terms of their experience, a well-known African proverb might well apply. That proverb runs: "Respect the old, for they have seen the eyes of the morning!"

It has been suggested that the Communist Party of India has been used by Comrade Dutt in support of his Minority formulation. What a crime! Most probably the colored Communists of India carry no weight with certain white Communists of Britain. What more illuminating examples of chauvinism can you find? While we here are still fighting imperialism, the Communist Party of India has for the first time in the history of the world won electoral victory under the capitalist system, and formed a government, even though it is in a small state.

Comrade Emile Burns in his *World News* article raises the question of our helping the so-called "backward peoples" of the world. The backward peoples of China and the backward peoples of Czarist Russia were the first to throw off the old regimes, and are now going forward with the most advanced ideology—the ideology of socialism—while the technically advanced peoples of Western bourgeois democratic tradition are still steeped in the mire of backward imperialist ideology.

And now India is following suit. The anti-imperialist struggle of the backward, mind you, Afro-Asian nations, from Egypt to Ghana, are today leading the progressive anti-imperialist ideological struggle.

So much for backwardness . . . Let us learn a few things from these so-called backward people also, before we give them "Big Brother" leads, advice, guidance, and leadership.

Talking of defense against American imperialism! Who saved the world from the threat of an atom bomb holocaust? The backward people of China and Korea! Clearly the freed colonial peoples are not that helpless. In their new world historic unity of Bandung, together with other socialist nations, including a Socialist Britain, they will know how to defend themselves against the threat of a new imperialism—they will not be in any mood to substitute new masters for old.

And comrades, let us not underestimate or sell short the progressive fight of the American working class and people, including the Negro people, upon whose heroic struggles the final curb to the American imperialist atom-maniacs will yet be given. The world is not as static as the Majority position assumes—that we will have a Socialist Britain, while things remain at a stand-still in the United States.

The descendants of Paine and Jefferson, of Lincoln, Frederick Douglass, and Gene Debs, and of William Z. Foster and Paul Robeson, who once defeated dominant British imperialism, will know too, how to defeat their own arrogant American imperialism which threatens not only colonial and national independence of all peoples, but their own progress to social advance.

It is most unfortunate that a cheap jibe, or shall I say, wisecrack, was thrown at Comrade Dutt, that he made use of the Minority formulations for his own pleasure. Most probably all the comrades who agree with the Minority position also indulge in these pleasures. Let me tell you comrades what you must already know, the contribution of Comrade Dutt in international affairs and especially on the colonial question may have given pleasure, and indeed a great inspiration to millions of oppressed peoples of the world, and to all progressive mankind.

Now comrades, before I leave this platform, I want you to know that I had given my name to speak on the Political Resolution because of my firm belief that on the crucial question of color discrimination, the colored people resident in this country are waiting for a lead by the British Communist Party. I was not given the opportunity to speak earlier. I hope that in the new draft there will be a rectification of this serious omission in the Draft Political Resolution. Such an immediate programme of united struggle and solidarity now is a prime precondition for future relations.

AMERICAN IMPERIALISM AND THE BRITISH WEST

POLITICAL AFFAIRS
APRIL 1958

Claudia Jones, a beloved leader of the Communist Party of the United States, was jailed under the infamous Smith Act, and upon release forced into exile; she is now living in England. The article which follows—one in our series relating the impact of American imperialism in various parts of the world—is especially timely. It was written, as Miss Jones comments, just before the March 25 elections to the Assembly of the West Indian Federation, whose formal appearance as a new member of the community of nations will occur this April. —The Editor

The election on March 25 of the first Federal Assembly in the West Indies marks a new political stage in the history of the Caribbean.

This period will also witness the advancing role of American capital investment in the forthcoming West Indian Federation. Increasing United States economic penetration is not, of course, unrelated to the struggle of the West Indian people for full political and economic independence.

Bearing in mind only highlights: there is the Texaco Oil purchase of Trinidad oil, the growing US investments in Jamaican bauxite and in British Guiana's aluminum deposits. Clearly the West Indian Federation is already heavily mortgaged to US export capital. Nor does it appear that this indebtedness to Uncle Sam worries John Bull unduly. Seemingly a sort of family arrangement has been worked out to prevent the burgeoning freedom struggle of the West Indian people from too rapid advancement or "getting out of hand." While the outward political responsibility remains with Britain, increasingly Washington controls the economic basis of the Federation.

This crucial interconnection was clearly shown when a *London Daily Express* staff reporter wrote that in talks he had had last October in Washington, a State Department official had pointed out that while American trade is less than half the West Indian trade with Britain, it is growing at a faster rate. And he added:

> The islands' three million people offer a reservoir of cheap labor to attract more American capital. A mighty American naval base mushrooming in Trinidad is encouraging the whole dollar flow to the West Indies. The US Defense Department makes no bones about it—the Trinidad base is now regarded as the Caribbean keystone to the Panama Canal. American forces are going to be there for a long time to come and businessmen look on the Trinidad base as a guarantee of military and political stability for the future.

This rather bald-face analysis likewise underscores the scandal of Chaguaramas, the Federation's capital site chosen after examination of other locations by a West Indies Commission. The United States blandly refused to cede Chaguaramas—site of the US Trinidad base—despite questions in Commons as to the original legality of the Churchill–Roosevelt ninety-nine-year lease (no legal authority exists for this and the other US military bases in Antigua, St. Lucia, and the Bahamas); despite special talks in London last summer between West Indian leaders and British and United States representatives; despite angry criticism of West Indian leaders that not even a by-your-leave request was ever made to the people of Trinidad as to the use of their land; despite an uproarious clamor of protest by important sections of the West Indian and British press criticizing the usual US high-handedness.

The growth of American economic and political influence in the West Indies was facilitated by the establishment in 1942 of an Anglo-American Caribbean Commission, renamed the Caribbean Commission in 1946. Presumably its function was "to advise and consult" the governments concerned on matters pertaining to "labor, agriculture, health, education, social welfare, finance, economics, etc." But with the help of this Commission, American monopolists have been seizing possession of the natural resources of the West Indies. For example, in 1955, they received the right to exploit the resources of Jamaica. Dominion Oil, a subsidiary of Standard Oil of California, operates in Trinidad. In 1955, Reynolds Metals started mining bauxite in St. Ann's Bay, Jamaica. These projects are financed by the United States government which, in 1951, advanced $1.5 million for this purpose through the Economic Cooperation Administration. Some idea of the inroads made by American monopolies into the British position may be gleaned from the fact that while British Union Oil spent £1 million since 1950 prospecting for oil in Barbados, when oil was found the concession was obtained by Gulf Oil of Pittsburgh.

For Britain, the West Indies is not only a source of cheap food and raw material, it is also a market for her manufactured products. Britain holds a predominant position in West Indian trade. Between 1948–51, she took 43.8 percent of the total exports of the area and supplied 37.2 percent of her imports. British trade superiority is facilitated by the imperial preference system. But despite all obstacles, American business has penetrated this market. The United States, as of 1955, was taking 7.1 percent of the exports and supplying 17.5 percent of the imports of the West Indies.

American capital has also penetrated West Indian agriculture. The notorious United Fruit Company owns extensive plantations—in Jamaica alone, fifteen thousand acres. Through the Royal Bank of Canada and the Canadian Bank of Commerce, which have branches on all the big West Indian islands, American capital exercises its influence on the economic affairs of all the British colonies.

Anglo-American Rivalry

Anglo-American antagonisms have particularly been reflected around the Federation issue—with Washington distinctly pooh-poohing it. Washington opposes any idea of strengthening Britain's position in the Caribbean. The US, moreover, has systematically encouraged opposition to the British Federation plan by neighbor states in the Latin and Central American Republics and by encouraging the opposition of certain sections of the West Indian bourgeoisie.

The danger of the new West Indies Federation falling into the pit of US imperialist domination cannot be sounded too often. For, faced with the immense task of solving the economic problems of the West Indies (the problem aptly termed by Labor Minister Bradshaw the "lame foot" of the Federation), many of the present national leaders in the West Indies look increasingly to the US for salvation based on a one-sided estimate of the relative progress of Puerto Rico and on the hope of a growth of tourism from Americans. A third factor explaining why the dangers of US imperialism are not fully grasped is the leaning among the West Indian masses towards the more prosperous United States—masses in revolt against British imperialism which they see as their ever-present and age-old enemy.

Still, a fourth factor is the view of many bourgeois-nationalist West Indian leaders that they can thus tactically bargain between the two imperialisms for greater benefits for the West Indies. Thus, as recently reported in the *London Times*, the Chief Minister of Jamaica, Norman Manley, publicly denounced the "parsimonious" handouts of the British Government to the Federation. He also criticized the saddling of the Federation of the military contribution of $325 million BWI for the West Indian Regiment. Dr. Eric Williams of Trinidad has spoken in similar terms. A £200 million loan requested as a minimum for a five-year period to launch the Federation has not yet been agreed to or satisfactorily settled by the British Government. Yet a recent issue of *Trumpet*, official organ of the People's National Party, the government party in Jamaica, revealed that Jamaica received from the USA a loan of $34 million—more than the total granted by the Colonial Development Corporation to all the West Indian islands.

Mass Struggle

The struggle of the West Indian people for the right to live and work and for national independence has taken on greater intensity in recent years with the spread of the national liberation movement in the colonial world. It is also one of the evidences of the deepening crisis of the British Empire under the growing influence of the liberation movement in the colonies.

Six times since the end of the war the British found it necessary to send punitive expeditions to "restore law and order" in the West Indies. In 1951, when Negro strikers in Grenada (pop. 80,000) demanded that their wages be increased—from 36 to 54 cents a day!—

two cruisers, a gunboat, marine, and police units went into action. In 1955, following the victory of the Peoples Progressive Party (PPP) in British Guiana, British Tommies and gunboats invaded British Guiana, deposing its legally elected legislators headed by Dr. Jagan and revoking its progressive Constitution as a "Communist-inspired coup." But four years later the people of Guiana, in a victorious mandate despite a party split, reelected Jagan, and the PPP now holds important elected ministerial posts.

Only a few weeks ago, as witnessed in Nassau, Bahamas, the same step was taken when a general strike exposed the shocking conditions under which the 90 percent colored population live.

The West Indian people have not taken lightly the extensive exploitation of their resources and human labor. Record profits have been declared by domestic and foreign capital interests in the sugar, oil, and bauxite industries.

But there have been many instances of working-class resistance: strikes among port workers in Jamaica, the workers of St. Vincent have been heroically struggling to win concessions from arrogant landlords in sugar. Throughout the West Indies, teachers, match workers, and waterfront workers were aroused to defend their interests. In Barbados, printers and port workers were locked in struggle with the powerful Advocate Printers. In British Guiana, the PPP victory forced revocation of reactionary laws which restricted the movement of their leaders. In Trinidad, store clerks, sugar, oil, and educational workers have similarly displayed commendable class consciousness in defending their interests in the face of menacing threats from employers and government.

These and other examples make it necessary to be mindful of the astute observation of Mao Tse-tung—namely, that imperialism is not prepared to permit the independent development of any new capitalist state, is out to stultify it, make it impossible for the native capitalist to carry out the bourgeois-democratic revolution. We know, of course, that as its foundations totter, imperialism seeks more flexible methods of governing the colonies and seeks to devise new means to camouflage its rule. Central, then, to Britain's desire to revise the status of her West Indian possessions is the spread of the national colonial liberation movement and the deepening crisis she finds herself in.

The New Federation

Exactly what will the Federation mean to the West Indies? To begin with, except for British Guiana, British Honduras, and the Bahamas, the remaining ten British colonial units, comprising approximately three million people, will be federated into a new national structure. This national structure will consist of an appointed or nominated Council of State. A bicameral legislature will consist of a nominated Senate of nineteen members, and a House of Representatives of forty-five members. The House is to be elected based on population with Jamaica, representing one-half of the Federation's population, having seventeen members; Trinidad ten; Barbados six; and two each from Grenada, St. Lucia, St. Vincent, Antigua, St. Kitts, Dominica, and one from Montserrat.

A Supreme Court of the Federation is to be established, having original jurisdiction in specified federal or inter-unit matters. It will also have jurisdiction to hear appeals from unit Courts of Appeal and recourse may be had to this court by British Caribbean territories not members of the Federation.

This new federal structure will in no way substitute for self-government in each unit, where territorial constitutions, already hobbled and proscribed by colonial administrative restrictions, must constantly be improved by the increasing struggles of the people and their political representatives.

Indicative of the measure of this struggle are the constitutional changes in Barbados where since October 1957, a Cabinet Committee excluding the Governor is the main instrument of Government. Similar changes have taken place in Jamaica, where, since November 1957, the Peoples National Party has been successful in its fight to put power in the hands of its Chief Minister, and to exclude the Governor from the Council of Ministers. But responsibility for criminal affairs will still remain within the control of the appointed attorney general. Although the Governor will not normally appear in the Council of Ministers, he will still have the right to summon Special Meetings to preside at them, and he will still retain his wide Reserved Powers.

The impact of these advances on other islands was recently summed up when the Bahamas Federation of Labor in the recent general strike demanded: "We want to be governed like our brothers in Trinidad, Barbados, and Jamaica."

Still another example of the fight for broader party representation was the sweeping victory of the Peoples National Movement (PNM), headed by Dr. Eric Williams in Trinidad, when the PNM was allowed to name two of the nominated members, thus creating a constitutional precedent.

But these examples are the exceptions rather than the rule. At present in most of the units there exists Legislative Councils of both Nominated and Elected Members and Officials. All the Governor-Generals hold wide Reserved Powers, as will Lord Hailes, new Governor-General of the WI Federation, who took office January 3, 1958.

It is no accident in face of this undemocratic system that for years the chief demand of the West Indian political movement and particularly its advanced sectors has been for greater internal self-government for each unit based on wholly elected legislatures.

Conflicting Views

So tenacious has been this key demand that it has now extended to the Federation itself. Some West Indian ideologists however, have counterposed self-government to Federation—as though the two concepts are mutually exclusive. Such, for example, is the view of W. A. Domingo, outstanding student of West Indian affairs. In his pamphlet, *British West Indian Federation—A Critique*, Domingo urges Jamaicans to reject Federation outright—primarily on the grounds that as the largest and most populous of the West Indian islands, she can easily achieve self-government without being hampered by the underdeveloped economies of the Leeward and Windward islands, dependent as they still are on grants-in-aid which are to be curtailed after the first five years of the Federal Government. He further holds that "to equate federation with self-government obscures the real issue—the right of every colonial people to seek and win control of their political life."

But no one who advocates a federated progressive West Indies *equates* these concepts. In fact, those who have consistently fought for a progressive federation structure have always accompanied this demand with one for autonomy of the island units as well. Besides, how can the unity of a people who have similar cultural and historical experiences be held to be violative of "a right" of self-determination if in seeking to control their political life, they strengthen their ties with others similarly situated? We can assume that Domingo's arguments, like other pre-Federation critics, had as their aim to modify the present federation structure. But to base one's arguments largely on the pragmatic grounds that Britain considers the West Indian colonies as "financial liabilities" and that they are of "no strategic value to England today," that Britain will "grant self-government" to the West Indian colonies, because of the "proclaimed official British policy to grant independence to the colonies" flies in the face of a fundamental, scientific assessment of imperialism today.

Still other political ideologists, including some progressives and even some adherents of Marxism, have denounced the current Federation proposals as a "fraud" and appear to be resisting its arrival.

Such approaches appear to be utterly unrealistic politically. For while serious limitations hedge the new federal structure, can it be denied that it is a political advance over the previous colonial status of three hundred years?

Basically, the struggle for the free West Indian market by both the foreign and local bourgeoisie is what has given the movement for Federation its urgency. John La Rose, leading Marxist of Trinidad's West Indian Independence Party, in his Report to the Second Congress of that Party, in July, 1956, places it this way:

The basic economic law of West Indian life which gives this movement such urgency is the struggle for the free West Indian market by both the local and foreign bourgeoisie (interlocked and not interlocked) caused by the inability of the markets of the local territories to satisfy the capacity for expansion and exploitation engendered by capital accumulation in their hands.

Both the foreign and native commercial bourgeoisie have expanded their interests beyond the confines of territories, ...

Both local and foreign banking and insurance institutions of finance capital (like Bookers Trading concerns, Barbados Mutual, etc.) have expanded their interests beyond the confines of a single territory . . . besides the activities of foreign banking and insurance institutions.

Both the local and foreign industrial bourgeoisie have expanded beyond the confines of a single territory, e.g., shirt manufacturers, biscuit manufacturers, gin and rum manufacturers, edible oil manufacturers, citrus juices, time clocks, cement manufacturers exporting to British Guiana, Barbados, Grenada, etc., and vice versa. Even at the level of small agricultural producers, e.g., Grenada, St. Vincent, this need is felt and exists as a powerful urge to Federation.

While not all political forces in the West Indies are prepared to formulate immediate demands they are nevertheless broadly united on the aim of Dominion Status. Thus it seems that here once again is reflected the inevitable process of development which cannot be halted—the quest for full national independence.

Consequently, the chief programmatic demand to overcome the limitations advanced by progressive and socialist-minded forces in the West Indies include:

1. Internal self-government for the Federation entailing a wholly elected Parliament (a nominated Senate is a retrograde step), full cabinet status based on the Party principle with the elected Prime Minister wholly responsible, and restriction of the Governor-General's powers to representation of the Sovereign as is the case of Ghana, or a republican form of government as in India, with the Crown as the head of the Commonwealth.
2. Civil liberties embracing the entire Federation including freedom to travel, freedom to organize and to discuss.
3. Protection of rights of minorities for cultural and other forms of development.
4. For full national independence for the West Indies.

❖ ❖ ❖ ❖ ❖

Despite the serious limitations it would be fundamentally wrong to assess the forthcoming Federation as being simply the brain-child of the Colonial Office. To understand the significance of this development it must be realized that what is taking place in the West Indies is the unfolding of the classical bourgeois democratic revolution, with, of course, its own special features.

Leadership of the national political movement is today in the hands of middle-class intellectuals who either come from the class of the national bourgeoisie, or are representative of their interests.

Because federation of the West Indies occurs at a time when the local capitalist class is developing, every nuance of the federal structure is, naturally, tempered by their influence. Motivated firstly by their own desire for improved status and a desire to be free of their inferior colonial status, essentially this influence is anti-imperialist and anti-colonial.

What unites the *all-class* struggle of the West Indian peoples is opposition to foreign imperialism. This stage of political development in general coincides with the historic aim and dream of the West Indian working class, its militant industrial and agricultural workers, who in the '30s hoisted the banner of Federation, with Dominion status and self-government for the units, to their standard. These and other demands have today been incorporated into the political platforms of the present national political parties and movements in the islands.

It is important to stress that leadership of the national political movement has passed relatively recently into the hands of the national bourgeoisie.

Prior to World War II, leadership of the national movement was in the hands of the working class, arising from the upheavals during the mass strikes of 1937–38. The working class spearheaded the mass struggle; their leaders won their confidence through their selfless and courageous actions. This was the period in which trade unionism rapidly developed in the Caribbean and a new sense of power was felt by the workers.

There then emerged the Caribbean Labor Congress, a united West Indian people's anti-colonial movement for Federation with Dominion status and self-government for the units. It comprised an all-class coalition in which the working class shared leadership with other anti-imperialist classes including important sections of the national bourgeoisie.

But this movement was split and declined.

Basic to the answer as to how this decline and split arose was the "divide and rule" tactic of imperialism, which, fearful of this forward development, facilitated the separation of the right wing from the left wing in accommodation with some of the bourgeois national leaders.

True, imperialism, faced with the mounting pressure of the national liberation movement, is seeking to develop the national bourgeoisie as a reliable bulwark to protect its interests for as long as possible even after national independence is won. But India's experience proves that that does not always work.

The working class was also handicapped in that it lacked a scientific approach to the national and class struggle, in many instances pursued sectarian policies, and consequently lost leadership to the developing middle-class intellectuals.

It is this background, given briefly, which largely accounts for the hesitations which have marked sections of the working class and socialist-oriented groupings in the West Indies in definitively committing themselves to the present Federation.

Here, a distinction is made between the justified reservations shared by all sections of West Indian opinion and the imperative task of the working class and its advanced sector to play its indispensable role in carrying forward the movement for West Indian national independence.

To sit it out, instead of entering fully as leading partners in the national struggle for independence is to abdicate a contribution they alone can make. The working class and the Left in such a role can encourage the progressive tendencies of the national bourgeoisie. It can steady the middle-class intellectuals towards firmer anti-imperialist stands (criticizing where necessary but not from outside this development).

Trade-Union Activity

A most imperative conclusion appears to be the need to coordinate and strengthen trade union activity. In recent months, support for the idea of a united militant trade-union movement on a federal scale has been underway in the West Indies. Such a trade-union movement would not only help to facilitate independence and national unity but would be the instrument for achieving improved living standards, higher wages, and in general defense of the workers' rights against pressure by US and British capital. Such a united trade-union movement would have a decisive effect on the policies of the two main federal parties—the West Indian Federal Labor Party and the Democratic Labor Party, who will contest seats for the Federal Assembly.

Together with improved living standards and economic advancement is the need for expanded educational development. Educational standards in the West Indies are today frightfully low—too low to fulfill the needs of a country aiming at nationhood.

A prime necessity is the development from the working class itself of a class-conscious cadre and leadership. This is especially important because of the mistaken conception current among West Indian intellectuals that political parties in the West Indies do not represent social classes. Buttressing this false theory is the fact that all mass parties in the West Indies have to rely on support of the working class.

Political pressure and leadership by the Left has already vitally affected the national political movement in the West Indies. One such contribution has been their pointing up the contrast between Soviet economic aid with no strings attached, and the historic significance of Bandung. Advocacy of such policies can help change the pace with which the national bourgeoisie and middle-class intellectuals press for full national independence in the West Indies.

While at this juncture the bourgeois national struggle is directed against foreign imperialism, without doubt as the development of the national bourgeoisie takes place, the internal class struggle will grow in importance and scope.

All political observers would do well to follow the course of West Indian development; in Britain this course has been forced on all political forces anew with the presence of eighty thousand West Indian immigrants now resident in Britain—the largest immigration of colonial people in recent years. Faced with impoverishment and unbearable conditions and barred by the infamous racially biased Walter–McCarran immigration laws which retards West Indian immigration to one hundred persons a years from all the West Indies to the USA, they have trekked in thousands to Britain, where they are confronted with an extension of their problems as colonials in a metropolitan country in the form of color prejudice, joblessness, housing shortages, etc.

Progressive and Communist forces in Britain, mindful of their own responsibilities and of the greed of the US imperialist colossus, are advocating economic assistance to the West Indies; solidarity with their trade-union and other struggles and full national independence for the West Indian people.

CONSCIENCE OF CARIBBEAN NATIONALISM: DR. ERIC WILLIAMS

WEST INDIAN GAZETTE
DECEMBER 1960

Dr. Eric Williams, Premier of Trinidad and Tobago, is an enigmatic man who has earned the approbation of his enemies, the devotion of members of his own ruling party, the People's National Movement, some times to the point of fanaticism, and the wide admiration of West Indians and other peoples on five continents. Revaluation of Dr. Williams' role is a constant among all West Indians as well as some Trinidadians— usually resulting in his ultimate favor—even if with some reservation.

Short of stature and proudly scholarly in his bearing, his appearance is witness to his long intellectual career which preceded his entry into Caribbean politics.

Dr. Williams' career spans an extraordinary gamut of experience. Author of *Capitalism and Slavery*, a major study of British economic history as well as a study of slavery in the West Indies, Dr. Williams also served for many years until his protest resignation from the US-Anglo-Caribbean Commission to enter politics in Trinidad. In an unprecedented sweep after forming his People's National Movement, he swept to power, capturing the Trinidad Legco, displacing the extended and overgrown administration of Albert "Bertie" Gomes. The average *PM*'er credits Dr. Williams with "opening the people's eyes." "Before EW," they will tell you, "we knew nothing."

Personifies Multiracial Society

It is said that Dr. Williams symbolizes the multiracial peoples who populate the Caribbean, not only by his own mixed Indian-Negro-

Chinese parentage, but more importantly in his personification of the dreams, hopes, and aspirations of those who desire an independent West Indies in which all of its many-peopled strain may enjoy the benefits yet to be fully realised. His *Economics of Nationhood*, presented at the West Indies Inter-Governmental Conferences last year, prepared by a panel of economists, had his personal supervision. In that document he advocates independent, truly interdependent West Indies with a Customs Union to meet the threat of a European Common Market, which, he believes, will impair imperial preferences to the detriment of the West Indies. Prerequisite, he insists, to the applause of most West Indian nationalists, is independence—political independence, although some express worry that his views are not sufficiently accompanied by a clear charting to economic independence and the necessary new alliances that will have to be forged by the West Indies for full nationhood. Williams, however, might well be termed *the conscience of Caribbean Nationalism*.

No Self-Ownership

Dr. Williams is at once politician and university lecturer, academician and government head of the richest West Indian unit, whose wealth springs from its great oil and asphalt reserves which West Indians do not themselves control, but which are in the newly transferred hands of US Texaco Oil and Gulf Petroleum (British) with Texaco holding the lion's share. To a query in a public meeting by a West Indian youth, no doubt fired by the example of national movements everywhere, Dr. Williams replied: There was "no need for Trinidadians to self-own their own reserves."

It may well be asked: What kind of nationalism is it that stops at some kind of halfway house of self-ownership of one's own productive resources? Or is the concept of self-ownership anathema ——.

Even if it is argued that the time is "not yet ripe:" that it is a question of stages, this question must ultimately be faced, and, moreover, prior to the achievement of political independence—lest the West Indies be consigned to some kind of "half-slave, half-free" limbo.

One gathers the certain impression that Dr. Williams has faced the question but has rejected it out of hand. With some adroitness, he builds an image of West Indian independence and freedom—but one sees the shadow—not the substance. Nor is argument of progress, which is being made everywhere, sufficient.

It is a curious kind of nationalism that is embarrassed by this question in a Caribbean surrounded by Cuba's powerful self-owning aura, so is the example of Guinea.

One cannot truly reject colonial control of one's political independence and simultaneously accept the BONDAGE of colonialist domination of one's productive resources.

An Ardent Nationalist Non-Socialist

Politically, Dr. Williams is an ardent nationalist. He specifically disclaims socialist leanings and can speak for hours without any reference to socialism—Caribbean or otherwise. Yet he is no doubt aware, as in his recent press conference when he unequivocally stated his position: "We'd have an international personality—like—if the Soviet Union offered us something—and we accepted it—we would get one."

Dr. Williams' pride in the Caribbean tradition and history is evident. He constantly inveighs West Indian students to research and to correlate the yet unwritten true West Indian history and to bring it up to date. Yet pride in his Oxford training which emanates from him, has led him to lay claim not unkindly to the idea that the West Indies should have achieved its independence long before the newly freed African states due to its long readiness for it.

He attributes the gap to the crab-like steps of the West Indies to independence to what he terms the well-known "colonial mentality," which he satirically holds West Indians seems to loath to shake off like a well-liked garment. Ever the scholar, the Trinidad premier can hold an audience spellbound for hours whether in Central Hall or in the University of Woodford Square, an institution which professor Gordon Lewis of Puerto Rico recently characterized as the outstanding mass educational media in the West Indies. Quick at repartee and quick, too, to deflect questions, Dr. Williams is an able speaker, debater, and can evoke and provoke new concepts such as: "Is it because we were the first of Her Majesty's Colonies, we must by that token albeit be the last to gain our independence?"

It is true to say that Dr. Williams seeks to establish a mo——
[missing line] beckons West Indians to make the leap swiftly. His

dream is a trilingual (English-Spanish-French) West Indies develop-ing and contributing despite its small size of 3.5 million peoples, and making a contribution to the councils of the nations.

His dream is a West Indies which will *"Dwell Together In Unity."* Whether that unity includes all ideologies or people who wish to pace the national movement along more militant lines the enigmatic Dr. Williams does not reveal. Yet on British Guiana in which he was accused by the *Trinidad Guardian* of "playing Indian politics" he stands to sponsor BG in the Federation and says they should join without any strings attached to their ideological leanings. He shows preoccupation with the confusion of political ideas in the West Indies. These for him are the differing constitutional Unit structure and the belief of some in the Caribbean in a "continental destiny of others even in an inter-continental destiny."

This clouds the political vision of West Indians—and their souls. The scholar in him mercilessly dissects the large *"record of degrada-tion of the human personality" in which Indians, Chinese, and Negroes in the West Indies earn as little as twenty-five cents a day.*

He satirically scorns the textbooks which still say "our ancestors had blonde hair and blue eyes."

A Confederationist Also

A strong federationalist, Dr. Williams seems to be today tending towards advocacy of Confederation—the ancient dream of Sam Simeon and other West Indian patriots. At London's Central Hall Lecture, before an audience of six hundred West Indians and friends, when he spoke on *The West Indies in the Modern World,* Dr. Williams repeatedly made reference to Martinique and Guadeloupe which lie between —— and Trinidad. Yet ——

[portion missing]

It appears he was not against the ideas so much as the prism in which it was projected.

An independent West Indies he holds would stand four-square for "release of my friend Kenyatta." "Where we stand on South African apartheid on the boycott was shown in Trinidad, in our streets on the wharf," he says with some pride.

The emerging West Indies, which Dr. Williams will help to shape, he sees as a "bridgehead between Africa and Asia" due to her multiracial heritage, a West Indies (with Martinique and Guadeloupe of seventeen million peoples, and independent West Indies), could not be indifferent to the presence in Caribbean waters of a threat to the sovereignty of any one of its sister states.

Mindful of the problem of migration to the UK and the "exiles" in London, the good doctor showed that he is not without humor. For he closed his talk with a tale of when he was a student in England, coming home one day from Brixton having had a haircut, a number of white Britons touched him. When he learned later it was "for luck" he commented wryly: *"With so many West Indians now in England, this should mean a whole lot of luck."*

ISLAND AFLAME–THE STORY OF CUBA

WEST INDIAN GAZETTE
1961

Something in the real story of Cuba has been told in the magnificent TV series on Cuba.

But for the most complete and graphic story yet filmed of this new Caribbean socialist country, termed on discovery by Columbus as "the most beautiful land human eyes have yet seen," one must see the new superbly-produced Soviet film of Cuba entitled *Island Aflame*.

Social Transformation

Told simply, warmly, and in intensely human scenes, the viewer sees the transformation of the lives of the Cuban people in this "Pearl of the Antilles" whose motto is "Patria o Muerte" (Homeland or Death). How a people is fused into fighters for social advance; how they come to be aware that the life of the seasonal sugar-cane worker who barely subsists and must migrate, can be changed and a new social system ushered in, and the fruits of the people's labor be theirs to enjoy and build upon; how a fearless and courageous leadership of the original 26th of July Movement with its assault on Moncada—a US-ruled military bastion was the tocsin for revolutionary struggle, led by Fidel Castro and his comrades, is effectively told and related to the story of Cuba *Island Aflame*.

Eight-Year Fight

Through the eyes of a youth, you see everywhere the fabulous beauty of Cuba's rich subtropical, mineral-rich, arable land and its even more beautiful multiracial, now free, people (so much like the West Indies in composition).

The film depicts the heroic eight-year struggle in the rugged Sierra Maestra mountains, led by Fidel and the revolutionaries. Unquestionably supported by the Cuban people, the downfall of the US puppet, Batista, who abducted the great wealth and shared the spoils of the people's labor, was merely a matter of time.

Old Cuba

It was a Cuba where the average per capita income was £2 per week, with the vast majority of people getting much less.

Over one million people out of close to six and a half million were then unemployed, or 25 percent of its population.

Only 11 percent of the people drank milk, 4 percent ate meat and 2 percent consumed eggs. The illiteracy rate was 41 percent. In the countryside, elementary sanitation, even of the most primitive, was unknown.

American imperialism ruled Cuba; its banks dominated its economy; its warships stood in Havana harbour (and yet today on Guantanamo Base or Cuban soil) ready to pounce and stop a flicker of resistance. And in its steps followed corruption, tyranny, racial discrimination, and foreign economic domination.

Socialist Changes

All that is changed now. With great struggle, sacrifice, loss of life, but above all its socialist programme, all reflect the complete identification of its leaders with the people and their needs.

Look at the Cuban peasants receiving their plot of land as the film shows, and ask whether they will ever give this up—ever! See the woman who gets her first home and inscribes on the wall *"Mi Casa es Fidel"* (my home is yours) as if you are a brother, as indeed he is regarded.

See the aged scrawl with pride her first written letter, trained by teachers whose apprenticeship included a training course in the Sierra Maestra.

See the pride of Cuba's multiracial peoples: Negro, Mulatto, Chinese, Indian, and Brown and White, and ask yourself if it is for imperialist indignity, racial discrimination, and prejudice that they would exchange their liberty!

The tourists still go there—but the people are for the first time tourists in their own sun-blessed land!

As sure as you sit in your seat—if not on its edge—you will know the earnest-faced young Cuban in his new school, will follow Cuba's eminent young leaders and their proud people's militia, in her defense, if needs be, today, for the danger still hangs heavy over her revolutionary gains—and surely on her morrow.

"And for what, if not for you, fought we in the Sierra Maestras?" asks the kind-faced Castro of the young.

What indeed!

Mexican authorities are stated to have strengthened the coastal and air defenses against smugglers schemes, supported by the USA, of secretly unloading weapons and enemies of revolutionary Cuba. The plan is said to be a new step-by-step invasion of the Cuban coasts by armed conspirators.

Some time in December West Indian Gazette *plans a film-showing of this film. Watch for the announcement in* WIG's *columns.*

LETTER TO MANU

AUGUST 31, 1961

Dear Manu:

I thought I'd better let you know that I'm prepared to accept your <u>recommendations</u> as to the <u>conditions</u> you proposed in the pub this evening re: your coming into the *Gazette* and *Afro-Asian Caribbean News*.

Namely, that our company in fact functions <u>more effectively</u> and that you, as a director, assume a specific role in its affairs on the publication as regards management and circulation.

I regret, as has unfortunately been the case for the past three years when your role became a cruel one that the discussion had more heat than light—but I suppose, that the recriminations will continue and only cease as a result of one of three lines of approach: (a) that on both sides a new relationship to the paper is affected which would occur if you do in fact assume these duties and responsibilities and that the responsibility for the paper is shared between us, (b) that there is recognition that unless the new course is begun the recriminations cannot cease, or (c) if no agreement can be arrived at any <u>business relationship between us</u> whatsoever is effected and a settlement arrived at.

Contrary to what you assume, I believe sincerely that you could play an effective and indispensable role on the paper in the <u>capacity you finally outlined re: circulation and business management.</u> I am prepared to not be involved in this phase except as <u>involves and affects decisions and policy after briefing</u> and <u>turn over these matters to you</u>. Having carried this phase of the work as well as the editorial aspect virtually since the paper's inception, I am more than mindful of the tremendous burdens accruing to both phases—both of which have suffered due to lack of assistance and proper departmentalisation. Were you, who have been associated with *WIG* from its outset to really plunge into its departmentalisation, [it] could be made a reality.

The question of confidence on my part in you should never arise again. I assure you, if I had any doubt about this, I'd never have considered it. From now on, if you agree to come in, some perspective should govern our approach—namely that we would allow a reasonable period of working together on which basis a proper evaluation of progress could be made rather than an expectation that miracles would be wrought or changes effected overnight on both sides.

I am prepared to meet these conditions.

Now my conditions are these:

1. That no personal matters be brought up in the office affecting us, either past, present, or future—before others or ourselves. For this can act as a demoralizing factor on those working with us and contribute to lack of authority generally.

2. Any disagreements as affects the work should be sorted out in a calm spirit of give-and-take, of mutual respect, politeness, and co-operation and lack of epithets of any kind (in any language). All characterisation of each other ("stupid," "What a man," "idiotic") should be completely dropped from our vocabulary. This may take, nay, will take great self-discipline, but it must be done. Any party violating it should be docked 6d each time to be placed in a "Speak Bitterness" box in the office, if this plank is violated.

3. That a clear time schedule for meetings between us that are necessary and office coverage should be worked out.

4. That the adjacent office be prepared as your office (I am making arrangements for the window to be opened and the place made habitable).

5. That once the broad scope of the work is set, reviewed, added to, and agreed mutually, the people are left to work on their own initiative and responsibility in implementing decisions.

6. That we seek to co-opt [or] bring in as soon as possible three other persons on a functioning editorial board.

7. That no reference as to how *WIG* functioned in the past on a subjective basis is allowed—but the problems it faces <u>viewed objectively</u> as possible and positive recommendations made to overcome what weaknesses exist and to buttress strengths where they exist.

8. That the first and urgent task before us is to view the present financial situation i.e. (a) the indebtedness of the paper, current payments due and revenues expected and the facilitating of its immediate collection; (b) repayment of all debts; (c) the bringing in of more capital into the paper; (d) provisions for regular salaries; (e) the employment of a full-time secretary; (f) the securing of our own press; (g) the determination of a permanent printer until that stage is reached; (h) the question of moving of our offices; (i) the securing of a site for next year's Carnival and independence Gala. John Eber has proposed that since it can coincide with African Freedom Day that we discuss some united approach.

Apart from current expenses which must be met in the next few days.

Payment due are:

Printing Sept. issue	150.	Income Due
Last payment Morris	59.	
First Payment (Kats)	25.	From Advertising
R. Ellington		
		Approx. 350
Phone (Urgent)	34.	
Light Balance Elec	11.	
		Owe on
Rent Theo 2 weeks	6	Outstanding
Misc (Ct. Debts Hem—ming)	20	Debts
Travel Credit	19.	
Total Due	314.	Total 1490.60.

This includes Acct. Miller

The truth is, my dear sir, that any responsibilities or liabilities you in fact are liable to, and that would sincerely hope that it is possible for us to finally agree and begin together to set the thing aright on a new basis.

I am sending this letter by hand through Gumbo.

Yours sincerely,
Claudia Jones

I'd appreciate it if you were to call me at Theo's on receipt of some —— message.

GOA—WITH INDIA

WEST INDIAN GAZETTE
JANUARY 1962

After 450 years of Portuguese rule, Goa, Daman, and Diu—integral parts of India's territory, have been again united with India. The people of Goa enthusiastically welcomed the Indian Army—their kith and kin—which liberated it.

Goa was not only a brutally repressed colony of Portugal; it had been converted into a naval base by the USA-backed NATO powers to be used as a bulwark against the people of Asia who had won independence.

Discriminating and repression was the daily lot of the Goanese people. Four Goans out of every ten are Roman Catholics, and in Panjim, eight hundred priests served that tiny province. Under Portuguese administration however, only three Hindues held senior official posts. There were six held by the Catholic minority and the pattern was repeated throughout the public service. The colonial connection between the Catholic Church and the Portuguese colonial administrators was indeed close in that colonial territory.

It was against conditions like these, and the constant repression of the Goanese National Liberation Movement, that the Indian Army, acting on orders from the Indian government, justly terminated the centuries-old, brutal, repressive, and cruel Portuguese rule of Goa.

After fourteen years of patient upholding of the principles of peace and nonviolence, often in the face of constant provocation and humiliation caused by Portugal and shame-facedly condemned and oft-times supported by her Western allies, the Indian government acted only when violence became unbearable and intolerable and a threat to international peace.

Calumny

Of course, it was to be expected that the papists of Angola and her tongue-in-cheek "democratic" allies would howl blue murder.

In fact, the USA has gone so far as to support Portugal's charges against India in the UN Security Council and has made use of the United Nations to obstruct the Indian people's liberation of their own territory. Never has there been such calumny in the popular press against the eminent leaders of India—Prime Minister Nehru, Defence Minister Krishna Menon, etc. They have gone so far as to insist that the philosophy and creed of the Indian people can best be interpreted not by the Indians themselves (or Nehru, Menon—or even Gandhi!) but by their pure imperialist selves!

But in contrast to their stands, there has been universal acclaim in India for this action. The only voice of disapproval has come, as expected, from the Swatantra Party, known to be notoriously pro-West, who claimed that India's action would deprive her of her "moral power to raise her voice against the use of military force."

On Nonviolence

Kingsley Martin, *New Statesman* editor, expressed an interesting view when he wrote of the Indian action in Goa:

> No doubt Nehru is right in claiming that India is completely united over action in Goa. Indians can make no sense of the criticism that he has betrayed the teaching of Gandhi. In fact, the Mahatma's teaching on the use of force was never simply or more wholly pacifist.

> Nehru is certainly right in saying that by using the army, he saved the bloodshed which further demonstrations would have caused; if there had been a measure of nonviolent resisters, the fury of Indians everywhere would have led to many more casualties that the very few who had lost their lives on what Indians regard as mere police action.

Nehru has recalled in a television programme that the Mahatma fasted in order to compel the Indian Government to pay a large sum of money to Pakistan, even though the two countries were at war. Gandhi was prepared for India to use force against Pakistan, but not for her to go back on her word.

Today Nehru stands for colonial freedom with a minimum of force, just as Gandhi sought Indian independence by nonviolence. (*New Statesman*, Dec. 29, 1961)

Wide Support

Apart from the discussion of the merits of how truly nonviolent the steps to Indian independence were, we know that all talk condemning India's action is mischievous and misleading. People everywhere will see through this game. Nor by this is meant only those who see the "doom" of the UN because India has acted firmly to remove a part of its territory from colonial orbit. In face of the sheer arrogance by certain UN spokesmen who claim that by the "peoples of the world" is meant only those of the West, the great majority of the peoples of the world—the Chinese People's Republic, United Arab Republic, Vietnam, the Soviet, Union, Tunisia, Cuba, Iraq, Ceylon, and Indonesia have greeted India's historic step. So have many Western democratic peoples as well. These nations and people, dedicated to ending colonial rule, have naturally applauded India's action over Goa.

No Violation of UN Charter

It is nonsense to assert that India has violated the provisions of the United Nations Charter. In fact, it is the colonial and imperialist powers which the UN General Assembly have twice condemned in resolutions urging the end of colonialism, who themselves—in Congo, Malaya, Kenya, and elsewhere have been the violations of the United Nations and its Charter.

Britain's hands, as Dr. Conor O'Brien's brilliant expose of the Katenga lobby in the Congo showed, are far from clean.

As put by the Indian Congress of Great Britain in its resolution supporting India's liberation of Goa, "No provision of the United

Nations Charter has been violated by the Government of India. In fact, colonial and imperial powers in the United Nations have hindered the ordered changes and ordered action against defaulters. The Government of Britain especially has actively sabotaged the high principles of the United Nations. Britain has even acted as an armed aggressor against the nations. How is it possible for her government, especially Conservative Government, to do any better?"

Strengthens African Freedom

Perhaps the most revealing comment expressing the underlying fear of colonialists and neo-colonialists was put by the *New York Times* when it wrote that India's action in Goa might lead to "intensifying the differences between the West and Asian-African bloc." "*Intensifying?*" This is nothing but a reflection of their fear that the majority of Africans and Asians will not compromise with imperialism with the NATO bloc supported by the shameful colonial system. As put by Hadelino Gwambe, National President of Mozambique's National Democratic Union, in a cable to the Indian Government: "Goa's liberation strengthens the national liberation movement in Africa."

And Radio Ghana, hailing Goa's liberation, voiced the hope that Angola and other African territories under Portuguese rule will soon be liberated.

VISIT TO THE USSR

WEST INDIAN GAZETTE
DECEMBER 1962

To visit the Soviet Union was long an ardent desire of mine. Like millions of ordinary people the world over, and like those too, with socialist beliefs, I wanted to see for myself the first Land of Socialism; to meet its people, to see for myself the growth of its society, its culture, its technological and scientific advance. I was curious to see a land which I already knew abhorred racial discrimination to the extent of making it a legal crime and where the equality of all people is a recognised axiom.

This desire was fulfilled when, following the kind invitation of the editors of the magazine *Soviet Woman*, I spent several months in the USSR, combining a needed holiday with a visit this summer. I talked literally to dozens of people; women textile factory workers in Moscow, footwear workers in Leningrad where I met enthusiastic "innovators" (workers who lighten the tasks of labor by inventing shortcuts to labor processes and thus hasten fulfillment of their socialist system of planned production). I talked with Soviet youth, women, men, and its remarkable children—children who are the pride and apple of the eye of the friendly and hospitable multiracial people and nation of the Soviet Union.

I talked with men and women from formerly oppressed republics that today are equal nations, whose societies proudly flourish as great industrial and agricultural centers in the Soviet Union and in whose nations academies of science exist and universities research the ancient histories of peoples for whom before the Revolution, not even alphabets existed.

I still remember the anticipation with which after crossing the continent via the Hook from Harwich, the train hurling across the lowlands of Holland through Germany West and East, and Poland, it arrived at Brest—the first Russian city—and thence to Moscow. The Moscow carriage in which my compartment lay has a wireless system. And, on entering Brest, Soviet songs in the rapid, politely, punctuated, Russian language, rose to my ears.

I Meet the Cosmonauts

I had arrived in late August, the very day on which the Muscovites proudly celebrated the return to earth of their twin space astronauts, Andrei Nikolayev and Ivan Popovich. The airwaves were naturally full of announcements and descriptions. I did not then know that I would have the privilege of meeting them in person as I later did when, holidaying in the fabulous Crimea, near Yalta, they visited our sanatorium one evening. The excitement of the assembled guests was so great that it seemed as if the very stately cypress that line the Black Sea Coast seemed to sway in welcome.

An International City

Moscow is one of the most splendid cities I have ever seen or visited. (The only exception for sheer beauty and architectural design is Leningrad, the famous city on the Neva, site of the cradle of the Russian Revolution, which was designed by Peter the Great.) Wide boulevards lend a sense of space, of bigness, that one later learns after one has "come, seen, and lived there" is characteristic of its people. Everywhere there is building going on; flats and apartments are being erected; everywhere one feels a sense of history in this ancient city and present capital of over two hundred million people in this land of socialism, now building communism—which simply means creating the material preconditions for a society in which each man will receive equal to his needs.

Moscow is also an international center. From my hotel lobby one could see and meet people from every corner of the globe. Not only visitors, diplomats, and tradesmen, but students from all lands are studying here. At another time, I will write of discussions and interviews I had with people from other parts of the Caribbean—from Martinique and Guadeloupe, from Cuba and Ecuador, from Colombia and Uruguay.

Many like myself, were first-time visitors to the Soviet Union who shared my enthusiasm and discovery of things Soviet.

At Peace with Themselves

The outstanding first impression (and first impressions are lasting) was the absolute "at peace with themselves" look of the Russians. And why not? We may ask. The Soviet men, women, and youth are the proud inheritors of their socialist form of society. I witnessed on November 7 in Red Square—commemorating the first forty-five years of existence—the famed international workers holiday of the great October Revolution.

The Soviet family does not have the same type of living concerns or anxieties as we have here or in our native lands. I saw not worried frowns, as are typical of most faces in England or elsewhere. For example, rents are very cheap. The building boom in which the aim in the next ten years is a "flat for every family" will soon overcome housing shortages which still exist. I visited two Soviet families in two widely separated areas. From the window of the balcony in one block of flats my host described to me how diversity in architectural design have led to greater differences in planning of new flats to make far more and more efficient and comfortable living space.

Free Education

The Soviet family is assured, moreover, that its children will receive free education, including university matriculation if the boy or girl qualifies. Great emphasis is put on technological courses. With Soviet science leading the world, not only as regards space science, but also as regards industry and agriculture, if the boy or girl does not qualify for an academic course, he or she can quickly qualify in a field where manual labor is on an equal par in Soviet socialist society contributing to man's progress.

What is more, as I saw in Leningrad and Moscow, every factory has training courses and apprenticeship systems. If a boy or a girl does not know at time of graduation what course to pursue, and chooses to go to work, it does not mean that his or her education stops there, but they qualify for highest skills while working by attending the many technical colleges which dot the Soviet Union.

An elaborate system of training courses, with time off to take exams to become highly skilled, exists there to say nothing of the special amenities, which women, and particularly mothers, receive. No apprehension hangs over the head of a mother who gets post and prenatal time off amounting to three months off.

Women Doctors

The second impression that is likewise lasting is the role of women in the USSR. A special article needs to be done on the rehabilitation of "people" in the USSR, shown in the widespread concerns for health and welfare of its people and its guests as well. Medical care is free in the Soviet Union and a wide network of medical personnel (who put the patient first!) and medical services exist to care for the health of Soviet citizens. What is outstanding is that the medical staff is peopled overwhelmingly by women physicians, pediatricians, etc. More than 90 percent of the doctors in the Soviet Union are women.

I remember while in Bodkin hospital, Moscow, for several weeks, having fallen ill shortly after my arrival due to my overdue need for a holiday, I spoke to a charming Soviet woman doctor, who was a house physician about this remarkable fact. We exchanged current experiences about this, my telling her that there existed an exact contrast of the medical consilium which discussed my health status. Whereas in the UK, there were two women doctors to twelve men, here in the USSR there were twelve women doctors out of the fourteen who stood around my bed. There vividly came to mind the wonderful story told years ago in the United States by Mrs. Eslanda Robeson who, visiting a nursery in Moscow, told us how she tucked a little boy under the chin asking: "What do you want to be, sonny, when you grow up—a doctor?" and the boy, replying: "No, that's for girls!"

Indeed, every Soviet youngster dreams of being a cosmonaut. Already four living examples are before him. I saw this when I visited the huge Pioneer Palace for Children, situated a little outside Moscow, where every conceivable aspiration of a child of school age is met. Children receive instruction in painting, ballet, printing, music, aeronautics, designing, radiology, domestic, science, and whatnot there.

Happy Children

Soviet children are among the happiest children I have ever seen anywhere. They are, first of all—children. Well behaved, talented, and above all—friendly.

We saw them at a reception of the Leningrad pioneers, along with other Latin American visitors, after we had paid a visit to the museum of the revolution. The children were having their pre-November 7 meeting and because we were guests (guests are invited to partake in everything—the night before we had been invited to witness a Soviet wedding by the uncle of a bride in the Palace of Marriages) we were invited.

It felt my honor to address the children, and even before I finished some of the sentences, particularly the one in which I remarked on the friendliness of Soviet children, and that I would tell West Indian, African, and Asian children of this friendliness, the children burst into applause. Yes, even if they have never before seen you, they smile with you. I later learned, that as is true of this remarkable country, everyone is studying another language. The Soviet youth are becoming bilingual. On tubes, on holiday jaunts, you frequently see an English grammar, a book on Tamil, or Swahili, or some other language tucked under arms.

When I commented to a Soviet youth about this, he said simply: "We want friendship and peace (*mir* and *drushba*) with the peoples of the world—all peoples." Another, who already had French as a second language, said to me: "Come back next year, I'll speak English fluently," explaining he was learning the language phonetically by linguaphone.

Learning Russian

The intensity of language training was demonstrated to me when I visited Friendship University—named after the heroic Patrice Lumumba. This is the unique university where some two thousand students are enrolled from at least seventy nations. I still recall the babble of tongues that reached my ears, all virtually unknown to me, when, following an interview with the vice director in the morning, I toured the University, and he invited me to interview the students at random. There I spoke among others to a young man, handsome and in Western clothes, who might easily have been from Port of Spain, Belize, or Kingston, or Harlem, USA, but language proved a barrier. He addressed my interpreter, though, in fluent Russian—which is the common tongue of the many-tongued students from Afro-Asian-Latin American countries, and the many republics of the Soviet union. The young man came from Mali, and so I later communicated to him in French.

Language instruction in Patrice Lumumba's Friendship University is highly intense, with phonetics, linguaphones, films, oral practice, etc. So the question of whether or not the Afro-Asian-Caribbeans have an aptitude for language study is augmented by the intensive and thorough course of study to enable them to get their instruction for the courses swiftly. I spoke to many students from Ecuador, Chile, Nigeria, Ghana, UAR, India, but a special article must be written on this.

Thirst For Peace

The third, and most outstanding of all the impressions gleaned while on this, my first visit to the USSR, was the thirst for peace, the commitment for peace by the peoples of the Soviet Union. I understood more profoundly, too, the measure of suffering and sacrifice which the people of the Soviet Union went through in the Second World War when their territory was devastated. Hardly a single family escaped some personal loss.

Soviet citizens were still speaking of the magnificent World Conference for Peace and Disarmament which had concluded its sessions the month before I arrived in Moscow. That conference and reports of its sessions were still filling the pages of many magazines in this high-reading public, where, every publication must limit its size of publication which is sold out, so high is the thirst for knowledge and information, especially as regards peace. For example, *Soviet Woman*, my hosts carried its September and October issues; statements and stories from American women who urged that swords be driven into plowshares and differences between nations negotiated instead of resorting to war, which today means a thermonuclear conflict. Though of varied political outlooks and differing social levels, they were united in their desire for peace.

Soviet's Support for Cuba

I was in the Soviet Union at the time of the US-spawned Cuban crisis and the tension felt throughout the world was felt there too. But in Moscow, while trade unions demonstrated their condemnation of USA war threats against little heroic Cuba, and the airwaves hummed with announcements on mobilization and the threat of war, the people of the Soviet Union stood firmly and calmly on the side of their government upholding its efforts for peace.

Following Bertrand Russell's splendid initiative and the actions of the Soviet Government, numerous of the Afro-Asian countries congratulated the Soviet head of state for the sanity and skill with which he upheld the people's desire for peace, for negotiations of outstanding differences, for peaceful competition and peaceful coexistence of the two world systems of society. Through it all, one is struck by the fact that Soviet citizens and their government make no bones about their determination to uphold the rights of the oppressed peoples and the constant and continuing support of the struggles of the new and yet-to-be freed peoples of African, Asia, the Caribbean, and Latin America.

Soviet Democracy and Culture

Whether visiting or enjoying my fill of the magnificent and realistic Russian or Soviet theatre, ballet, or operatic art; whether visiting the ancient museum which chronicle the history of Russian painting; or the Hermitage in Leningrad where great treasures in world paintings abound; whether visiting the over-full attractive shops where, while shortages still exist, the basic consumer goods are on the shelves and the well-dressed and well-shod Soviet citizens are buying them quickly; whether speaking to ordinary Soviet citizens or to intellectuals; or to Communist Party or newspaper editors; whether flying in superb Illuyshins over the Sea of Atovsk to the sub-tropical Crimea so reminiscent of the Caribbean; the universality of the Soviet people's desire for peace strikes you anew. They convince you that their vital system of socialism (which has caused so much fierce controversy in the world by the representatives of dying systems of society), because it abhors the exploitation of many by man, can best flourish in peace and in peaceful competition with other peoples and systems.

And the thirst to know about other peoples and systems is clearly to better be able to understand and to develop with them, in peace and friendship.

One is finally struck by the collective breadth of knowledge which the Soviet youth strive for and possess. They discuss Shakespeare and Somerset Maugham with you—and with themselves.

They have read the novels and writings of many nations, which are widely translated into the various Soviet languages. They are anxious to read the authors of newly independent countries, the better to know the peoples with whom they will now come into contact. I searched a giant bookshop in Leningrad to find a copy of *The Leopard*, by the well-known Jamaican author Vic Read—only to find it was completely sold out. But other titles were on the shelves, Tutuola's *The African Princess*, a charming children's tale; *The Bee and the Earthworm* by a Chinese author, Yeh Pen-wing.

The famous books by Dr. W. E. B. Du Bois and his author-wife Shirley Graham are also there. I had to promise to make recommendations as to authors and books for republication from the Caribbean.

This was the most wonderful holiday visit and trip I have ever experienced. In the next issues of *WIG*, I shall be writing of my visit to Patrice Lumumba University. At Proletarskaya Pobeda ("Victory of the Revolution") Shoe Factory, a piece which I have subtitled "All God's Children Got Shoes," since not only were these of God's children wearing shoes—the ancient dream of all oppressed people, as the Negro spiritual says, but producing them. I shall write of my visit to Children's Pioneer Palace and Camp Artek, famous international children's camp, my visit to Sevastapol, to a textile factory, and something of the Crimea. And I shall relate too, how the slogan of the Seven-Year Plan "Today the Innovators; Tomorrow the Collective" is the essence of Soviet successes and the cornerstone of its society.

Sevastapol—Hero City

Perhaps it was at Sevastapol, one of the framed hero cities of the Soviet Union, and later at Leningrad when I visited the famed "Alley of Heroes" where 670,000 people died of starvation, that I understood most deeply both the depth for peace and the suffering which the peoples of the Soviet Union have gone through to preserve their way of life, and their very existence, and to guarantee the defeat of Hitler fascism.

Every blade of grass, every stone, has its own tale to tell in blood and suffering of the Soviet people. It is all demonstrated in the splendid duorama drawn up by splendid Soviet graphic artists; but everywhere among the people of Sevastapol one finds here a mother; there a wife, here a son—some one of whose kin fell at Sevastapol.

Of Supermen and Human Beings

Soviet people discuss this; and they discuss, too, the strenuous efforts being made to eliminate the "cult of personality." There is evidence everywhere that the current criticism is being used as a weapon to broaden ever further the rights of the Soviet people, even as they strenuously work to support the rights of people and formerly oppressed nations who are only now beginning to enjoy those rights. Soviet people discuss also with some impatience their weaknesses. "If you know better, teach us," they say. Something of what Anton Chekov once described as a "national trait" of the Russians—their "self-abnegation" is evidenced here. When a visitor comments on some out-standing achievement or trait or heroism, the Soviet man or woman will say "Perhaps we are too close to ourselves to see what you see." The man who spoke had fought in the Second World War, had lost nearly his whole hand in the struggle, and was now a political leader in his native Ukraine. Their impatience is for greater, swifter progress, so that to the stranger, who is amazed at their great achievements in every sphere, they look almost as superman.

It is less than half a century since these former overwhelmingly peasant people took their own destiny in their own hands and created a socialist society. If they seem to be supermen it is because these extraordinary human beings transformed their society, and in that process, transformed themselves.

It was in one of the many beautifully decorated bookshops where books are displayed in loving designs that walking one day with my interpreter, I was drawn to a magazine which had on its cover the picture of Antoine Gizenga, the jailed Congolese deputy to Patrice Lumumba, whose fate is as yet unknown. Asking for a translation, my interpreter quickly translated and summarizing remarked: "The essence of it is that we stand for immediate freedom." Where, in any other capital in my part of the world, I asked myself, would such a magazine be featured in over a dozen bookshops at the same time?

I think often of any interpreter's remark as summing up the sig-nificance of the Soviet people and its socialist system. It is that "in essence they stand for the immediate freedom of all the oppressed." It is no wonder that most Africans, Asians, Negro Americans, and Latin Americans—in fact, peoples from every land whom I met there, all remarked unanimously of this fact which they feel as they live or visit among the people of the Soviet Union.

THE CARIBBEAN COMMUNITY IN BRITAIN

FREEDOMWAYS
SUMMER 1964

Claudia Jones, born in Trinidad, lived in the United States for many years where she played a leading role in youth and civil rights activities. Deported under provisions of the McCarran Act, she now lives in London where she edits The West Indian Gazette.

Over a quarter of a million West Indians, the overwhelming majority of them from Jamaica, have now settled in Britain in less than a decade. Britain has become, in the mid-1960s, the center of the largest overseas population of West Indians; numerically relegating to second place, the once superior community of West Indians in the United States.

This new situation in Britain, has been inimitably described in the discerning verse of Louise Bennett, noted Jamaican folklorist, as, "Colonization in Reverse."

Immigration statistics, which are approximate estimates compiled by the one time functional West Indian Federation office (Migrant Services Division) in Britain, placed the total number of West Indians entering the United Kingdom as 238,000 persons by the year 1961. Of these, 125,000 were men; 93,000 women; 13,200 were children; and 6,300, unclassified. A breakdown of the islands from which these people came, showed that during the period of 1955–1961, a total of 142,825 were from Jamaica; from Barbadoes, 5,036; from Trinidad and Tobago, 2,282; from British Guiana, 3,470; from Leeward Islands, 3,524; from the Windward Islands, 8,202; and from all other territories, the sum total of 8,732.

Distribution of the West Indian population in the United Kingdom indicates that by mid-1962, over 300,000 West Indians were settled in Britain. The yearly immigration and the growth of community settlement illustrates the rate of growth of the West Indian settlement. For example, the emigration of West Indians to the United Kingdom in mid-1955 totalled 24,473 and by 1961, this figure soared to 61,749. Corresponding to the latter, was the fear of family separation due to the then impending Commonwealth Immigrants Act.

In the industrial city of Birmingham, by mid-1955, 8,000 West Indians formed the community there, while in mid-1962, this figure stood at 67,000. Similarly in London, where in Brixton the largest settlement of West Indians exists; the mid-1955 figure of 85,000 had by 1961 grown to 135,000.

West Indians were also to be found in the North of England (Manchester, Nottingham, Wolverhampton, Derby, and Leeds) and in such cities as Cardiff, Liverpool, Leicester, Bath, Oxford, Cambridge, and in other provinces. *What constitutes the chief features of this unprecedented migration to Britain? To what factors may we ascribe this growth of overseas West Indians away from their original homelands?*

Emigration from the West Indies has served for over two generations as a palliative, a stop-gap measure to ease the growing economic frustrations in a largely impoverished agricultural economy; in which under colonial-capitalist-imperialist relations, the wealth of these islands is dominated by the few, with the vast majority of the people living under unbearable conditions.

It was the outstanding Cuban poet, Nicholas Guillen, who noting a situation (also observed by other West Indian writers) in which the young generation, most of it out of work, "chafing at the bit," seeing as their only hope a swift opportunity to leave their islands, lamented thus: *"Scant, sea-girt land, Oh, tight-squeezed land ..."*

Indeed, as with all migrant populations here is mirrored in extension the existing problems of the nations and territories from which the migrants originally spring. West Indian emigration to the United Kingdom is no exception to this phenomenon. Furthermore, this emigration, as with many other Afro-Asian peoples, has occurred almost immediately prior to the achievement of political independence in two of the largest of the West Indies islands. *It is because prospects have not yet qualitatively improved for the vast majority of the West*

Indian workers and people, inhibited by the tenaciousness of continued Anglo-American imperialist dominance over West Indian economic life, that this emigratory movement of people from the West Indies continues. History will undoubtedly evaluate this development as, in part, attributable to the demise of the West Indian Federation and the consequent smashing of wide hopes for the establishment of a united West Indian nation in which freedom of movement would have absorbed some of our disinherited, disillusioned, and unfilled people who were compelled to leave their homelands in order to survive.

Up to a decade ago, West Indian immigration was directed to America rather than to Britain. But this was sharply modified when, in 1952 the United States Federal Government enacted the racially based McCarran–Walter Immigration Law, which unequivocally was designed to protect the white "races' purity," and to insure the supremacy of Anglo-Saxon stock; limited to one hundred persons per year allowed to emigrate to the United States from each individual Caribbean territory. Henceforth all eyes reverted to Britain. This is not to imply that West Indian immigration to Britain was wholly nonreciprocal. Another influence was that post-war Britain, experiencing a brief economic boom and full employment, needed overseas and cheap labor to staff the semi-skilled and non-skilled vacancies, the results of temporary postwar economic incline. Britain sought West Indian immigration as an indispensable aid to the British economy; indeed, encouraged it!

The presence of West Indian immigrants (who together with other Afro-Asian peoples total nearly a half million people) represent less than one percent in an overall Anglo-populous of fifty-two million. But even this small minority has given rise to a plethora of new sociological and analytical works such as *"Newcomers"; "Colored Immigrants in Britain"; "The Economic and Social Position of Negro Immigrants in Britain"; "Black and White in Harmony"; "Colored Minorities in Britain"; "Colonial Students"; "Report on West Indian Accommodation Problems in the United Kingdom"; "Race and Racism"; "Dark Strangers"; "They Seek a Living, and the Like."*

Extreme manifestations of the racialism which underlie the present status of West Indians in Britain were graphically witnessed in late 1958, when racial riots occurred in Notting Hill and Nottingham. These events, which followed the as yet unsolved murder of a St. Vincentian, Mr. Kelso Cochrane, claimed world headlines. Clashes even occurred between West Indian and other Afro-Asian migrants with white Britons. The firm handling of the provocateurs by the authorities, following the wide protests of immigrants, labor, Communist and progressive forces, and the intervention of the West Indian Federal leaders, for a time quelled the overt racialists, and the "keep Britain white, fascist-propagandists." But the canker of racialism was now nakedly revealed. It exposed also the smugness of official Britain, who hitherto pointed to racial manifestations in Little Rock and Johannesburg, South Africa, but continued to deny its existence in Britain.

Today, new problems, underscored by the Tory Government enactment, and recent renewal of the 1962 Commonwealth Immigration Act (one which ostensibly restricts Commonwealth immigration as a whole, but in fact, discriminates heavily against colored Commonwealth citizens) has established a second-class citizenship status for West Indians and other Afro-Asian peoples in Britain. Accompanying the general social problems confronting all new migrant workers, West Indians, stemming as they do in large measure from African origins, are experiencing sharper color-bar practices. In common with other workers, the West Indians take part in the struggle for defense and improvement of their working and living standards. But the growing intensity of racialism forces them, as it does other Afro-Asians, to join and found their own organizations. In fact, their status is more and more a barometer of British intentions and claims of a so-called "Multiracial Commonwealth." As put in one of the recent sociological studies of the absorption of a West Indian migrant group in Brixton, financed by the Institute of Race Relations and the Nuffield Foundation:

> Now that the whole equilibrium of world power is changing, and the Commonwealth is, by virtue of conscious British policy, being transformed from a family based on kinship, to a wider multiracial familia, the presence of colored immigrants in Britain, presents a moral and a practical challenge. The people of these islands face the need not only to reformulate their views of Britain's role and status in such a Commonwealth, but also to apply the new relationships in their dealings with colored Commonwealth

migrants here at home. And not only the color-conscious migrants themselves, but the newly independent Afro-Asian countries and the outside world as a whole, show an inclination to judge Britain's good faith in international relations by her ability to put her own house in order. (From *Dark Strangers,* by Sheila Patterson)

The Commonwealth Immigrants Act

Far from heeding the advice even of sociologists whose studies themselves show a neo-colonialist bias in its precepts (the study is full of pragmatic assertions that xenophobia is the "norm" of British life, and hence, by implication "natural," etc.), the Tory Government has shown utter disdain for putting its own house in order.

Faced with the coming general elections in October, having suffered from local government defeats, mounting criticism rises towards its ruinous domestic and foreign policies. Internally, these range from housing shortages and a Rent Act which has removed ceilings on rentals to the failures of providing new houses, high interest rates on loans to the rail and shipbuilding closures, mergers, and the effects of automation.

The external policies of the present British Conservative Government also suffer similar criticism. As a junior partner it supports the United States imperialist NATO nuclear strategy, continuing huge expenditures for colonial wars in Malaysia, North Borneo, and Aden. Its subservience to US imperialism is also demonstrated in the case of its denial of long-overdue independence to British Guiana, on whom it is imposing the undemocratic system of Proportional Representation, which aims further to polarize and divide the political life in British Guiana in order to depose the left-wing, thrice-elected People's Progressive Party under Dr. Cheddi Jagan. As an experienced colonizer shopping around for a scapegoat for its own sins, the British Tory Government enacted in 1962 the Commonwealth Immigrants Act. The Act sets up a voucher system allowing entry only to those who have a job to come to. Some of its sections carry deportation penalties for migrants from the West Indies, Asia, and Africa, whom it especially circumscribes. Its passage was accompanied by the most foul racialist propaganda perpetrated against West Indians and other Afro-Asians by Tory and fascist elements. Thus, it coincided with the futile efforts then engaged in by the British Government to join the European Common Market. It was widely interpreted that these twin events demonstrated the dispensability in Britain's eyes of both the needs of the traditional market of the newly independent West Indian territories for their primary products, and the labor supply of West Indians and other Afro-Asian Commonwealth citizens. On the other hand, the doors would close on colored Commonwealth citizens, while open wide to white European workers.

The pious and hypocritical sentimentality accompanying the bill's passage was further exposed when the Tory legislators removed the non-Commonwealth Irish Republic from the provisions of the Act, revealing its naked color-bar bias. The result, following a year of its operation, showed that 80–90 percent of all Indian and Pakistani applicants were refused entry permits; and West Indian immigration dropped to a little over four thousand qualifying for entry. The latter occasioned cautious queries, whether the West Indians had either turned their backs on Britain or had become bitter with the Act's passage.

What the figures showed, of course, was that the main blow fell as intended, most heavily on the *colored* Commonwealth citizens. So much for the facile promises of the then Home Secretary, now Britain's Foreign Minister, Mr. R. A. Butler, that *"we shall try to find a solution as friendly to these people as we can, and not on the basis of color alone."* (my emphasis: CJ)

All Tory claims that the Act would benefit either Britain or the immigrants are, of course, easily refuted. The most widely prevalent Tory argument was that colored immigrants were "flooding Britain." At the time of the Act's passage, the 1961 British population census showed a two and a half million increase, during the very period of the growth of the immigration of West Indians and Afro-Asians, and this increase was easily absorbed by the British economy. The colored migrant is less than one in every hundred people. Yearly emigration of Britons shows that for every single person entering Britain, three leave its shores.

The shibboleth that "immigrants take away houses and jobs," when viewed in light of Tory responsibility for high interest property rates and the Rent Act, makes this claim likewise ludicrous. As for new houses, there is no evidence that West Indians or other colored immigrants have taken away any houses. Allowed largely only to

purchase old, dilapidated short-lease houses, it is the West Indian building worker, who helps to construct new houses, who makes an invaluable contribution to the building of new homes.

Even the usual last retort of the racial ideologists that West Indians and other colored citizens "lower moral stands" also fails to stand up. The world knows of the exploits of Christine Keeler and the British Ministers of State, an event which occasioned a calypso in the widely read *West Indian Gazette*. There has been no notable increase in jobs as a result of this Act. In fact, rail and shipbuilding closures, mergers, and automation, continue apace. It is widely admitted that withdrawal of colored workers from transport, foundries, and hospital services would cause a major economic dislocation in Britain, and that they continue to make a contribution to the British economy. Vic Feather, leading trade-union official, reiterated strongly this view at an all-day conference recently in Smethwick, a Birmingham suburb, where a local election campaign slogan was that to elect Labour meant *"having a nigger for a neighbor."* One finally observes regarding the asserted economic social burden of the migrant, that a "tidy" profit has been made by the Ministry of National Insurance from contributions of the surrendered cards of thousands of immigrants who returned home after a few years in Britain.

In the eyes of the world, the Tory record does not stand any better when it is known that nine times they have blocked the Bill to Outlaw Racial Discrimination by the Labour member for Parliament from Slough, Mr. Fenner Brockway. The main provisions of this bill would be to outlaw discrimination in public places, lodgings, inns, dance halls, and other leases; and also put penalties on incitement to racialism. The Bill has now gained the support of the Labour leadership who promised if they achieve office to introduce such a measure (although there are some indications that it may be watered down), as well as from leading Liberal MP's and even from some Tory MP's. Thus, there has been witnessed a reversal of the former open-door policy to Commonwealth citizens, and speciously to colored Commonwealth citizens. The result of all this has been a new degrading status and sufferance accorded to colored immigrants who are likewise saddled with the responsibility for Britain's social evils.

There is a reluctance on the part of virtually all sections of British public opinion to assess the fundamental reasons for the existence of racial prejudice. The citizens of the "Mother of Democracies" do not yet recognize that the roots of racialism in Britain are deep and were laid in the eighteenth and nineteenth centuries through British conquests of India, Africa, and great parts of Asia, as well as the British Caribbean. All the resources of official propaganda and education, the superstructure of British imperialism, were permeated with projecting the oppressed colonial peoples as "lesser breeds," as "inferior colored peoples," "natives," "savages," and the like—in short, "the white man's burden." These rationalizations all served to build a justification for wholesale exploitation, extermination, and looting of the islands by British imperialism. The great wealth of present-day British monopoly capital was built on the robbery of colored peoples by such firms as Unilever and the East Africa company, to Tate and Lyle, and Booker Brothers in the Caribbean.

These artificial divisions and antagonisms between British and colonial workers, already costly in toll of generations of colonial wars and ever-recurrent crises, have delayed fundamental social change in Britain, and form the very basis of color prejudice. The small top section of the working class, bribed and corrupted, and benefiting from this colonial robbery have been imbued with this racialist "white superiority" poison. On the other hand, progressive opinion rallied with the migrants' protests at the Commonwealth Immigrants Act, for the Labour Party leadership had voted in opposition to its enactment; yet allowing its subsequent renewal to go unchallenged, for the professional and other black-coated workers predominated in the migrant groups from Trinidad and Tobago, while skilled workers were more numerous from Jamaica and Barbados. Considerable downgrading of skills frequently occurs, and many unskilled workers have been unable to acquire skills, many from rural areas having formerly no industrial experience at all. But even where qualifications exist, many find it difficult to obtain jobs commensurate with their skills. Some employers have a secret quota system for the employment of colored workers, based on the chauvinistic view that *"too many colored workers,"* even if qualified, will *"rock the boat."* Others, even when inclined to take on colored workers, have had to face English workers, in some cases, trade unionists, who have a definite policy of keeping out colored workers. Even Government Employment Exchanges accept orders from employers not to submit "colored" applicants for work. But this too, is being resisted and demands are being made for the Ministry of Labor to rescind these instructions.

In the background is the countrywide pattern of industrial-labor relations; the traditional view of "keeping the labor force small," the better to bargain with the employers, and the real fear by trade unionists that non-union labor will undercut wages. Then, too, there is the ambivalent right-wing trade-union view which seeks to reconcile the principles of trade-union brotherhood and non-discrimination with the antipathies of a large and vocal proportion of its rank-and-file members.

Even in the early stages of the present West Indian immigration to Britain, struggles had to be waged for the acceptance of West Indian workers into the jobs they now hold. In the transport system, despite the agreements between the British Transport System and the Barbados Government to train and employ workers, sharp struggles by progressive trade unionists, led by Communists, had to be waged for hiring and upgrading of West Indian workers for their right to work in booking offices, or as shuttle-plate workers in railway depots, or for West Indian women to be employed as "clippies" or bus conductors.

Many of these gains are today under fire. A recent vote by the London busmen served notice that they opposed the hiring of any more West Indian workers. What is more, a growing "Blacklist for Jobs" exists, as an article in the *Sunday Observer* states. The article noted that thousands of West Indians born and educated in Britain will "not be content to do shift work on buses" in a society which, "despite their high academic levels treats them as less than human beings," (the article detailed the difficulties experienced by school-leavers particularly in white-collar jobs). In banks, sales staffs, insurance companies, and newspaper staffs, a policy of "tokenism" is operative. As one executive put it: *"If you have one in an office and she's pleasant, she fits in; but you put two or three there and you may find yourself losing some of your white staff."* Facing stiff competition for jobs, they have it both ways: if undertrained and if efficient (the too-well-trained, may be rejected) in either case, they may face a color bar.

Excluded from skilled jobs and forced into lower paid ones, still another disability must be faced in the field of housing accommodation. In addition to the problems occasioned from the general housing shortage, the West Indian immigrant and other colored Commonwealth citizens are widely rejected as tenants of advertised flats and lodgings on the basis of a color bar, and are obliged to pay higher rents, even than white tenants. "So sorry, No Colored, No children," "European Only," "White Only," signs dot the pages of advertised flats and lodgings. A "color-tax" meets the West Indian purchaser of property, often inferior lease-hold ones. No wonder estate agents and unscrupulous landlords, some of them colored themselves, have not been averse to exploiting for huge profits this housing shortage. "Rachmanism" is a synonym in present-day England for this type of practice, alluding to the fortunes made by the man so named in North Kensington in the very area of racial riots of a few years ago. Through exorbitant rentals, resale of properties, the shortage of housing is widely exploited and the West Indian, Afro-Asian, as well as white workers are the victims.

A Commons inquiry is now pending since the revelation of collusion of estate agents with Big Business when a restrictive color-bar covenant was discovered in Loriel Properties on whose board of directors are two Tory Cabinet Ministers, a leading Conservative Member of Parliament, who led the racist attack in the House of Commons on the Commonwealth Immigration Act. This company has shareholders among the nation's leading universities at Oxford and Cambridge and most of the other directors hail from The Establishment. Thus, the real origin of color-bar practices and policies stems from the City's imperialist financial barons to whom it is highly profitable, both ways. The Commons inquiry, it should be added, has been initiated by Mr. Fenner Brockway who has nine times tabled his anti-discrimination bill to ban discrimination in public housing, leases, inns, pubs, hotels, dance halls, etc. These and other examples more than confirm the urgency for this type of legislation in present-day Britain. Education policy is yet another field in which inroads are being attempted by the racial propagandists. Stemming from their central campaign, now sanctioned by the Commonwealth Immigration Act to oust West Indian Immigrants from Britain, they have fastened on the growth of communities where children of Afro-Asian-Caribbean immigrants are at school. Encouraging the idea of schools segregation, they have attempted the organization of parents to get them to move their children to other schools. In Southall for example, where, in two wards five thousand Indian families live, this type of segregation propaganda began to make headway and the local Council, despite the relatively good stand of the Board of Education, began to weaken. Following an appeal however, from the Education Committee to the Minister of Education, Sir Edward Boyle told four hundred parents, "there will be no segregation in our schools." A basis was adopted to spread the children over several schools so that there will be no more than one-third Indian children in the schools. Despite this, new calls are being heard for establishment of separate classes for colored children on grounds of "language difficulties," despite the well-known adaptability of children to become bilingual. This approach is being strongly resisted by West Indian, Afro-Asian, educational, and progressive groups in Britain. For it is feared that such a wedge may establish an American "Jim Crow" pattern of "separate but equal education," an animal (as we have learned from the Negro liberation struggles that just don't exist). This fear was confirmed anew when a recent White Paper issued by the Commonwealth Conservative Council suggested that children of immigrant parents be regarded as "immigrants" despite being born in the United Kingdom.

Consequently, whether as tenants waging anti-discrimination struggles, clubbing together to purchase homes to house families, the large majority of whom were separated for years until the necessary finances were raised; whether as workers fighting for the right to work or to be upgraded; or as cultural workers engaged in the attempt to use their creative abilities on stage, screen, or television, or to safeguard their children's right to an equal education; or as professionals, students, or in business pursuits; the West Indian immigrant community has special problems, as a national minority. While the workers are heaviest hit, the disabilities cut across class lines.

Future Perspectives

Conscious, therefore of the need for alleviation of their second-class citizenship, determined to live and work in human dignity as is their natural right, the resourceful West Indian migrant, in common with all peoples involved (either consciously or not) in anti-imperialist struggles, are also thinking about their ultimate direction. That they are only now at the stage of tentatively formulating their views may be ascribed to three main factors: (1) to the constant pressure and concern with daily problems of survival, (2) to the groping in their own minds for the fundamental significance of their national identity, and (3) to the lack of an organized perspective for a progressive, united West Indies at home. Linked to the first factor is the urgent necessity to organize and unite the West Indian community in Britain around their fundamental demands. The level of organization in Britain is not yet commensurate to fulfill this urgent need. The West Indian worker, in common with all workers, is confronted with the necessity to engage in struggles, supported by their allies, for his own survival in a new environment. This also means engaging in the general struggle for peace, trade unionism, democracy, and social change. While clinging strongly to his own roots, he is mindful of the conditions at home and the reasons for his emigration, and mindful, too, of the disabilities which face him there. But his economic situation is relatively better and he views as a practicality that his children will grow up in England. If to this is added the recognition that as with all migrations, this, too, will form a permanent community, it is only natural that steps should be taken to implement the recognition: that with permanency comes the growth of new institutions with all its accompanying aspects.

It is true, of course, that some measure of organization exists. West Indians are organized largely in social and welfare groups in the United Kingdom, established originally to meet the needs of incoming migrants. Only a smattering have thus far joined political movements or play an active role politically. This is undoubtedly attributable to the false twin ideas that they should only become politically active with their "return home," or the apolitical view that they should eschew politics. More fundamentally, it is traceable also to the lack of previous political activity at home and the fact that for most West Indians their political baptism is occurring in their new environment. There exists such organizations as the Standing Conference of West Indian Organizations, a council composed of fifteen social and welfare groups in London boroughs, as well as Freemason Lodges in areas of large West Indian settlements. There are also similar organizations existing in the Midlands, all of which have close supervision by the Migrant Services Division of the Jamaica, Trinidad and Tobago, Barbados, Leeward and Windward Islands government offices in Britain. In addition there are a growing number of inter-racial committees and groups engaged in dealing with the problems of West Indians and other migrants, besides the student organizations.

There are also special organizations based on island origins beginning to develop. The Church forms a center for many religious West
Indian groups, choirs and the like. Yet questions are now arising as
to whether these organizations fully meet the present needs of this
community. This is evidenced in the concern being expressed by West
Indians, as to whether integration in British life should be the sole
aim in Britain or whether the self-organization of West Indian should
not likewise be emphasized. Questions are being posed too, as to how
to harness the national identity of West Indians towards this end.

An interesting example of attempts to concert these trends among
West Indians on the basis of reliance on their own efforts, was shown
in Bristol last year, when in midst of the MCC [Marylebone Cricket
Club]–West Indian Test Match tour, a young university student graduate led a successful struggle following threats of a bus boycott by West
Indians when one of their number was refused a job by the Bristol Bus
Company. Here was witnessed too, the classical intervention of "do
good" liberals who "advised" the young West Indians militants not
to be too "hotheaded" and, themselves sought to designate who were
the "good boys" and the leadership to be followed. But this ruse didn't
quite succeed. Their action, widely publicized in the press was won
when following the intervention of the then High Commissioner for
Trinidad and Tobago, Sir Learie Constantine, and Mr. R. C. Lindo,
Jamaican High Commissioner, supported by Mr. Robert Lightbourne,
Jamaica Minister of Trade and Industry, trade-union and student
groups, the bus company climbed down and revoked its stand.

A major effort designed to stimulate political and social thinking has been the launching, six years ago, of the progressive news-
monthly, the *West Indian Gazette.* This newspaper has served as a
catalyst, quickening the awareness, socially and politically, of West
Indians, Afro-Asians, and their friends. Its editorial stand is for a
united independent West Indies, full economic, social, and political
equality and respect for human dignity for West Indians and Afro-
Asians in Britain, for peace and friendship between all Commonwealth and world peoples. It has campaigned vigorously on issues
facing West Indians and other colored peoples. Whether against
numerous police frame-ups, to which West Indians and other colored
migrants are frequently subject, to opposing discrimination and to
advocating support for trade unionism and unity of colored and

white workers, WI news publications have attempted to emulate the path of progressive "Negro" (Afro-Asian, Latin-American, and Afro-American) journals who uncompromisingly and fearlessly fight against imperialist outrages and indignities to our peoples. The *West Indian Gazette* and *Afro-Asian-Caribbean News* have served to launch solidarity campaigns with the nationals who advance with their liberation struggles in Africa and in Asia. The present circulation and readership of the WI publication would be larger but for the usual welter of problems faced by most progressive journals. A campaign of support for financial aid among its readers and friends has recently been launched to help its expansion to a weekly and to establish its own printing plant. It counts among its contributors and supporters many West Indian writers who live in England, trade unionists, and members of Parliament.

Underlying what may be termed "the search for a national identity," is the concern of West Indians to understand their historical and cultural heritage. This concern which arose with establishment of the now defunct West Indian Federation has become more widespread. The consequent polarization of West Indians into Jamaicans, Trinidadians, Barbadians, Grenadians, etc., has certain unrealities in England where existing problems among West Indians are shared in common. A consequence of emigration to England, has been that Afro-Asians and West Indians have come to know one another as they might not have previously, separated by the distance of their homelands.

Here, reference is not to some pseudo-intellectuals who, ignorant or unaware of a scientific definition of nationhood, deny the lack of a national identity on the spurious grounds of lack of a separate (not common) language. But rather to the leadership needed to acquaint West Indians with their own history, and by a social interpretation of that history, better to arm them for future struggles by imparting a pride in their origins, struggles, and future. This lack of historical perspective is at root, as Dr. Eric Williams correctly noted, from a society which eulogized the colonialist, and whose knowledge of West Indian history was limited to that of Anglo-Saxon conquests, Sir Walter Raleigh, Captain Morgan, and the feats of royalty. The task remains to enhance the knowledge of the true history: of the Morant Bay anti-slavery rebellion, the glorious Maroons, the early anti-colonial struggles of Captain Cipriani, or of Critchlow's trade unionism, or of the significance of the movement towards closer West Indian Federation, all of which early struggles created the preconditions leading to the contemporary struggle for nationhood, which thus is something less than that for which West Indian patriots fought and dreamed. Such an understanding would likewise help to create awareness of the need for support and aid to the bitter struggle being waged for British Guianese independence against US imperialist intervention which fears social change along socialist lines.

Related finally to the continued lack of an organized perspective for an advancing West Indies, is the indication of floundering in West Indian political life since the Federation's demise. The present political parties in the Caribbean advocating a socialist alternative, the only ultimate course for the West Indies, are still small and ineffective. But they represent the hope of the future, if only because they challenge the perspective of the present bourgeois-nationalist leaders, who heading a titularly independent West Indies, continue to proclaim their reliance on the West, not only geographically, but in political and social aims even to the shame of all West Indians, and Jamaicans in particular, of the unprecedented offer of Jamaica's soil for a US nuclear base.

Such advocacy may ultimately inspire West Indians at home and abroad to leap the shoals of struggle necessary to transform the economy of the West Indies, and consequently to establish a socialist West Indian nation that will play its role in the community of nations.

Such a perspective would win inspiring participation among West Indians in Britain, who adjure the gradualist view voiced by many of their Ministers that the pace of West Indian advancement will be "slow" and that the West Indian immigrant would do well to consider themselves primarily citizens of Britain and to cease to worry about their national identity. This idea is likewise based on the view held towards immigration by many bourgeois nationalist West Indian politicians who encourage migration as a "safety-valve," fearing the growth of militancy for social change, at home, more than they do the loss of their most valuable citizens.

A special importance attaches itself to the Caribbean, where there is evidenced the two paths to national liberation: either the path of obsequiousness to US imperialism and neocolonialism or the high road to socialist advance as exemplified by Socialist Cuba. Particularly in the Caribbean, where United States imperialism threatens Socialist Cuba; infringes on the national sovereignty of all Latin American peoples; intervenes in the internal affairs of British Guiana and Panama; and whose pretensions of a "free America in a free world" stands exposed before the massive hammer blows of the mounting Negro liberation struggle, which, as shown in our merged protests, Afro-Asians, and Caribbean peoples, held a Solidarity March to the US London Embassy in support of the Negro peoples' demands; the struggle for national liberation proceeds with singular emphasis.

THEY CRY PEACE— AND THEIR CRY IS HEARD!

WEST INDIAN GAZETTE
AUGUST/SEPTEMBER 1964

Claudia Jones, editor of the West Indian Gazette, *flew to Japan, as a delegate at the historic Tenth World Conference against Hydrogen and Atom Bombs. She served as a vice-chairman of the Conference Drafting Committee. The* WIG *editor writes: "The Tenth World Conference and its principled stand in defense of world peace and national liberation underlies the new energy and clarity with which the magnificent peace partisans of Japan and the world would ensure victories in the urgent struggles ahead against US imperialism and for world peace."*

The Conference held in Tokyo from July 27 to August 2, was attended by two hundred foreign delegates from fifty-two countries and nine international organizations and [an] unprecedented number of delegates. From every prefecture of Japan, and its decisions are bound to exert far-reaching influence on Japanese and world peace movements.

Still ringing in my ears was the prolonged mutual ovations of the overseas and Japanese delegates and shouts of "*HEIWA!*" (PEACE!)— the Japanese greeting, she reports.

The delegates unanimously adopted the Five Resolutions, including the APPEAL FOR INTERNATIONAL UNITED ACTION FOR PREVENTION OF NUCLEAR WAR AND FOR TOTAL BANNING OF NUCLEAR WEAPONS. A second document pledged to FIRMLY SUPPORT STRUGGLES OF ALL THE PEOPLES OF THE WORLD—particularly in Asia, Africa, and Latin America, "who constitute over two-thirds of the world's population" and whose liberation is the firmest guarantee for the achievement of world peace.

REPORTS ON TRIP TO CHINA & JAPAN

AUGUST 7, 1964

Ed. note—The following text was pulled from a series of typewritten drafts, heavily annotated by Claudia Jones. We have tried to reorganize the pages and transcribe it to the best of our ability. Her handwritten annotations are in italics, and missing or illegible words are denoted with ——.

Hiroshima—August 7—Amidst thousands of people, among whom were atomic sufferers and leaders of the Japan Council Against A and H Bombs, I stood with over 163 overseas delegates from every continent of the globe—from Asia, Africa, Latin America, Europe, and Oceania to commemorate the Nineteenth Anniversary of the United States imperialist nuclear bombing of Hiroshima.

Before the stone obelisk, arched and defiant as the bones of the three hundred thousand victims of this blatant crime against Japan and humanity, the people murmured "Mo Govenda!" (NO MORE HIROSHIMAS!). Each and every one of us carried a rose or some flowering which we laid as we marched past the monument *to gather with a contingent of over three thousand Japanese delegates,* nearby which Buddhist monks intoned prayers for the dead, amidst incense-offerings, the families of victims and the atomic victims, themselves form an integral part of Japan's massive peace movement.

We had come to the Tenth World Conference Against A and H Bombs *from fifty-two countries and eight international organizations and thirty-five thousand Japanese delegates,* which a few days earlier had closed its historic five-day session in Tokyo. Still ringing in my ears were the prolonged ovations *and shouts of* Heiwa! *(Peace!)* to the delegates in the final session which unanimously adopted the **final** *Resolutions and Allied for* International United Action to Prevent Nuclear War and asked for the Total Banning of Nuclear Weapons, *and for* —— [illegible] *of Unity,* in a second document pledged to firmly support the struggles of All the Peoples of the World—particularly Asia, Africa, and Latin America "who constitute more than two thirds of the world's peoples."

A Special Resolution Against New War —— [provocation by?] *US Imperialism Against the Democratic Republic of Vietnam, the appeal for international united action calls for the organizing of rallies of one* —— *people by the 11— [th?] World Conference Against Atomic and Hydrogen Bombs.*

These ovations were to be echoed and re-echoed in the huge mass meeting organized by Gensuikyo (Japan Council Against A and H Bombs) of thirty-five thousand Tokyo peace fighters; in Osaka where another thirty-five thousand overflowed in two halls, and in Kyoto where a similar audience in a standing ovation cheered unanimously in adoption of the appeal and the specific demands in support of the national liberation and peace struggles of the peoples.

Japan's peace movement is a massive, deep, day-to-day movement which relates, perhaps more consistently than anywhere else in the world, the interrelationship between the struggle for peace and that of national liberation. In the words of the second document, the delegates signalized their concern and condemnation against the thrust by US imperialism to extend the special warfare in South Vietnam, supporting the demands of the Democratic Republic of Vietnam for withdrawal of all US troops and other military personnel, for the peaceful reunification of Vietnam—North and South and for allowing the Vietnamese people to settle their own affairs without any foreign interferences.

Despite the ban by the Japanese Government of several delegates, including some of the delegates from the People's Republic of China, the Democratic Republic of Korea, East Germany, the persistence of the leaders of Japan's peace movement supported by the delegates, won through in part. *Some of the Chinese delegates and those from the (check name) National Liberation Front of Vietnam were finally allowed into Japan.* The delegation of the Liberation Front of Vietnam were to receive *cheers* again and again as they spoke, and pledges of support against the *brazen* US attempt, signalized in the recent bombing of the Republic of Vietnam, to extend the war in Southeast Asia, thus threatening the peace of *Asia and* the world.

It was from the fronts of great struggle, from Congo (Brazzaville), Congo (Leopoldville), Panama, *Angola,* Indonesia who fights to crush "Malaysia," that the comprehension of the delegations and the Japanese peace fighters were manifest in the enthusiastic greeting and response *to their speeches.*

It was the Peoples Republic of China, who is *widely regarded by Asian, African, ——[American?]* and Caribbean delegations, and *who* leads *the fight against* US imperialism and support for all national liberation struggles that the ovations were the loudest *(second only to Vietnam!)* and outpouring from the assembled and massive outpourings of the people in Peace Marches in Hiroshima, Nagasaki and in Kyoto.

It was *the delegates* from the lands of Africa—South West Africa, Southern Rhodesia, the Kamerun, Reunion, *St. Tome and Principe,* Northern Rhodesia, Angola, and other lands were delegates from Ghana, Algeria, Zanzibar, Jordan were also present that the audiences signalized again and again by their applause their understanding, their support in the words of the document: (Quote here from the second document, the section on Africa.)

This unity had to be *(——)* fought for in the International sessions. From the start of the consultative sessions, and throughout, the unity of the World Conference and Gensuikyo itself had been threatened by the action of three prefectures (wards) of Gensuikyo led by the right wing of the Japanese Socialist Party. The disagreement was a principled one. As against Geneuikyo's stand which refused to cede to the demand that there was no difference between just and unjust war, and hence their refusal to uphold any stand that opposed possession of nuclear arms by all countries; the Japanese Socialist right wing wanted this condemnation in the Gensuikyo programme. As against the principled stand of the Gensuikyo to oppose the chief enemy of peace—US imperialism, the Japanese socialists and those who supported them by attending their conferences and leaving Gensuikyo's including the delegations of the Soviet Union, India, and the World Peace Congress delegates, and some scattered African and Latin American delegates who were brought by these delegations, without invitation to this Tenth World Conference, these "peace advocates" emphasized nuclear war as the danger, not those who wield it and threaten peace, i.e. US imperialism.

The conference debate came to a climax when after detailed democratic debate, the Conference Presidium, upheld unanimously by delegates refused to allow those who wanted sit here to be —— delegate/observers, or finally when they were forced to concede on the —— of such a stand, to serve on the leading Tenth World Conference committee—namely; Steering, Presiding, Drafting Letter were sent by the delegations of the Soviet Union, India, and the World Peace Congress delegation and the other scattered individual representatives and a press conference held by Mr. Zhukov, leader of the Soviet Delegation that "they were forced to leave due to the "undemocratic procedure" and "discrimination" of "not allowing them to serve on committees." Despite numerous appeals from all delegations who attend the Tenth World Conference to the Soviet delegates to declare their stand as to whether they were going to attend the splitters conference, they made no reply. But later they attended a rally in Tokyo by the splitters organized by the Japanese Socialist Party right wing of three thousand people. Gensuikyo's audience in Tokyo Gymnasium was over thirty thousand.

It was in the international conference sessions where reports showing the counter-struggles of the peoples of the Caribbean, Guadeloupe, and Haiti, Panama, and Nicaragua, the opposition by the beacon light of the Caribbean—socialist Cuba to the US Yankee Imperialism, in Colombia, Peru, Venezuela and elsewhere that one learned more deeply of the principled stand of the Tenth World Conference against A and H bombs. It was in the group meetings and the women's panel where I spoke and attended with delegates from France, Indonesia, People's Republic of China, Belgium, Hawaii, United States, and Korea that one saw the torrent for peace which issues forth from the mothers, wives, and sisters of Japan.

To learn how to build a peace movement, one must study the Japanese experience. Here is a peace group, which links the campaign for dried milks dumped by Americans in Japan with opposition to the use of Japan as a base for organizing war against Vietnam and Southeast Asia and Malaya project. Another peace group has as a delegate the atomic victim, who but from Gensuikyo did not know what to do with her life. The atomic sufferers deserve a special story, they are woof and weft of the massive —— movement whose heroic —— is to be found everywhere in the fight demanding: NO MORE HIROSHIMAS! Here is a teacher who speaks of the Japanese minorities some of whom may be likened to the untouchables of India as regards their class position, telling of how learning and working with the children of the Bokura, teaching them peace songs, they now have a peace group which raised a few thousand yen to support the Tenth World Conference. Here is a group whose main activity is in defense of a member of the Japanese Self-Defense forces who was transferred to another prefecture, they think, unjustly. All of them come from the Million Gathering withheld and organized in preparation for this Tenth World Conference. Projected for the Eleventh World Conference is a billion peoples gatherings and heightened struggles, a signal of which is to stop the war in Vietnam now!

And their cries for peace are strong: they cry peace to stem the US imperialist mercenaries whose monument of lust is witnessed in the obelisk at Hiroshima, and the monument to children, who died or live maimed by their thrust. It is heard in the live, throbbing, fighting Japanese peace movement with whom all the continents and peace fighters signalized their programmatic support and agreement. It is heard in the voice of the Japan Council Against A and H Bombs and in the movements of the people whose struggle for national liberation is an Integral contribution to peace.

Coming next month: features on Women, Workers, the Japan Council.

DR. LUTHER KING'S WARNING

WEST INDIAN GAZETTE
DECEMBER/JANUARY 1965

Dr. Martin Luther King, widely regarded as a "moderate" in his native America, where he is a leader in the mounting Negro proples struggle for equality and freedom, had some excellent, and, for some, very radical things to say when passing through London on his way to Oslo to receive his Nobel Peace Prize.

What he said on racial discrimination caught the nation's headlines, and intrigued the overwhelming majority of Commonwealth citizens from Asia, Africa, and the Caribbean. As well it might. For his visit came in the midst of a debate on removal of the Commonwealth Immigrants Act, challenge to its renewal was virtually absent either by the Labour Government or by the Tory Opposition which introduced it. Yet, undoubtedly this color-bar act has accelerated racialism in this country and has led to the imposition of a second-class citizenship status for Commonwealth colored citizens in Britain.

We take it that Dr. King's main whiplash was against racial discrimination. Hitting out at the Commonwealth Immigrants Act, he told Britain:

> While I cannot speak on specific issues, there are some things which we have learned in the United States that, I think, have some relevance here. As far as housing is restricted and ghettos of a minority are allowed to develop, you are promoting a festering sore of bitterness and deprivation to pollute your national health and create for yourselves a serious situation.

Second, equal opportunity for education, training, and employment must be made available without regard to class or color, if the nation is to prosper in spirit and truth.

Third, the presence of immigration laws based on color are totally out of keeping with the laws of God and the trends of the twentieth century. It will eventually encourage the vestiges of racism and endanger all the democratic principles that this great nation holds.

We will not now quibble about Dr. King's reference to the "vestiges" of racism, or, as a few of our intellectuals seem preoccupied with "meditating about their navels," whether or not the American Negro struggle in all its aspects parallels our situation here. We can agree that there is enough that is similar from which to draw certain lessons. One such lesson is the necessity to uphold a principled stand on every issue of discrimination facing our people—even if some of our proclaimed friends do not, and, even if all struggles are not won at one fell stroke.

In this connection, it is interesting to note that in most of the press coverage of Dr. King's warnings, stress was laid not on its essence, i.e. his criticism of racial discrimination, but rather on the so-called issue of "growing ghettos."

Of course, Dr. King could not have known that there are some, who, pleading their friendship with Commonwealth immigrants, seek to obscure the main issue of racial discrimination by counterposing the so called question of growing "ghettos"

Of course, there is an underlying method in their madness. If the root causes of racial discrimination are obscured, the "scapegoat theory" remains untouched and can, like Damocles' sword, be hung over our heads again and again. Discrimination, however, is man-made and is based on the exploitation for profit at the expense of colonial and newly independent peoples as an integral part of the imperialist system, which oppresses other nations using racialism to disrupt working class unity.

Ghettos of course are abhorrent and should be fought. But the best way to fight these is to end discrimination in housing.

Recently, the Rev. Stephen Pulford, sixty-nine-year-old Rector of the Church of England near Ross-on-Wye, Herefordshire, said that colored people should be given return tickets to their own countries from Britain. He presumed the slogan raised in the Smethwick election campaign: "If you want a nigger for a neighbour, vote Labour" to be an accurate gauge of the feelings and fears of the British people as a whole. In true Southern Dixiecrat fashion, invoking the name of God, he talked about opposition to mixed marriages, repeating the worn-out racialist cliches "that colored people come to Britain to batten upon the welfare state," and that "this country is already overcrowded and Britons are queuing up for houses," etc. This minister made these points in a letter to a local newspaper in Leyton where the British Foreign Secretary Mr. Patrick Gordon Walker, defeated at Smethwick, proposes to stand for his Commons seat.

There has also been a recent rash of suggestions as [we] witness the proposals to "Buy-for-Whites" houses in Smethwick, hearteningly condemned by Labour councilors in Smethwick, and the proposal which for built-in racially restrictive covenants to presumably overcome the problem of overcrowding, for which it is alleged Commonwealth immigrants have a special penchant. Then there are the prevalent views which seek to muddy the waters further by counter-posing inter-nation differences among Commonwealth citizens as being synonymous with White supremacy."

What is all this but an attempt to divert the concern from the spawners of racialism and racialism itself onto the heads of Commonwealth citizens from Asia, Africa, and the West Indies? The so-called issue of "ghettos" has been blown up far beyond all proportions. Commonwealth citizens if they live together in the same street or house are only doing what most people with similar cultural and traditional backgrounds normally do in family groups. Why should those, except of an apartheid mentality, fear this? Moreover, they do so usually after having the bitter experience of being faced with color-bar adverts and refusals to give them housing if it is available. The attempt by the racialists to buy houses does not have as its aim the overcoming of crowding. If it did, they would fight for a proper housing programme to build the homes needed for all Britons. Its aim is to break up and squeeze out Commonwealth citizens who by banding together have been enabled to purchase houses or rent them at the most exorbitant "color tax" prices and rentals.

Suspicion is therefore rife as regards the "holier than thou" attitudes of those who would distort the essential warming made by Dr. King which finds an echo in the hearts of all Commonwealth citizens. Some of those who are preoccupied with "ghettos" are the main perpetrators of racialism.

Accompanying this trend is the usual concern voiced by them about fears of unity of colored Commonwealth citizens, and the implication of such unity, as related to what is termed "black supremacy."

The shoe is on the other foot. The lessons [of] the American Negro struggle are that whatever advances towards equal rights and integration have been made, they have been accomplished in unity and struggle. As Paul Robeson observed recently on the militant Negro struggle, "We can't say 'Great God Almighty we're here at last, but we're moving.'"

Commonwealth immigrants, too, can move if they but heighten the trend for unity and organization.

That is why Dr. Martin Luther King's answer had to be a dual one, namely, the necessity for all decent Britons to challenge every case of racial discrimination and for the Commonwealth citizens to organize and unite—the better to effectively challenge the disabilities confronting us.

THE WEST INDIES AND THEIR FUTURE

WEST INDIAN GAZETTE
JUNE 1961

Books—Towards A WI Confederation

The West Indies and Their Future—by Daniel Guerin (Dennis Dobson, 18s)

"Scant, sea-girt land
Oh, tight-squeezed land."
—Nicholas Guillen

Daniel Guerin's book, *The West Indies and Their Future*, is peppered through its two hundred compact pages with lines from Caribbean poets and writers who cry the urgency of West Indian independence and economic freedom. It is a cry not alone against overcrowding, poverty, and our heritage of colonialism; but a cry for unity of all Caribbean peoples. That he approaches his subject not merely from the artificial colonial divisions that have plagued the West Indies for three hundred years, but from an overall survey of the Caribbean— the West Indies (British), Martinique and Guadeloupe (French), Curacao (Dutch), etc.—is one of its chief virtues.

Another contribution is that Guerin, in his description of the liberation movements and their growth discusses them in toto, irrespective of the imperialist powers who have dominated them for the last three centuries. As such, Mr. Guerin's book in its first half is a revealing and damming exposure of imperialism and its harmful results on peoples and populations.

Sharp Contrasts

"In no other part of the world," he wrote, "is there a sharper contrast between the bountiful generosity of nature and the wickedness of society . . . between the glittering wealth of the few and the unfathomable poverty of all the rest."

Under his chapter headings "Where Splendour and Misery Sit Side by Side," "Demographic Pressure," "The Mischief of Single-Crop Agriculture," "Concentration in Agriculture," "The West Indies Have Not Been Industrialised," "The Cost of Living is High," The Colonial Pact Lives On," etc., one may glean the reason for this situation. It is a condition in which the fabulously wealthy planter benefits from the contact, rife unemployment, the high cost of living, and the racial divisions and racial prejudice which, despite pretty phrases, they yet spawn.

In the second half of the book he describes the growth of the national liberation movements, and interestingly he concludes:

> . . . The real aims and contents of the movements vary much less, from one island to another than party labels would lead one to suppose. The movement everywhere expresses a dual awareness, firstly racial, then social, a common revolt against the supremacy of the white sugar planters; and its militants are more preoccupied by the immediate and peculiarly Caribbean aspects of their struggle than by extra Caribbean ideologies . . .

> Regardless of whether one declares himself a reformist and the other a revolutionary, they are both, basically, prisoners of the same contradiction: authority has been delegated to the both, they hold office, one on the governmental plane, the other on the departmental and municipal planes, that within the framework of the colonial capitalist regime: their common problem is how to do anything to relieve the poverty of the masses without yet being able to render the sugar plutocrats harmless. The "cold war" which split the Caribbean into two examples, just as it did the whole world, has managed to drive the

men towards opposite poles they will meet again along
the same road leading to the same historical destination.

Evidence of this hope on Mr. Guerin's part, and that of all thinking
West Indians, is documented in his chapters: "The Dawning of a
Social Consciousness," "Self-Government and Assimilation," "The
Failure of the Middle Classes," "Dark Men Become Aware of Their
Race," "Racial Prejudice," etc. But as his condition he warns against
bartering West Indian Independence and through anti-communism,
set the stage for American Intervention in Caribbean Politics.

About the future, Mr. Guerin goes beyond a federation formed from
the ex-colonies of any particular Power; he advocates a confederation of
all the islands with a population of around seventeen million persons.

As befits his thesis which is frank and realistic throughout, Guerin
urges that there be no self-deception. Thus, in the last lines of his
book he writes: "The West Indian Confederation has a slight chance
of being born within the framework of the present capitalist and
colonialist society; sixteen years ago, in 1945, the Caribbean Labour
Congress forcefully affirmed 'that there is no hope for the West Indies
unless they become a Socialist Commonwealth.'"

The great new wealth of the West Indies is its people. Trade
Unions and Intellectuals, men and women. Its cultural renaissance, its
crop of writers, artists, etc. gives hope for the unfolding of this perspective. Mr. Guerin, a Frenchman by birth, does not deal much with
Cuba which has brought that hope nearer, but it is the —— virtue of
his book that in contemporary developments, the vision of Jose Martí,
San Simon, Captain Cipriani, Albert Marry show, and other founding fathers of West Indian and Caribbean unity is gaining ascendancy
in the minds and hearts of the Caribbean peoples.

THESE ARE THE FACTS: BEHIND THE CONGO UPRISING

WEST INDIAN GAZETTE
SEPTEMBER 1960

It is barely two months since the Congolese people won their independence from the Belgian Government. Since then, that embattled young African Republic has experienced military intervention by its former enslavers; downright attempts to sabotage its right of self-determination by the Belgian conspiracy to split away the Katanga province using the puppet Tshombe; internal and external plots to thwart its will to implement its own national destiny.

But during that time, too, there has emerged to the admiration of all the world, even their enemies, a new stature of African leadership, of African-Asian unity as evidenced in the Summit at Leopoldville, a growth of world opinion in their favor as shown in the recent UN Security Council Second Resolution (after unusual delays) to enter and occupy the Katanga Province, and thus to keep the peace not only in the Congo but perhaps the world.

Because we are witness to one of the most intense and critical struggles for national independence of a new African state, the outcome of which may lay the pattern for African states with a similar colonial heritage, it is worthwhile to examine the facts behind the upsurge in the Congo.

For over half a century, the Belgian imperialists ruthlessly ruled the people of the Congo.

When it is considered that under Belgian rule about 90 percent of the Congolese were not allowed to receive any elementary education worth mentioning and that the illiteracy rate is one of the highest in the world, one begins to glimpse the factors behind this upsurge.

The fact is that far from being *"unready"* for independence—the favorite cry of those colonialists and pro-colonialists who wish to hold back the tide of African national independence—the Congolese people are today showing they have long been ready and ripe for it.

Secondly, insofar as secondary education is concerned, the possibility of entering the professions was completely out for any Congolese.

There was not a single Congolese Doctor educated under the Belgians. They were truly the *"hewers of the wood and the drawers of the water."* No Congolese soldier ever rose higher than an ordinary noncom.

Is it any wonder at the very first opportunity they rebelled against continuing serving under Belgian officers once they had tasted the —— [fruits?] of their political independence?

Shacks for Homes

Living conditions? "Shacks, covered with leaves," is how Mr. I. T. A. Wallace Johnson, elected member of the Sierra Leone House of Representatives now in England, recently described the African quarters. "Only the few with money could even afford to put corrugated iron roofs on their homes."

Rough tracks were the substitute for good roads.

Nor was there proper sanitation or a sewage system in the African areas.

Under these conditions disease flourished: malaria, leprosy, yaws, etc., were—and are—still commonplace among the African population, having been denied adequate medical treatment.

Congo Women Violated

Early European writers visiting the Congo half a century ago, expressed their shock at the conditions in which Congolese women and children were forced to pave the streets with their bare hands.

It is these past conditions that are implanted on the minds of thousands of the Congolese people as they stride towards national independence and freedom.

Some people, unaware of these conditions, are apt to raise eyebrows when, as was true a few weeks ago, the press produced banner headlines of a number of alleged cases of rape.

Of course the enemies of national liberation always produce such charges, but forget that for many years, European men in the Congo have used African women as they pleased.

And this is a fact of history the Congo people will never forget.

Recently this bit of history was recalled when according to a *London Times* report the Belgian Minister of Information asserted in a Brussells radio speech that the instances of alleged rape were triggered off by the violation of African women during the Belgian occupation. General Alexander, C-in-C of the Ghana Armed forces, reported in Leopoldville that every attempt to trace the cases of alleged rape have come to naught.

Comparison to South Africa

Thirdly, the degree of discrimination and segregation in the Congo rivaled South Africa. It was common practice of the early European settlers to burn Congolese shacks to the ground when the population refused to honor some absurd order. Also, there was the practice where the Congolese people were barred from the market places while the European wives went to shop!

Only *after* the first choice of all goods were made would the Africans be permitted to do their own marketing. The 8 p.m. curfew for all except servants in the European part of the town and the practice when open wagons were the only means for Africans to travel in by rail were only some of the humiliations suffered by the Congolese.

It was not so long ago that a favorite form of punishment by the Belgian colonialists was the cutting off of the feet and hands of those (including children) who rebelled against the aforementioned practices; and for women, it meant the severing of a breast!

In view of this sordid and shocking colonial past, what must one take of the current argument that the Congolese people *"have no right to rule"* and *"unready to rule"* etc? These arguments bring to mind the old adage of the American Negro which runs, "If you'd get off our backs, perhaps we'd have a chance to rule ourselves."

Wealth of Katanga—Their Concern

Needless to say, the underlying concern of such arguments has to do with the priceless uranium and copper-mining wealth of the Congo.

It is the exploitation of African labor that has produced this great wealth, bringing the Belgian dollar reserves to more than ninety million pounds yearly! As well known by political economists, not only is the powerful Belgian Union Minière a controlling factor, but the British have their control through Tanganikya Concessions and the Americans through the Rockefeller family.

That is why when papers like the *Daily Express* show their concern for the puppet Tshombe and their obvious ire and bias against the young Congolese Republic and its leaders that their real aim unfolds.

That aim is unquestionably to perpetuate the state of things as they were in which huge profits accrued to the European monopolists at the expense of the lives of the Congolese people.

UN Resolution Unenforced

In order to break up the new Republic of Congo, the Belgian armed forces spread a reign of terror, firing on the people with guns and rocket planes. A puppet government was set up in Katanga.

Against this armed aggression by Belgium, Premier Lumumba appealed to the United Nations. The UN resolution passed in the Security Council on July 19 said that the Council "decides to authorize the Secretary-General to take the necessary steps, in consultation with the Government of the Republic of the Congo, to provide the Government with such military assistance as may be necessary until, through the efforts of the Congolese Government with the technical assistance of the United Nations, the national security forces may be able, in the opinion of the Government, to meet fully their tasks."

UN troops which were sent to the Congo from the Belgian armed invaders are being used against the Congo Government. They have been given orders to shoot Congo troops if necessary, in order to prevent the Congo Government from controlling its own airfields.

It was not for nothing that the Soviet Union opposed the inclusion of NATO countries troops who are allies of the Belgians in the UN missions. The Soviet Union alone of the great powers have consistently supported the Congolese people and Government.

At the last session [of] the Security Council on Congo, Antoine Gizenga, the Deputy Premier suggested: the UN action should be conducted in cooperation with the Central Government who should be constantly informed of the movement of UN troops and that the policing of the airports and seaports should be in the hands of the Congolese National Army. Mr. Gizenga further demanded that the UN force should entirely disarm all Belgians in Katanga as well as total evacuation of Belgian troops from Congo including Kitona and Kamina Bases.

Despite the fact that the Secretary-General has promised the evacuation of the Belgians within a week he only talks of "non-combatants." In the meanwhile, Tshombe with the help of his Belgian masters is raising a so-called "International Legion."

Hence all democrats and fighters against colonialism must be vigilant and alert. There is a need for sustained exposure of the colonialist and imperialist tactics and continued support to the Congolese people and their government in their critical struggle for the consolidation of their independence.

WIG EDITOR VISITS ASIA

WEST INDIAN GAZETTE
NOVEMBER 1965

Last summer, for two and a half months, *WIG* Editor Claudia Jones traveled thousands of miles to Asia where on invitation of the Japan Council against A and H Bombs she participated as a delegate in the Tenth World Conference against A and H bombs. There she served as a Vice-Chairman of the Conference's Drafting Committee which called for the total banning of nuclear weapons and which took a principled stand in support of the anti-imperialist struggles of the world's peoples, particularly in Asia, Africa, Latin America, and the Caribbean.

Visiting five cities, she saw the massive and heroic Japanese peace partisans, including atomic victims, who met in their thousands in peace marches and mass meetings in Tokyo, Osaka, Kyoto, Hiroshima, and Nagasaki.

Later, on invitation from the China Peace Committee of the People's Republic of China, she witnessed the life and society of the 650 million people of the new Socialist China, visiting six cities—Peking, Shanghai, Yenan, Anahan, Sheyyang, and Canton.

There, *WIG* Editor Claudia Jones met and spoke with the Chinese Government and Communist leaders including Chairman Mao Tse Tung, Marshall Chen-Yi, Madame Soong Ching Ling, with People's Commune leaders and peasants, students and youth, women, and children.

What is it like to visit Asia—to see life and industry of the Chinese people, who recently celebrated fifteen years of socialist liberation?
Probably the first West Indians to visit Asia who has had the opportunity to see Chinese socialism at work first hand, Miss Jones

writes of her observations in interviews, talks, and visits with China's leaders and people.

In her series, China's internationalism and firm anti-imperialist stand becomes obvious.

ENDNOTES

Foreword

1 Gerald Horne, *Powell v. Alabama: The Scottsboro Boys and American Justice* (New York: Watts, 1997).

2 Gerald Horne, *Black Revolutionary: William Patterson and The Globalization of the African-American Freedom Struggle* (Urbana: University of Illinois Press, 2013)

3 Gerald Horne, *White Supremacy Confronted: US Imperialism and Anti-Communism versus the Liberation of Southern Africa, from Rhodes to Mandela* (New York: International Publishers, 2019)

4 Gerald Horne, *Black Liberation/Red Scare: Ben Davis and the Communist Party* (London: Pluto Press, 2016)

5 Gerald Horne, *Paul Robeson: The Artist as Revolutionary* (London: Pluto Press, 2016).

Introduction

6 Carole Boyce Davies, "Piece Work/Peace Work: Self-Construction versus State Repression," in *Left of Karl Marx: The Political Life of Black Communist Claudia Jones* (Durham, NC: Duke University Press, 2008), 221.

7 Augusta Strong, "Hundreds Say Goodbye to Claudia Jones, Who Sails Today," *Daily Worker*, December 9, 1955.

Jim Crow in Uniform

8 Ed. note—Jones is referencing "Mobilization Day"
9 "The American Negro in the War," by Emmett J. Scott. [from original]

An End to the Neglect of the Problems of the Negro Woman!

10 Today, in the rural sections of the South, especially on the remnants of the old plantations; one finds households where old grandmothers rule their daughters, sons, and grandchildren with a matriarchal authority.